MW00605250

Praise for Loved So Much It Hurts

"Rebecca's personal journey of faith in God in the midst of pain, fear, and a life-threatening disease inspires us all to believe in the Great Physician to do the impossible in our lives. If you are needing hope beyond what you can see for healing, Rebecca's story and heart for God will be the spark you need to rise above—and partner with God for divine healing."

Veronica Karaman, Performance Coach and Author, The Champion's Way: Training for Reigning in Life, Leadership, and a Fulfilled Calling

"Rebecca Olmstead's Loved So Much It Hurts is a rare glimpse into an overcomer's victory found on a steep uphill journey of daunting pain and loss. Her heartwarming stories of reliance on God's Word, and gratitude for His steadying hand, reveal a surprisingly refreshing relationship with the Holy Spirit. The authentic day-to-day struggles and touching family memories in Loved So Much It Hurts will validate, strengthen, and inspire you to find Christ-courage on arduous steps of your own path."

Lynn Hare, Author, The Quest for Self-Forgiveness
Lynnhare.com

"I couldn't put Loved So Much It Hurts down until I read it through! It was like reading a diary or listening to a best friend. I loved the focus on God and how Rebecca never once fell into unbelief, and He came through in her behalf. It was compelling to see what this next day would bring, and how He was faithful to always be there with Rebecca."

Anita McCall, Author, Overcoming the Spirit of Offense: Understanding How Offense Operates, in Order to Be Able to Overcome It

"This is not an ordinary book, it's a life-transforming masterpiece in God's hands. As He revealed Himself to Rebecca, who has gone through tremendous pain, loss, sickness, and much sufferings, He will show up in everything you are going through in your life., Watch Him work miracles and wonders by just trusting in Him."

Pastor Stephen N. and Hannah Mwathi, Kenya, Africa

"Rebecca Olmstead has written a must-read guide for those who are suffering from cancer, tumor, and like diseases. As she shares her life experience throughout the book, she shows the way to help decrease pain and even get healed through faith in God and prayer."

Habte Bekana , Author, 'ጠል Chopa Dew', & Computer Engineer, Ethiopia

"Loved So Much It Hurts .... what a wonderful title to an inspiring book written by my beautiful friend Rebecca Olmstead .... Rebecca's journey thru her diagnosis of cancer and recovery is very touching .... her honesty and transparency in the pages of this book will encourage you to look beyond your circumstances to the one who created us intricately and wonderfully .... Rebecca's journey was fraught with fears, pain, and questions, all of which have led her to a deeper understanding of God's grace and unending love .... her passion for life and unfailing desire to know God more intimately are breathtakingly apparent .... her encouragement from friends and family within the body of Christ as she laid herself bare was a rare and wonderful insight into the functioning of love within the Body of Christ .... this love is available to all who may read her testimony in this book .... God is not a respecter of persons, so if you are going through difficult circumstances or are looking for a deeper relationship with the Father, this book will inspire you to go deeper and ask of Him .... ask of Him, and He will show you great and mighty things ...."

Jennifer Dennis, Mt. Gambier, South Australia

"I feel that the world is very busy with work, family, and life, and it is very difficult to make time for anybody. I don't know about the busy life in America, but there are many people in Pakistan that spend all day in work, and they are very busy and show little interest in reading books. I am also included with them, because I am a pastor and my days are spent on God's work. I have many books, but I don't read them. But, when I started to read Sister Rebecca's book, I felt joy and I took more interest in reading it. Before reading Loved So Much It Hurts, I believed reading books was a waste of time, but Sister Rebecca's book has changed my heart. There are many things I was taught from this book, as the Bible says in the book of John. I teach these things to people after learning from it, like that love is better than hatred, and my family and church people have received blessings as I took blessings from this book. I pray to God that this book becomes more precious in the future. I believed that this book is very blessed and will bless people as they read it. I have many more words I could share with you, and I just want to say I pray you to write more books like Loved So Much It Hurts, and to bring people towards God. God bless you."

Pastor Amir Pavez, Pakistan

LOVED SO MUCH IT HURTS

Purpose in the Pain

Second Edition

Rebecca Olmstead

LOVED SO MUCH IT HURTS

Purpose in the Pain

Second Edition

Rebecca Olmstead

Thunder and Fire Press

Thunder and Fire Press

Printed By: Thunder and Fire Press
Thunder and Fire Press is a division of Watch God Work Ministries
contact@watchgodwork.com
Printed in the United States
ISBN: 978-1-7370218-0-3

This book is dedicated with love to the warriors I came to know and love on CarePages and CaringBridge and their wonderful families. You have taught me so much about grace, faith, and courage, and I would not be the person I am today, had God not placed each of you in my life at just the right time. You will always have a special place in my heart.

Daniel Saenz
Camilla Andrea Duarte
Kathy Dulski
Vinny DiGerolamo
Joshua Dean Mueller
Tyler Fisher
Brian Ernst
Derrick Ide
Jonathan O'Malley
David Buck
and Mikayla Rietgraf

These heroes are mentioned throughout my story, and their photographs and tributes can be found at the back of this book.

Contents

FOREWORD

*L*oved So Much It Hurts *is an excellent and important discussion of the issues of finding personal and professional support in a critical and extremely difficult time in one's life, the assessment of a new malignant diagnosis. That early diagnostic process can be extremely challenging for the patient and their family depending on your personal strengths, your health, the details of your tumor issues, and health care providers.*

The oncology provider needs to manage patient issues according to the patient's needs for support and comfort. Providing personal or spiritual support has clearly not been a strength of most Cancer Centers until very recently and is now a resource being carefully evaluated because of its critical contributions to successful patient care. Accommodating patients and their personal and family needs will hopefully receive greater support in future health care coverage, as a critical determinant of successful care.

Despite our greatest efforts to be empathetic and supportive of our patients, our efforts are never adequate, especially in the early "diagnostic" phase of patient evaluation. I always think that despite our best efforts to be empathetic to our patients during the stressful times of tumor imaging and tumor "staging," we never do an adequate job. Obviously, a patient's ability to tolerate that stress is directly related to the support of their family and friends, their level of clinical discomfort, and their spiritual beliefs and strengths.

Rebecca has done a great job of describing those challenging times and the personal and spiritual resources that kept her in balance during those difficult days. She clearly could have never made those long trips, driving 5-6 hours to Seattle, from Walla Walla, without Chuck at her side, the support of her family and friends, and her spiritual

1

support. Her "Shelter in the time of storm" was her way of describing those critical resources that allowed her to make all those trips and experience a positive outcome that probably would not have happened without her personal and spiritual strengths.

Patients with musculoskeletal tumors or a malignant sarcoma have some of the greatest challenges of all tumor patients because of the relative rarity of those tumors and the need to travel for good care because of the diagnostic challenges associated with those kinds of tumors. Sarcomas are a malignancy of the connective tissues that "hold you together" (i.e.: nerve, artery, tendon, bone, etc.) and represent the only solid tumor malignancy that can occur in any patient age and in any location, with a hundred different "subtypes." A sarcoma is typically a difficult diagnosis to make by imaging (i.e.: MRI, CT, and/or PET) and a difficult diagnosis to make under the microscope, even for the experts. Malignancies of the breast, lung, prostate, kidney, colon, or thyroid are far more common and more easily diagnosed. Having such a difficult tumor in such a difficult anatomic location (i.e.: pelvis or sacrum) can create very challenging diagnosis and treatment issues for any surgeon or oncologist.

There is no doubt that having significant family and spiritual support is an essential requirement for a successful patient outcome and assists with the stressful times of imaging, biopsy, surgical resection, chemotherapy, radiation treatment, and clinical follow-up.

Recognizing our patient's' personal and spiritual strengths is an important assessment for all providers. The extreme example is the patient who appears for their first or second visit to the Sarcoma specialist by themselves, with no family or friend accompanying them.

Rebecca has also done an excellent job of describing her resources for her experience and how essential they were for her. It is likely that her family and Chuck, her friends and spiritual partners, served as her rock, her "Shelter," and allowed her to recover so completely and as quickly as she was able. She actively requested and recruited those partners, and finding a way to have those resources for all of our patients would be a wonderful goal for all of our Cancer Centers.

Congratulations, Rebecca, on your excellent story and for showing the way for current and future cancer patients, no matter where they live.

Love and Regards,

Chappie Conrad, M.D.

Ernest U. Conrad, III, M.D.

Professor of Orthopedics

Director of Division of Orthopedic Oncology

University of Texas, Mc Govern School of Medicine

Houston, Texas

ACKNOWLEDGMENTS

When I was diagnosed, writing a book was the last thing on my mind. Yes, I was a writer, but that seemed of little consequence with the "C" word looming over me. It wouldn't be the first time God's plans for me were beyond my comprehension, and I dare say it won't be the last. So, first and foremost, I give God the glory for being the Author and Finisher of my faith, and for allowing me a small part in His big picture.

I also want to express my deepest love and gratitude to my husband, Charles Glen. God knew exactly what He was doing when He put you in my life. I can't imagine my world without you, my best friend, biggest fan, partner in crime, and love of my life. I thank God for you every day.

The hardest part of this journey for me was leaving my children for such long periods of time. But God loves my kids even more than I do, and He provided just the right people to watch over them. Thank you so much, David and Shawna Corbett, for making a home-away-from-home for our baby, Gracie. And to Dad and Mom (Chuck and Lois Olmstead), Aunt Vicki Ruley, and Grandma Helen Clough, for the care, feeding, and taxiing of our older kids. You were all such a blessing!

God also blessed me through this journey with a wonderful group of caregivers. I'd like to thank my doctor, his nurse, Diane, the radiology department, and receptionists of Adventist Health in Walla Walla, Washington. And then in Seattle, my hero, Dr. Ernest "Chappie" Conrad, and his posse, along with the nurses, techs, reception, kitchen, and housekeeping staff of Seattle Cancer Care Alliance and University of Washington Medical Center, who amazed and blessed us with their kindness, professionalism, and compassion. I never thought it possible to enjoy hospital food, but—when I could eat—I ate very well.

And many thanks to my dear friend and fellow author, Helen Heavirland (Helen H. in the book), without whom this book would have never seen the light of day. And my dear friends and fellow authors in my writers' groups, Walla Walla Christian Writers, and Christian Scribes, Shirley Waite, Laura Bradford (Laurie B. in the book), Laurice Shafer, Libby Swenson, Sally Daley, Shirley Ruble, Cleona Bazzy, Charles Edwards, and Donna Ritchie. Your tireless reading—and rereading, encouragement, and pushing to "dig deeper," not only helped me make the book better, it helped me heal.

To my beta reader and wonderful friend and mentor, Helen Clough, for your help and encouragement, and to my initial editor and grammar cop, Sue Miholer: thank you both so much.

*"I thank my God upon every remembrance of you, always in
every prayer of mine making request for you all with joy, for
your fellowship in the gospel from the first day until now, being
confident of this very thing, that He who has begun a good
work in you will complete it until the day of Jesus Christ."*
Philippians 1:3-6

INTRODUCTION

*I*considered myself a Christian all my life. Raised in the church, I attended church activities during the week, participated in youth groups, sang in the choir, started singing solos at the age of eight . . .

Even during my rebellion as a young adult, I felt the hand of God in my life. I knew deep down that I could never live without Him. But, returning to the fold only stirred my longing. I was adrift in a sea of religion—and I was dying of thirst. I needed more of God.

From my youth, I'd heard and read about the great men and women of God in the Bible. I knew, theoretically at least, that intimacy with the Creator comes at a price. Did I decide to ignore this fact? Or, did I just want Him so badly I didn't care about the cost? I was like an Israelite at the foot of Mt. Sinai, but unlike those trembling in the shadows, I wasn't hiding. I was determined to see God face-to-face—or die trying.

PART I

"And we know that all things work together for good to those who love God, to those who are the called according to His purpose."
Romans 8:28 NKJV

Chapter 1

A BEND IN THE ROAD

Dr. Monroe closed the door of the exam room behind him but came no farther.

"Hello," he said, glancing briefly my way. His normally bright face was strained as he bent over my latest MRI results. After a moment, he pulled himself up to his full six feet and cleared his throat.

"Well," he said gently, "there's something there."

Just say it. I tried to shift away from the pain within the confines of the wheelchair; they no longer made me climb up onto the exam table. I was tired, tired of the pain, and I just wanted answers. I wanted a label for my condition that could be targeted and eliminated.

"It's a tumor, isn't it?"

For an instant, his professional objectivity failed him, and he sighed. "Yes," he said. "You have a tumor."

Wait, what? That wasn't what he was supposed to say. I only said it to deflate the two-ton elephant in the room. I only said it because I thought voicing such an outrageous possibility would make the truth come easier. I only said it because I knew God would never allow such a thing to happen. Not to me. Not now.

For the first time in my life I was happy. Secure. I'd tasted it all: abuse, fear, divorce, poverty, grief . . . But I'd made a decision to trust the Lord, and He'd brought me through the fire, blessing me beyond my wildest imagination. He'd given me a wonderful husband, financial security, even the house of my dreams. So great was the Lord's faithfulness, I couldn't help but ask for more of Him—oh, boy.

Suddenly, it all came clear. I'd become so desperate for God I'd forgotten the four years that had gotten me this far. The painful and terrifying stripping away, teaching my heart to trust Him alone. Jesus' words echoed in my mind.

> *"And whoever does not carry their cross and follow me*
> *cannot be my disciple."*
> Luke 14:27

It was time to count the cost. But I was too far gone. I'd tasted and seen that the Lord is good, and I could no more turn back than cut out my own heart.

My stomach turned over as I recalled all I'd been through since the first of September when my health took a sharp decline. Chest pains, H. pylori, chronic fatigue. Then came the back pain—the pain that drove me to my chiropractor. But the ice treatment he prescribed was like throwing gasoline on a fire, igniting the nerves in my hip, sending flames up into my back and down my leg into my ankle. No amount of ibuprofen or acetaminophen helped, and soaking in a tub of hot water brought only temporary relief. Walking on my own became impossible, and sleep was sporadic at best. In the blur of pain and exhaustion came visions of animals gnawing off their own limbs to escape a trap. But my trap was my own body.

My G.P., Dr. Monroe, thought I'd strained a muscle and prescribed a muscle relaxant and Vicodin for pain.

As much as I wanted to believe my problems were as simple as a strained muscle, deep down I knew it was more. Increasing pelvic pain, along with constant bladder and colon pressure, led me to my gynecologist. But she found nothing. Never before had I been disappointed at receiving a clean bill of health from my gynecologist. I was getting desperate.

When I returned to Dr. Monroe two days later, my pain brought tears even to his nurse's eyes. I was given Demerol and Phenergan to get me through an x-ray. But, like everything else I'd done, the x-ray shed no light on the cause of my pain. Dr. Monroe added oxycodone to my pain regimen and ordered bed rest and heat—a moot point, since I could barely make it to the bathroom and back to bed, and my heating pad and tub were my best friends. If I didn't improve in a month, he would order an MRI.

I worsened. Hot enemas eased the pelvic pain, but nothing eased my guilt—we had a three-year-old, a tween, and two teens at home, and my husband, Chuck, was shouldering the full load on top of running our contracting business. For three days, Chuck spent his lunch hours at Dr. Monroe's office, hounding him for more medication. Then he took me back, insisting Dr. Monroe either order an MRI or admit me to the hospital for pain management.

Dr. Monroe added morphine and alprazolam, an anti-anxiety medication, to my growing list of drugs, and ordered an MRI to be done immediately. Immediately . . . I went hot and cold all at once. I'm claustrophobic. That long narrow tube might as well have been a coffin.

I looked to Chuck, my chest tightening. "I can't do it."

The nurse, who'd watched the blood drain from my face, was quick to respond, "I'll ask Dr. Monroe for something to help you relax."

With a shot of lorazepam, and an extra dose of oxycodone on board, I tried to convince myself I'd be all right. Chuck wheeled me across the parking lot to the hospital, but the drugs were no match for the adrenaline coursing through my veins. As slowly as he walked, each crack and bump in the pavement shot arrows of pain through my spine. I fought growing waves of nausea as cold sweat broke out on my skin. In spite of the warm September air, my body shuddered, and my jaw clenched. My chest slowly turned to lead, and the circuits in my brain began to melt. Reason ground to a halt.

As I bumped through the doors and halls of the hospital, walls, faces, and voices swam around me. In the radiation department, I clung to Chuck as he helped me out of my damp, sticky T-shirt and sweatpants and into a gown. His comforting words bounced off me, and my replies were labored and disjointed. My gown was already damp when he wheeled me into the scan room.

"How are you, today?" the tech greeted us.

"Not so great," Chuck answered. "Could she go in feet first? She's claustrophobic."

The tech grimaced. "No, sorry. It isn't set up like that. But, don't worry. We'll get you through as quickly as possible. And I'll give you a panic ball to press if you have any trouble. Just give it a squeeze, and I'll get you out, okay?"

I nodded, and Chuck kissed the top of my head. "You can do this," he said. He helped me onto the table and tucked a warm blanket around me. The tech handed me a set of headphones.

"What kind of music would you like?"

"Christian," I said. *Maybe that will help*, I thought, somehow managing to get the headphones in place.

"I'm sorry. I don't think we have any Christian music."

Hope faded.

"Classical?" I tried again.

"That we have."

"I'll be right next door," Chuck said, kissing me again.

The tech strapped me to the table and placed an oxygen mask on my mouth and nose and a panic ball in my hands. How do they expect people *not* to panic with their arms bound to their chests?

"Are you comfortable?" he asked.

"Are you kidding?"

He smiled back. "Try to hold real still, now," he said, oblivious to the storm raging in my brain.

Right.

The oxygen from the mask couldn't make its way through the lead in my lungs. I tried to focus on the music, think of my Gracie's sweet face, my glorious Cape Cod honeymoon, anything but where I was. I tried to pray, but the words wouldn't come. The table began to move, a shroud of darkness closing over my face, and an icy wave rolled over me. *You're going to die.* My hand closed tightly around the panic ball.

"Are you all right?" the tech's voice sounded in the headphones.

"No. I have to get out. *Please.*" The table began to move back down the tube, and I tried to resist the urge to fight against my bindings as tears rolled into my ears. *Get me out!*

Chuck was quickly at my side, taking my trembling hands in his, his touch hot against my icy skin.

"They're going to have to knock me out," I told him in ragged breaths. "I just can't do it."

The tech explained how long it would take to get an anesthesiologist to come and that his next patient was waiting, but my usually compliant attitude failed me. I wasn't going back into that tube awake. Chuck wheeled my gurney into the waiting area and relief washed over me. During the next hour, the adrenaline subsided, and the lorazepam began to work.

I could feel Chuck's warm hand in mine as my heavy eyelids closed. "I think I can do it now," I told him.

"Are you sure?"

I nodded.

"Well, I'm going in with you this time, whether they like it or not."

I smiled and squeezed his hand.

When Chuck wheeled me back into the scan room, the lorazepam had wrapped my brain in a warm, thick blanket. The paralyzing terror ebbed from my flesh, and I praised God for it. Chuck remained at my side, stroking my hair and talking to me gently, and soon it was over, and I was on my way home.

But my euphoria was short-lived. I had just settled on my heating pad when the phone rang.

"Mrs. Olmstead," came the voice on the other end, "we found something at the bottom of the MRI. We need to get a lower picture."

Something? What did that mean? *Something?* I'm just celebrating my victory over the MRI. I have a plan for surviving that now—but *something?* What am I supposed to do with that?

The next morning, I was back at the hospital. My newfound weapons, lorazepam and Chuck, made another trip through what I'd come to call the "torpedo tube." bearable. I hadn't gotten both shoes back on before I received orders to report to Dr. Monroe first thing the next morning. Knowing what it took to get to the front of the line, I made a mental note to be thankful the next time it took so long to get an appointment.

Now, here I sat, looking into Dr. Monroe's troubled eyes. And here was that word—"tumor."

After what I'd already been through, I didn't even want to imagine what lay ahead.

I'm not very excited about this, Lord. Not at all; in fact, to be honest, it really stinks. But I will trust You—not that I'd know what else to do. I praise Your name.

As Dr. Monroe spoke, I thought, *Aren't I supposed to be breaking down? I must be in shock. People don't take this kind of news so calmly.* I looked to Chuck for a reality check but saw the same calm on his face I felt in my heart. I just thought, *Okay, what do we do next?*

"I'm sending you to a neurosurgeon," Dr. Monroe said.

Surgery? All I needed was surgery? Not the best news I could receive, but certainly not the worst. And Walla Walla had three of the best neurosurgeons on the West Coast. One Chuck had worked with in the hospital, and another, the father of our daughter's best friend, would waste no time telling you so. "Self-confidence," "arrogance"—call it what you will. I called it, "good for me." These men did brain surgery, for heaven's sake. My derriere wouldn't even be a challenge for them. Thank you, Lord!

"They're going to need another MRI," Dr. Monroe continued.

My heart sank.

"You'll have this one at St. Mary Medical Center. They need one with contrast fluid."

I tried to swallow the lump in my throat.

"What does that mean—exactly?"

"Well . . ." Dr. Monroe relaxed his stance. "They'll give you an IV and then introduce a contrasting dye into your veins as they take the pictures."

I looked to Chuck, as if he could somehow save me from this fate. But he just smiled reassuringly.

I sighed. "Oh, goody."

We checked into St. Mary's at 5 a.m., as ordered, and waited in a dark, empty radiation department for the staff to arrive.

"Where is everybody?" I asked.

"I don't know," said Chuck. "They told us to be here at five. Why don't you lie down, and I'll try to find someone."

I curled up on two armless chairs, breathing through the pain and nausea, praying the extra alprazolam wouldn't wear off before my scan. After a futile search, Chuck settled beside me to wait, getting up occasionally to search the deserted halls.

An hour later, I was called back for my scan. The technician's brusqueness made me wonder what I'd done to inconvenience her.

"You can wait out there," she dismissed Chuck at the door. I smiled. She didn't know my husband.

"I'll be going in with her." His tone was surprisingly pleasant, considering how long we'd been waiting. My smile grew.

"We don't allow anyone back here during testing," she said, more annoyed now at having to deal with this ignorant man.

But Chuck wheeled me on past her. "Well, there's a first time for everything," he said cheerfully. "She'd like Christian music, if you have it. If not, classical will do."

The openness of the scan room eased my anxiety some, but I began to question the cost of our victory over the tech when she wheeled in the IV equipment. It's never a good idea to antagonize someone who is accessing your veins. I shot Chuck a worried glance, and he took my shaking hand in his. I steeled myself, thankful I had big bright targets for the needle. The searing pain of the needle was soon replaced by the chill of fluid surging through my veins.

I whispered a prayer of thanks as I went into this tube feet first. With the tumor so low in my spine, the top of my head extended out of the tube. I didn't have to endure complete enclosure. My eyes were still in the tube though, so I didn't dare open them. I was visualizing the high ceilings, relaxing beneath my husband's touch, when my peace was shattered by the blare of brass in my ears.

I jumped. "Too loud!" I couldn't raise my own arms to save myself. "It's hurting my ears!" Chuck pulled my headphones off and ran back to the tech, who either hadn't heard me or didn't care. The blare, still clearly audible, subsided.

"Sorry, honey." Chuck replaced my headphones, and I tried to relax once more. Between, "don't breathe" commands and the break to release the contrast fluid into the IV line, I did my best to sleep. But time crept more slowly as the pain from lying on the hard table intensified. With the scan finally over, I would have ripped the IV needle out myself, if not for my husband.

"It's almost over, honey. You'll be home in bed soon. Your pain meds are overdue. If I'd known we'd be here so long, I'd have brought them. I'm so sorry."

After a ten-minute drive home with far too many stops, bumps, and turns, I retreated to my bed and heating pad and concentrated on relaxing every muscle to allow my pain meds to work faster.

According to Dr. Monroe, all three neurosurgeons would confer with their own radiologist over my MRI. Together, they would decide on the best course of action and which of them would perform the surgery. All I had to do now was wait for the call from the surgeons' office with my surgery time. It was all downhill from here. But, when the phone rang the next day, it wasn't the surgeons' office calling. Dr. Monroe wanted to see me again—now.

When he met us in the exam room, Dr. Monroe's expression was no less strained than it had been two days earlier. He didn't mince words this time.

None of the doctors here will do the surgery. We're sending you to Seattle Cancer Care Alliance."

Chapter 2

THE LONG JOURNEY

*C*ancer?

"You'll be in good hands," Dr. Monroe assured me. "Dr. Conrad is one of the best in his field."

I was already in the best of hands—God's hands. But, once again, His plan for my life was looking less and less like my plan. Feeling a bit like Gideon, I wondered if He'd chosen the right warrior for this particular battle.

That night, a video of Dr. Conrad on the SCCA website revealed a warm and caring physician. We knew he'd been handpicked by God. It was as if God was telling us that, like Gideon, we would not be the ones doing the fighting in this battle.

We had one weekend to prepare for my Seattle appointment. Chuck rushed to complete service calls and bids, rising early and working late Friday and Saturday. In his "spare time" he organized my appointment times, made hotel reservations, shuttled busy kids, and arranged for their care in our absence. My uselessness weighed heavily on me, as did the heartache of leaving my kids, not knowing when—or if—I'd see them again. Rachel was 15, Aaron, 13, Daniel, 11, and Gracie, only 3. She'd been my appendage from conception. Would she understand I wasn't leaving her by choice? Would she understand if I didn't come back?

On Monday, October 5th, Chuck worked at a breakneck pace, making a last-minute delivery, collecting all of my medical records from doctors and hospitals, lobbying for stronger pain medication, gathering supplies, and packing for both of us.

At 5:30 p.m. I put on my best "brave" smile as we gathered in the driveway. I held each of my kids long and hard, and they didn't resist.

Feeling me tremble beneath my thick coat, Rachel spoke softly in my ear. "You're going to be all right, Mama."

I smiled and kissed her. "I love you, Gooseberries." I kissed each one of them again. "I love you very much."

"We love you, too, Mother Gooseberry," they chorused.

"We'd better get going, hon," Chuck said, helping me into the Tahoe.

"Be good," I called to the kids as Chuck tucked the blankets around me in my back-seat nest. "I love you!"

The door closed between us, and my tears began to flow. I was grateful to be lying down so the kids couldn't see their mother crumble. It was all too real now. No longer just words and plans and "ifs." The five-hour drive to Seattle was only the beginning of our journey, and we had no idea where it would lead. But God wasn't just waiting at our destination, He was right in the back seat with me. That much we did know.

I lay as still as possible, dreading each turn of the wheel and adjustment in speed that pushed and pulled at my aching body. Nerves, guilt, pain, and medication ripped at my stomach, and the nausea patch behind my ear was losing its battle. As if that weren't enough, the tumor compressed my colon and bladder, giving the constant sensation of needing to relieve myself. The delicate balance between pain and nausea control was disrupted by frequent stops, Chuck helping me into public restrooms, holding me while I vomited, preparing hot enemas for my pain, and just keeping me upright. It's funny how insignificant etiquette can be sometimes.

Time slowed to a crawl as the effects of my medication ebbed. The pull of inertia roused me from precious sleep as the Tahoe came to a stop once more.

"Another rest stop so soon?"

Chuck looked back. "No. Sorry, honey. There's an accident up ahead."

I felt a rush of adrenaline. How long will we be stuck here? What if I need a restroom? I repositioned myself on my pillows, my hip throbbing. "Is it time for my meds?"

He reached back for my hand. "Just forty-five minutes, honey. Try to go back to sleep."

I closed my eyes and prayed until sleep returned. Farther down the road, another car accident delayed us further. With two hours added to our trip, Chuck was forced to stop for a power nap to avoid falling asleep at the wheel and becoming a third accident.

We rolled into our hotel at 1 a.m.—in spite of a homicidal GPS telling us to, "Turn left, here," into brick walls and nonexistent streets. With Chuck bearing most of my weight, on top of his own fatigue, it was a slow trek to our seventh-floor room.

"Why didn't I think to rent a wheelchair?" Chuck puffed.

"Seriously? I think you had enough on your plate. I should have thought of it."

He opened the door to our room, and my gaze fell instantly on a big Jacuzzi tub in the far corner.

"Surprise!" Chuck sang.

My eyes began to well. "Oh, honey—can we afford this?"

He wrapped his arms around me and kissed my forehead. "Anything for you, babe. Besides, after that drive, I could use a hot soak myself."

He filled the tub and got me safely situated before going back for our luggage. "Thank you, Jesus," I said as the soothing heat penetrated my throbbing muscles and bones. It wasn't long before my body was weighted with sleep and my eyelids refused to stay open. Reluctantly, I traded my warm sanctuary for bed. I thought I could sleep for days, but the wee hours were punctuated by the alarm clock signaling medication times, and at 6:15 it was time to rise and—well, rise. I tried to choke down the oatmeal and mint tea Chuck brought up from the buffet, but nausea and nerves won out. I did not want to be there. I should have been home, planning a birthday party, baking a cake, decorating the house . . . but here I was stepping back into the elevator, off to meet another fate.

My chest tightened in the dark, low-ceilinged parking garage. I rolled down my window and closed my eyes until I felt the warmth of the sun on my face. All too soon we were swallowed up by another "cave" beneath Seattle Cancer Care Alliance.

From the closeness of the garage to the confinement of the elevators, I stifled the urge to cry, or vomit, or both. The dark cloud lifted when the elevator opened to the third-floor lobby, large and bright in shades of aqua and tan. Couches and recliners faced floor-to-ceiling windows. Beyond the windows, brightly colored sails danced on the sparkling water of Lake Union.

A smiling receptionist handed me a stack of paperwork to complete while we waited, and I looked from the stack to Chuck. We both laughed. I had a hard time remembering what day it was, and they wanted my entire medical history? We found a couple recliners and began working our way through the stack, giggling most of the time—me at the difficulty of the questions, and Chuck at my unconventional answers. But the laughter did little to calm my quavering flesh.

At 10 a.m. they called me back. The nurse took the unfinished stack from Chuck so he could help me walk. As we slowly made our way, a beautiful, well-dressed young woman passed us, smiling brightly in spite of the sequined cap covering her baldness. My gaze moved across the room, seeing for the first time the other souls populating the reception area. An elderly man, shrunken and bent, his face heavy with fatigue. Beside him, sat his companion, speaking words of encouragement. A middle-aged couple sat side-by-side, he flipping silently through a magazine, and she staring blankly out the window. Misery, annoyance, resignation, peace—it was all there on the third floor.

The nurse ushered us into the exam room, closing the door behind her. "Have you heard about our patient blog?"

"No." Chuck helped me onto the exam table.

"You can create your own blog at CarePages to keep friends and family informed of your treatment. People can leave messages for you, and you can meet and talk to other patients all over the world. It's a great support network."

"Oh!" My husband, an electronic guru, brightened. "That'll make things easier. Thank you."

"No problem. Now, you'll be getting a lot of information today—too much to take in at once." She handed him a tape recorder. "You'll need this." Chuck's brightness dimmed, and we exchanged questioning looks. "The doctor shouldn't be too long, now." She smiled warmly and left us alone.

"Well, I guess we'd better finish this," Chuck said, waving the stack of papers at me. The questions were no easier to answer, but somehow they'd lost their humor.

"Rebecca Jo . . ." Chuck waited until I made eye contact before going on. "I'm not going anywhere. No matter what."

There was a knock at the door, and Dr. Conrad and his team crowded into the room. I wondered if they had stopped outside to put on their game faces. Not a hint of emotion escaped their stony expressions as Dr. Conrad delivered my prognosis. Was this the same man we'd seen on the video? He explained that at the time of my last MRI, there were three masses growing out of my sacral nerve root. He was fairly confident the largest was a nerve sheath sarcoma, a rare and aggressive cancer.

"There's a small chance we'll obtain a preliminary diagnosis of benign," he said, "but we won't know for at least a week."

Dr. Conrad described the treatment plans for each scenario, much like an auto mechanic explaining the options for repairing a transmission. "If the biopsy comes back benign, I'll remove it surgically. If it's malignant, you'll have to move to Seattle for at least eight months."

I looked at Chuck. *Move?* The possibility of losing our home and business and uprooting our kids had never occurred to me.

"You'll have to undergo chemotherapy for a few months to shrink the tumor before I can remove it," Dr. Conrad continued. "We'll follow surgery up with radiation to destroy any remaining cancer cells. In either case, I'll have to remove the affected nerves. This will cause paralysis from the waist down on your right side. You'll lose motor skills and bladder and bowel function. To what extent, I can't be sure. You'll most likely need urostomy and colostomy bags, but there is a possibility the remaining nerves will take over some bladder and bowel functions. Only time will tell."

As I tried to envision the worst-case scenario, my heart was breaking for Chuck. He had watched his first wife of twenty-five years endure dialysis, two kidney transplants, and numerous surgeries as diabetes slowly stole her from him. What must this be doing to him? How could I hold him to the promise he had just made? I looked at his face for some sign of the disappointment I had caused him. He just smiled back at me.

"I want you to check into the University of Washington Medical Center right away," Dr. Conrad said as his team filed out. "We'll make the arrangements and get your scans set up. See you soon."

Alone once more, I looked at my quiet husband and forced a grin. "Did you get all that?"

"Huh?"

I nodded toward the tape recorder still in his hands. Chuck looked down at it in surprise. He hadn't even turned it on.

My gaze dropped, and I breathed a heavy sigh. "I'm sorry."

"What for? I'm the one who forgot to turn it on."

"You know what I mean."

"Hey." He came to my side and took my hand. "I meant what I said. I'm not going anywhere. God is in control. He won't give us anything we can't handle—together."

I studied my husband's' determined blue eyes, and I knew he was right.

*C*huck typed the address of the medical center into the GPS. *"Looks like it's pretty close." When I didn't reply, he went on. "First class all the way, huh? Valet parking and all. I didn't even know hospitals had valet parking."*

Instinctively I reached for the hand of my best friend, resting on the console between us. For six short years, I'd held that hand. Its warmth and constancy comforted me. I didn't want to think about letting it go now.

In minutes, we were pulling into the hospital. Chuck turned the Tahoe over to the valet, helped me into a waiting wheelchair, and whisked me off. Soon I was tucked into bed. I felt as if I'd wrestled a grizzly. I was tired and heavy, and I hurt all over.

"Get some rest, honey," Chuck said. "I'll take care of the paperwork."

I smiled at this. "You're the only one who knows the answers anyway." His laugh warmed me as I dissolved into the pillows, pain meds, and a giant, water-filled heating pad.

Lord, I don't know what You're doing, but I'm going to trust You.

Beside me, the clicking of my laptop began to fade. "What do you want to call your CarePage, honey?" My husband's voice came on a foggy wave.

I chuckled. "What else? 'Watch God Work.'"

Chapter 3

HIDE AND SEEK

CAT Scan
Tuesday, October 6, 2009
Posted by Chuck

Rebecca's CAT only took about 10 minutes from start to finish. The MRIs took almost an hour. The CAT machine has a larger opening as well, so it's not as stressful for her. She's back in her room and ready for some sleep. She had to drink a solution for the scan that has her stomach upset. Hopefully, that will go away soon.

Biopsy Scheduled for Thursday
Wednesday, October 7, 2009
Posted by Chuck

Dr. Conrad's orthopedic fellow doctor woke Rebecca up this morning. She went over what was going to happen during the biopsy on Thursday. They'll make a small incision in her lower back. This will give better access to the tumor. Then they'll use a needle to get a sample. The doctor didn't know what time the surgery was scheduled. Most likely late in the day. Rebecca will be all the way out, which made her feel better.

Thursday Morning
Thursday, October 8, 2009
Posted by Chuck

The same doctor as yesterday came in at 5:45 a.m. to wake Rebecca up. A quick check, and everything is ready to go.

Rebecca's in more pain today. They should be bringing more medicine soon. God is in control, and we pray for His work to be done. May He bless each and every one of you.

Will Work, Beg, or Borrow for CHOCOLATE!
Thursday, October 8, 2009
Posted by Chuck

Rebecca is very hungry; nothing to eat for 12 hours. She will do just about anything for chocolate. Her pain is rising, but she just received more pain meds. Waiting for them to kick in. Hopefully, they'll be coming to get her soon for surgery.

She's looking forward to going home to a couple freezers full of new beef. If Rachel isn't eating it all—at least not all of the steaks. Rebecca's brother, Howard, picked it up for us. Thanks, Howard.

Some more flowers came a little while ago. They're beautiful. Thank you, Judy and Jesse. Everyone, thank you so much for all of the support, prayers, and messages on this site. Also, thank you, everyone, for looking after our kids.

We love you all,

God bless.

Away to Surgery
Thursday, October 8, 2009
Posted by Chuck

Rebecca is going down for surgery. It's 2:30 p.m., and the surgery was scheduled for 11:40 a.m.

The kids called. Rebecca was able to talk to them before surgery. My niece, Shawna, called at lunchtime with Gracie laughing in the background. Rebecca loves hearing her children's voices. Praise the Lord. His timing is always the best.

I laid in pre-op, beneath an inflated heating blanket, shuddering violently. I was scared. Dr. Conrad stepped in to check on me, and Chuck asked him to pray with us. After the prayer, the doctor looked down at me with a smile.

"Are you nervous?" he asked.

I nodded.

He bent down and gently kissed my forehead. "Don't be," he said with a grin. "I'm the best there is."

I don't think Dr. Conrad makes a habit of kissing his patients. In fact, it probably surprised him as much as it did me. I do believe that, at that moment, my Heavenly Father used a receptive messenger to let His child know everything was going to be all right.

Of course, God has a sense of humor, too. I would awaken from surgery to find the "small incision" for the biopsy measured nine inches down my backside and that an inch of my tailbone was missing!

Praise God Our Lord
Thursday, October 8, 2009
Posted by Chuck

I just talked with Dr. Conrad. The surgery is over. He doesn't think Rebecca has a tumor. He found a blood clot. We'll know in five to seven days, when the tests come back. Praise God! Dr. Conrad said blood clots can show up as tumors. I'll be able to see Rebecca in an hour or two.

Thanks, everyone, for your prayers. God is great, and we need to trust in Him and praise Him in all things!

Back in Her Room
Thursday, October 8, 2009
Posted by Chuck

Rebecca just got back to her room. She's a little sick to her stomach, and she hurts from the surgery. She's praising God for the news about the tumor.

They've given her a "happy pain pump." She can't wait to talk to everyone tomorrow. Praise the Creator of everything, our Lord and God.

God bless, and we love you.

Praise God Our Lord—Update
Thursday, October 8, 2009
Posted by Chuck

Today a miracle of God happened; He changed a tumor coming out of a nerve into a blood clot. I know what you are thinking: yeah, sure, that didn't happen. The doctor just made a mistake. Well, I'm here to tell you it is a miracle!

Two MRIs at WWGH showed a tumor. This was read by the radiologist at WWGH. Dr. Monroe sent the scans to Dr. Camp and his team. Three surgeons and their radiologist saw a tumor and ordered another MRI, this one using contrasting dye to give a better picture of the tumor. This was again read by Dr. Camp's team, and they decided it was too difficult for them to tackle and sent us to Dr. Conrad at SCCA.

A CAT scan was done here at the UW with contrast that showed a tumor, read by a different radiologist and Dr. Conrad's team. Everyone who looked at these films saw a tumor! If all these experts saw a tumor, it must have been a tumor. If it sounds like a duck, quacks like a duck, and looks like a duck, it's a duck!

Then what happened? God happened. In His grace, He decided to change this tumor into a blood clot. Why did He do this? I can't say for sure.

I do know a lot of people have been praying for Rebecca. This glorifies God. I also know both Rebecca and I have been praising God for this tumor. We didn't know how He was going to use this for His glory, but we knew He would use it. I praise You, my Lord and God. May the name of the Lord be shouted loud and clear from the highest mountaintops for all mankind to hear!

Rebecca and I asked for healing, but most of all, we asked that God's glory would shine, and His will be done. We also asked for the courage and strength to praise Him in all things, even if the worst happened.

Did the worst happen? No. Did the best that Dr. Conrad say would happen, happen? No. What happened was not something I expected. It was something that only happens to other people. You read about them or see a movie made about them, but not you. But it did, God healed my wife today. He blessed me six years ago when I married Rebecca, and He has blessed me again today.

Praises be to God the Father, and His Son, Jesus Christ, in whom all things are done, and to the Holy Spirit. Amen!

Friday's Schedule
Friday, October 9, 2009
Posted by Chuck

Today's goal: PAIN control!!!

Dr. Conrad's team was just in to see Rebecca. We won't see Dr. Conrad today. Rebecca is in a lot of pain. Most of it from the surgery. During surgery, they took a sample of bone and some of the blood clot and sent it for testing. The doctors were very surprised at not finding a tumor. God wasn't.

Rebecca has two drain tubes in her back that are also causing pain. They should come out in a couple of days.

Praise our Lord and God!

She'll also have an MRI today. Keep us in your prayers.

MRI Is over for the Day
Friday, October 9, 2009
Posted by Chuck

Rebecca just finished her MRI. I guess the doctors are trying to find the tumor that isn't there anymore. Her pain is better than this morning. She's going to eat some soup for lunch.

Thank you for your prayers.

Chuck

As happy as I was about the news, I was overjoyed when Chuck told me he was going to bring the kids for a weekend visit. I hadn't even been away a week, but I missed them terribly. Then reality struck. Having my kids with me, meant Chuck being gone.

"It'll only be a day," he assured me. When you're confined to bed, a day can feel like a year. The thought filled me with dread, but I decided having my kids with me was worth it. What could happen in one day?

It didn't take long to find out.

A few hours after Chuck left, my pain management specialist stepped into my room. He introduced himself and then stood at the foot of my bed, silently reviewing my chart. He flashed me a suspicious glance before returning to my chart.

"This can't be right," he said. "No one needs this much pain medication."

I was confused.

He turned an intent gaze on me. "Do you have a history of narcotic use?"

Confusion gave way to shock. "No."

I had no idea of the doses I was taking, only that it was what I needed to endure the pain. "My pain has been increasing every day since September." But the doctor's eyes narrowed. He shook his head and grunted.

"No one needs this much pain medication." He slapped my chart shut and left me alone.

Tears spilled from my eyes. I was mortified. A doctor, who was supposed to care for me, didn't believe me. I may as well have been five years old again—and he may as well have been my mother.

Then came a terrifying thought—this man had the power to take away the only relief I had. I wiped my eyes and reached for the phone. I had to talk to Chuck.

"Okay, honey. Calm down. I'm just an hour from home. I'll call your nurse as soon as I get there. I'll take care of it, I promise. I won't let them take your medication away. Try to get some rest, and I'll call you as soon as I talk to them."

I had no doubt my knight would come to my aid. He would soon be back at my side with our kids, and all would be well. Peace filled me, and I said a prayer of thanks. Now I could rest. Or so I thought

MRI Shows Mass Is Still There
Saturday, October 10, 2009
Posted by Chuck

We will praise our Lord and God in all things! Yes, including this news. He has a plan. We just don't know what it is. Yet. We know we are loved by our God, and He will not give us anything we can't handle!

I just talked with Rebecca. Dr. Conrad's team came in and told her the MRI still shows the mass. They're not sure why they didn't see it during surgery, except it's in a very well-protected part of her body. This makes it very difficult to get to. They'll be doing the PET test on Monday.

Definition: Positron Emission Tomography, also called PET imaging or a PET scan, is a type of nuclear medicine imaging.

I'll be heading back to Seattle with the kids for the weekend and bringing them home on Monday. Keep us in your prayers, and special prayers for Rebecca as she is by herself for most of today.

Thank you, Lord, for being with Rebecca as her family is traveling to be with her. In Your Son's name, Jesus Christ, I praise You. Amen.

Blessings to everyone.

Chapter 4

GOD'S GRACE IS
SUFFICIENT

Back in Seattle
Saturday, October 10, 2009
Posted by Chuck

Hello, everyone. We're back in Seattle. Rachel gave me a break by driving all the way to the hospital. She's growing up so fast.

Rebecca is off the pain pump and back on tablet medicine. This is letting her get more sleep. She's having a nice visit with all the kids. The Internet connection isn't working in her room, so I had to find a hot spot to send this update and receive your messages.

Bless each of you for your support. It means so much to us. I think Rebecca will feel much better tomorrow after a restful sleep.

*I*t's hard to believe sometimes that God is concerned with the mundane details of our lives. I mean, He is God. He has a lot on His plate. Yet, He continued to remind us that where His kids are concerned, no detail is beneath Him.

I needed to see my kids, and Chuck knew it. But, neither of us knew that the weekend he had chosen to bring them for a visit, the Washington Huskies were playing at Husky Stadium. Traffic was a nightmare, and parking was practically nonexistent. Chuck was praying for a room as he pulled into the first hotel. Having four kids along, he was kicking himself for not calling ahead. It did not look good. The clerk was quick to tell him how lucky he was. They had the last room available in the area—and it was big enough for all five of them. As Chuck relayed the story in amazement, we both knew luck had nothing to do with it.

With my kids gathered around my bedside, I felt I could finally breathe again. I put all my energy into smiling through the fog of medication. I greedily hugged each of them and tried to focus on each card they handed me. I so wanted to set their minds at ease, but I could see the truth in their young, worried eyes. I wasn't fooling any of them. Three-year-old Gracie, desperate for Mommy, clawed at the bed until Chuck lifted her up for a snuggle. This appeased her only a moment. There were far too many things on my bed to look at and touch, and her weight and wiggles exhausted me. Chuck took her down the hall to visit the fish tank while I talked with our older kids. I wanted to hold on to every detail, their faces, their voices . . . but even this precious time would soon fade into oblivion, until I found their cards a year later.

Quick Turnaround
Sunday, October 11, 2009
Posted by Chuck

I brought the kids back to Walla Walla today. Gracie was starting to get a cold, so we came home early. She can't be around her mom with a cold.

Rebecca has a PET test at 7:30 tomorrow morning. I'm headed back tonight, so I can be there for the test.

Rachel came through and let me sleep coming home. Yes, she drove to Seattle and back. No problems.

More updates tomorrow. Thank you for your prayers.

PET Test Today
Monday, October 12, 2009
Posted by Chuck

I made it back to Seattle at 1:45 a.m. Rebecca didn't sleep much. She was worried about the test, and she's still in a lot of pain.

They came in at 7:30 and took her to the PET test. They injected radioactive glucose for this test, and then she had to wait about an hour and a half before they moved her to the PET machine; it looks like a CT scanner. This test took about an hour and 15 minutes. Set-up time added 30 minutes on top of this. Rebecca's pain got so bad lying on the hard surface, her nurse had to come down from 6 SE (Rebecca's wing) and give her more pain meds to get her through the test. We'll get the results tomorrow morning.

Internet is back up and working. Shawna, sent more pictures of Gracie; Rebecca loves to see pictures of the children. Thank you so much, Shawna!

I've read Rebecca all of the postings she hadn't seen, and it lifted her spirits.

Yesterday, she had PT (physical therapy) and walked out of her room and down the hallway about 80 feet, then back to her bed. She'll be having both PT and OT (occupational therapy) every day.

Thank you so much for your messages and prayers.

New Pain Meds
Monday, October 12, 2009
Posted by Chuck

Rebecca had a shower and is on new pain medication. It's making a big difference. Her pain level has gone from an eight down to a two. Praise the Lord our God! She's had a good dinner and is missing everyone. She talked on the phone with all of the kids, and they are fine. We're looking forward to being home with everyone again. I pray we have a game plan tomorrow, when the test results come in.

May God bless you all. Your prayers are felt.
Our love for you all.

Waiting for PET Results
Tuesday, October 13, 2009
Posted by Chuck

Rebecca had a very good night. She wants to go for a walk around the hospital, maybe get some fresh air.

One of the doctors was in this morning and changed the dressing from the biopsy, which is healing very well. She said the PET test results are not in yet, but we should hear later today. Then they'll have a game plan for us.

Rebecca says hi to everyone, and she misses you all.

God bless you all. I'll update you on the PET results as soon as we get them.

Up and About
Tuesday, October 13, 2009
Posted by Chuck

Rebecca just finished her physical therapy. She did very well! She walked all the way around the unit, about 125 yards, and up and down five stairs. She stopped to look at a quilt hanging on the wall by the nurses' station. She also saw the fish tank Gracie had told her about when she was visiting last weekend.

Rebecca is giving me a bad time and joking with the hospital staff. It's good to see her feel so much better.

May the grace of God fill your lives. Thank you for all of your support.

"Be still and know that I Am God!"

I'm Finally Getting to Post a Note!
Wednesday, October 14, 2009

Unfortunately, some kind of gremlin got into my computer and is messing up my keyboard. It's putting letters there that I'm not wanting to type. It's possible it could be the elephant tranquilizers they're giving me. Personally, I'm blaming the gremlin. I just want you to know what a blessing you are to me and my family—and I know I'll be home any minute.

Thank you, love and blessings,

Rebecca

Who Carries You?
Wednesday, October 14, 2009
Posted by Chuck

Dr. Conrad's intern came in and said the PET results are back and show the mass is active. Before we can know what to do next, we'll need the pathology report. This should be by Friday. It's a frozen sample and takes longer to get back. This will give the best results.

We do know God has put us here for His glory. That may show up as prayer and praise coming from all over the world, or it might be to witness here in the hospital with the staff who are taking care of Rebecca. I'm not sure we'll ever know in this life what His plan is. I know we will when we face our Savior. Until that day, we must trust in Him in all things and praise in all things.

We are seeing God show up in the care of our family. Rachel, Aaron, and Daniel are being cared for by my mom and dad, and Gracie is being cared for by Shawna and her husband, David. I thank God they are able to do this for our family. Rebecca and I are being cared for with all of the prayers and praises from family and friends. We are in the loving hands of Jesus Christ. When we are not strong enough to go forward, He is carrying us.

Rebecca is such an example of the grace and love of Jesus to me. She keeps me centered and focused on what's truly important. It's not the things we own or the house we have, but the peace of Jesus that matters.

I've walked this path before. That time, I was in denial of my need for Jesus. I could do it on my own; who needs God? As I look back now, I see all of the times He carried me. This time I'm able to truly feel His love and the calm in my soul. This can only come from the Holy Spirit. This isn't a normal human feeling. It's supernatural.

In closing, our Lord God is worthy of all of our praise! I pray you are blessed by your faith in our Lord Jesus Christ.

Praise the Lord! Dressing Is Gone!
Thursday, October 15, 2009
Posted by Chuck

Dr. Conrad's intern came in this morning and removed all of the dressings from Rebecca's biopsy incision. The incision is itchy, so this made Rebecca very happy. The pain medicine has been increased and is helping her rest better. She'll have more physical therapy today, and she's looking forward to it.

The biopsy pathology isn't back yet. Hopefully, tomorrow we'll have a game plan. Will Rebecca be starting on chemotherapy? Will we be able to do this in Walla Walla, or will Rebecca need to stay in Seattle? With all of these unanswered questions, I do know we are in the good hands of Jesus Christ.

I hope everyone has a great day. Look out—you may have a God sighting, or better yet, be part of a God sighting. Praise the Lord.

Thank you, and God bless you all.

I could see in Chuck's face that something was troubling him.

"Please don't worry, honey," I told him. "It's going to be all right."

"I know it is." He rose from his chair and took my hand in his. "I have to go back home," he said. "I can't keep the business going from here, and that's all we have."

I knew he was right, but that was the last thing I wanted to hear. We didn't know yet what my future held, and I couldn't bear the thought of being there all alone. Especially after what had happened the last time. Not that I doubted God's presence or ability, but in my physically and mentally diminished capacity, Chuck embodied the strength and knowledge I lacked. He was my life raft in this turbulent sea. How would I stay afloat without him?

Fear crept over my flesh, but before it had a chance to settle, my mind was filled with the voice of God.

You're going with him.

Hallelujah! Hallelujah!
Thursday, October 15, 2009

How does that little ditty by Handel go? . . . Oh, yeah . . . Hallelujah! Hallelujah!

My surgical team just left. They came to let me know I can go home tomorrow with Chuck!

Dr. Conrad is still convinced it's just a blood clot, though the biopsy will reveal all next week. We'll be returning to Seattle on October 27th to go over everything, including a game plan.

Praise His Name, all ye people, shout to the Lord with a voice of triumph!

I love my medical team! I love you all! But the King of Kings is the love of my life!

Isaiah 45:5–7: *"I am the Lord, and there is none else, there is no God beside me: I girded thee, though thou hast not known me: That they may know from the rising of the sun, and from the west, that there is none beside me. I am the Lord, and there is none else. I form the light, and create darkness: I make peace, and create evil: I the Lord do all these things" (KJV).* Amen!

I know this journey isn't over yet, but I know who is at the wheel. And He loves me very much, as He does all of you.

God is good!

I can't wait to see you all again. Please pray for safe and comfortable travel. God bless you!

Chapter 5

HOME SWEET HOME

Home Sweet Home
Saturday, October 17, 2009

Hello Everyone,

As thrilled as I am to be home, I've learned that merely being here doesn't constitute being well.

It was a difficult trip for us, the nausea, the inability to get comfortable, and, of course, the strange looks we got in the public restrooms since I'm not quite independent yet. But I was able to get some sleep, which helped immensely.

Our wonderful children, with help from some very special angels (who are excellent cooks, by the way), were waiting with a beautiful candlelight dinner complete with purple roses.

However, once the pain meds wore off, reality came into sharp focus. It takes two people to get me up and down the stairs (twenty steps to be exact), so I've decided my room is just fine for now. I'm so happy we chose a king-sized bed. Believe it or not, it's quite comfy, with four kids sprawling with pillows, blankets . . . and Mom and Dad. Ahhh, this is the life.

I think the stress is finally catching up with Chuck. He may be getting a cold. Gracie, too. So, please keep them in your prayers.

If there's anyone in Walla Walla who has some home-care equipment not currently in use, such as a walker, bath bench, wheelchair, etc., I'd be very grateful for the short-term loan of such things. Also, for any helpful hints, such as organizing medicine, or just getting around, and pain control.

God bless you all for your prayers, encouragement, meals, help with kids, and, of course, the chocolate.

Love and blessings,

Rebecca

y husband is a very analytical man with an affinity for spreadsheets. When he took over the administration of my medication, the first thing he did was create a color-coded schedule. When he presented me with his masterpiece, my jaw dropped. My regimen included a short-term and long-term oxymorphone, a pain patch, an anti-anxiety medication, ibuprofen, acetaminophen, and three anti-nausea medications. No wonder the pain specialist thought I was an addict. I was taking something every two to three hours.

Chuck also became my taskmaster, forcing me out of bed for "therapeutic" walks around the house. But, when I wasn't hobbling around like a drunken duck, pain kept me tied to my bed. I snuggled with Gracie, watching movies that to me seemed freakishly psychedelic, trying to sleep, and praying tomorrow would be better. But each day there was one beautiful time on Chuck's spreadsheet when all of my medications coincided. I lived for that time—two whole hours when pain loosened its grip just enough for me to remember why I wanted to live.

Monday
Monday, October 19, 2009
Posted by Chuck

We haven't had any update from the doctor yet, and we're still waiting for the appointment time for October 27th. But she's doing some physical therapy, walking down the hall, and leg stretches. The main challenge has been pain control.

I've been able to get back to our business for the first time in over two weeks. Your prayers for God's provision for our business would be appreciated.

May God bless you and your families.

Love,

Chuck and Rebecca

Better All the Time
Wednesday, October 21, 2009

Good morning!

God is amazing! I actually slept through one of my medication times this morning! And it wasn't pain that woke me, but the realization that I'd forgotten something. I had a very comfortable day yesterday, which was nice, but I just feel like sleeping all the time. I've been told on many occasions that's exactly what I need, so I'm trying not to feel guilty. I've learned that God is like a driving instructor with the controls on His side of the car. If He says, "Slow down," and I don't respond, He'll do it for me. How awesome to be loved like that!

Love and blessings,

Rebecca

Appointment Time Is Set
Thursday, October 22, 2009
Posted by Chuck

We just received the appointment time for Rebecca at SCCA with Dr. Conrad. It's on Tuesday, October 27, 2009, at 10:45 a.m. We'll be going to Seattle on Monday, and hopefully will be back home late on Tuesday.

Rebecca's pain has come way down. She's stopped her pain patch and is cutting back on the long-term pain pills. She's going to try and use only the short-term pain pills. Two of these are over-the-counter. We've been very blessed by this reduction in pain.

God is great. May He bless every one of you.

We'd like to thank all who continue to pray for us. We feel your prayers and are being blessed by you.

Chuck and Rebecca

Getting Ready to Go Back to Seattle
Sunday, October 25, 2009
Posted by Chuck

Please pray for our travel to Seattle. May it be nausea-free, pain-controlled, safe, and only for two days—and most of all, good news. Also, keeping our kids safe, and my mom and dad's safe travel between LaCrosse, Washington, and Walla Walla to watch our kids.

Gracie's having a hard time with us leaving this time, so we'd like special prayer for her to not miss Mom and Dad too much.

Vicki, thank you for being the kids' taxi service all week, checking on Rebecca every day, and for the special treats you brought.

Rebecca has stopped all of her long-term pain medicine—a patch and tablets three times a day. It took a couple of days for the long-term meds to get out of her system. Now she's only on the short-acting pain tablets. She can take one to four tablets every three hours. She has been taking about two tablets every three hours today.

Rebecca was able to make it downstairs last night for our weekly family pizza and movie night. We had a fire in the fireplace, and she enjoyed this time with our kids very much. She came downstairs again, today. I built another fire, and her brother, Howard, and his wife, Linda, came over for a visit. It was good to see them.

Rebecca did several trips around the downstairs with her walker, and she did great. Between walker "races," we watched four episodes of the '60s TV show, *The Invaders*. I also did something I've never done for anyone in my life! I made Rebecca chocolate tapioca. I can't stand tapioca, so this was a big deal for me—it must be true love!

It was good to be back at church tonight, even though Rebecca couldn't go. I'd like to thank everyone who has brought meals, and for your prayers.

Tonight, Helen H. stopped by with a loaner wheelchair. This will make the trip to Seattle much easier on Rebecca, when we need to stop. Rebecca enjoyed Helen's visit very much. Helen, thank you for the wheelchair and for praying with us.

Most of all we thank our Lord and God, Jesus Christ, for in Him all things are done. May you come to know the love of Jesus and the comfort He brings to your soul. May God's full blessing fall down upon you all.

Travel Day
Monday, October 26, 2009

Well, today's the day! I'm feeling much better overall. It seems getting up and around actually reduces the pain, but I have to be careful not to overdo, or the opposite happens.

We'll be leaving for Seattle this afternoon after celebrating Aaron's 14th birthday at his school and taking Gracie to her favorite cousin, Shawna's. This is the part I hate—leaving my babies. Please pray for our separation anxiety. And safe travel with little or no pain. Most of all, we're believing in God for a clean bill of health from the doctor.

God has been so good to me through this. It's not always easy to see through the medication and pain, but, with Chuck's help, I can see now just how awesomely God has worked in the whole journey.

One of the biggest blessings, I have to say, has been my knight in shining armor, Chuck. I couldn't have asked for a better husband to help me through this. And the rest of our family and friends have really shown me who Jesus is. Thank you all, so much.

Well, we'll talk to you from Seattle.

Love and blessings,

Rebecca

On our initial trip to SCCA, I went straight from the exam room to the hospital for a thirteen-day stay. Now we were returning for the results of my biopsy, and as we prepared for this trip, my anxiety rose.

What if I was admitted for surgery right away again? I couldn't stand the thought of another long separation from my kids. I needed more time.

God knew the outcome of this trip—of this whole journey, and I trusted His will. But, the holidays and the rest of the kids' birthdays were only months away. I wanted to be there for them. I wanted to make more memories with my children, in case . . .

God had so graciously granted my last request—would He grant me one more?

Chapter 6

THE GOOD NEWS, AND
THE BAD NEWS

We Are Back in Seattle
Monday, October 26, 2009
Posted by Chuck

We're in Seattle. It was a very rainy drive over Snoqualmie Pass, but we were ahead of the snow. Rebecca was able to sleep most of the way. What a blessing from our Lord and God.

Rebecca is talking to the kids. They're having a good time with their grandpa, my dad. Hopefully, we'll be able to post the results tomorrow before we leave Seattle. You can't tell how I want tomorrow to go, can you?

May God bless everyone, and thank you for your prayers.

Love from,

Chuck and Rebecca

Headed for the Doctor
Tuesday, October 27, 2009
Posted by Chuck

Rebecca had a good night's sleep. We've had breakfast and are heading for our appointment with Dr. Conrad. We're praying for good news. But whatever the news, God already knows what's going to happen. It's all part of His design. We praise Him in all things.

May God's blessings go to all of you.

*E*very muscle tensed as Dr. Conrad and his team came into the exam room.

"So," he said, "do you want the good news first or the bad news?"

Then, seeing the anxious look I shot my husband, he continued. "The good news is it looks like you have a low-grade tumor."

"What does that mean?" I asked.

"That means it's not very aggressive. It's slow-growing. And I'll be able to get it all in surgery. The bad news is, I won't be able to operate for six weeks."

I hadn't realized I was holding my breath until I felt myself exhale. I beamed at Chuck, and he smiled back.

"So, what's the bad news?" Chuck asked.

I was going back home. God had answered one more prayer.

The Results Are In
Tuesday, October 27, 2009
Posted by Chuck

Praise our Lord God, for in His will all things are for His glory! Yes, all things, even when the news is not everything we were hoping for.

We met with Dr. Conrad this morning, and Rebecca has a low-grade peripheral nerve sheath tumor. He believes it to be a low-grade cancer but said the final pathology would tell us for sure. He said this was very good news. No radiation or chemotherapy will be needed.

He'll be doing the surgery to remove the tumor in six weeks. This is the soonest he can get her on the schedule. She'll be in the hospital for about a week after surgery. We'll come back to Seattle on a Monday and see Dr. Conrad and his team on Tuesday. Then Rebecca will have another MRI, and surgery will be on Thursday.

We're still praying for God to remove this tumor before we come back. If not, then to guide the doctors, as they are His instruments in Rebecca's healing. However God decides to heal Rebecca, we are blessed by our Lord, Jesus Christ, in every part of our lives. We all know what He did in six days. Can you imagine what He can do in six weeks? We need to pray, praise, and hold on to Him.

Rebecca is soooo glad the stitches are out!

We'll be heading back to Walla Walla this afternoon. Please keep us in your prayers.

With love and blessings,

Chuck and Rebecca

No Place Like Home
Wednesday, October 28, 2009

Good Morning Everyone,

It's so good to be home again with my kids. Our family has been so gracious in the love they've shown the kids. They've truly made some forever memories.

Even though waiting six weeks for surgery will mean six more weeks of dealing with the pain, it's six weeks of being with my kids, so I don't mind. I also truly believe God will do some amazing things in the coming six weeks.

The trip home was as good as could be expected. Being in the same position for long periods of time makes the pain worse, so traveling and sleeping nights aren't my favorite things.

Right now, Gracie and I are enjoying a morning together alone. The older kids are at school, and (praise the Lord!) Chuck is on a job. Gracie has been talking about visiting her friend, so I don't know how much longer I'll have her. I can't really keep up with her anyway, but it's nice to have the company.

We've decided to come at the next six weeks from a prayer and nutritional position, so we ask for your continued prayers and any cancer-related diet information you can share.

I can't stress enough how much all of you have meant to us through this. I know the Lord will bless you greatly in return as He receives the glory for His amazing love.

God bless,

Rebecca

Keeping the Faith
Sunday, November 1, 2009

I'm bummed about missing church last night. I was sure I'd be up to it, but yesterday wasn't one of my better days. So far, today isn't looking much better. I have a feeling it may be a medication issue, so hopefully, I'll get it sorted out soon. I really don't tolerate nausea well. Or that spaced-out feeling. This is the hard part—trusting in the wisdom and timing of God, when all I want is to feel "normal" again.

How wonderful it will be to get my new body that will never feel pain, fear, or confusion. But, for now, I choose to believe that God is carrying me through this, that He has a purpose, and that it's for my best.

The strangest thing for me is my total loss of interest in food. Food has always been a comfort to me. Without my appetite, and with Chuck gone much of the day, I'm having to learn to rely solely on God for my comfort.

And I wish I could be more energetic for my kids. I'm so grateful to our friends for providing Gracie with some fun distraction.

I've almost finished my antibiotics for my incision, and Chuck says it looks good. It's still sore to sit or lie on, but getting better.

Thank you all for your continued prayers. Your messages really make my day.

God bless,

Rebecca

Talk about Power
Monday, November 2, 2009

If any of you ever wonder if your prayers have an effect, let me assure you—they do. I was really down yesterday when I updated the page and reached out to you all. By evening, I was feeling so much better, I couldn't believe it. I was watching movies with my kids after a restful nap, and even my dinner tasted good. This may sound minor to some, but it's not to me, and I'm praising God for my prayer warriors. I slept well last night and feel well this morning. I still don't have an appetite, but I'm not as nauseated as yesterday, praise God.

Chuck has been busy with small jobs, but even in this, God will provide. Sometimes we have no other choice but to keep our eyes on the Lord, which, coincidentally, is exactly where they should be.

Never doubt for a minute whether the words you lift up to the Lord on the behalf of others do any good. If the Creator of all things cares about my appetite, there isn't anything He doesn't care about. Thank you, Lord!

Love and blessings,

Rebecca

Chapter 7

THE WAITING

News Flash!

Thursday, November 5, 2009

We finally heard from Seattle today. My pelvic CAT and MRI are scheduled for Monday, November 30th, at 1:20 p.m. My meeting with Dr. Conrad is Tuesday, December 1st, at 11:15 a.m. Surgery still has to be scheduled, but we should hear soon.

I got out to parent/teacher conferences this morning and then went on a service call with Chuck. It was good to get out, but it sure took it out of me. I slept the rest of the day. My medication is still in pretty good balance. Last night I took a bad turn, but we thought I might need a new ear patch for nausea, and once we changed it, I did better.

I thank God for each day I feel like just a person with a backache. It makes me feel that God is in control, and I'm really going to get through this all right. And I continue to thank Him for the love He shows me through all of you.

If it's God's will, I'll be back home for Rachel's sweet sixteen. I had big plans, but I'm learning Someone else has plans of His own. Luckily, He's a much better planner than me.

Praise the Lord!

Love and blessings,

Rebecca

Oops!
Saturday, November 7, 2009

I took a spill early this morning that caused some bleeding and bruising to my drainage spot. It's pretty sore. That'll teach me to go to the bathroom without my walker!

Chuck stayed busy today, Rachel got to school, the boys got to basketball practice, and Gracie and I watched some movies together. I felt pretty good all day.

This evening, Bruce and Helen brought over a wonderful dinner to share and stayed to watch a movie. It was so good to have a normal family night.

I have much to thank God for tonight, including your encouragement and prayers.

God bless,

Rebecca

My New Career
Saturday, November 7, 2009

In all my years on stage, I've passed for many characters, from maid to princess, but this morning I topped them all.

When my pain medication ran out, I had to see an on-call doctor here to get more, since a prescription for this medicine can't be called or faxed in. Chuck and I must look like pretty shady characters—as in drug dealers or addicts. Never mind the amount of drugs I've *stopped* taking, the doctor just couldn't believe the amount of this one medication I would need until the surgeon could mail in another prescription. Apparently, he's never had a tumor in his sacral nerve root.

Our story must have been quite convincing (I'm sure all the paperwork didn't hurt), because he finally relented—praise God! He had to let us know before we left, though, that it was the largest quantity of this painkiller he'd ever prescribed in his career. I wanted to congratulate him, but I just whispered a prayer of thanks and got out of there.

My prayer today is that I get to church. The sitting I had to do at the doctor's office and pharmacy was quite painful and tiring, so, hopefully, I'll get enough rest to make up for it.

Cheers for now,

Rebecca

Lesson Learned—I Hope
Monday, November 9, 2009

Note to Self:

You are not a doctor, nor do you play one on TV. The next time you get the brilliant idea to decrease your pain medication, *call You're your doctor!*

I have a love/hate relationship with narcotics. I love them when I'm in excruciating pain, but when it's time to say bye-bye—oh, boy.

I have, however, finally learned (I hope) that there's a right way and a wrong way to say good-bye. I, of course, did it the wrong way—again. It was just one itty-bitty pill, and I felt great—for a day. Then I had an anxiety attack and have spent the day dealing with anxiety, nausea, dizziness . . .

Fortunately, I had an appointment with my hero, Dr. Monroe, who explained the correct way to lower my dosage for this medication. God bless you, Dr. Monroe!

I just thought I would share that with any of you who may, like me, think you know what you're doing, or perhaps think doctors are too busy to be bothered with such trivial things. Don't play with your medicine! Doctors actually go to school for this stuff.

If you are an individual who enjoys withdrawals, please feel free to disregard this warning.

I'm feeling better, but I don't even want to think of what would have happened if I didn't have so many people praying for me. I even got my prescription filled without getting fingerprinted!

Thank you and God bless,

Rebecca

Cross My Heart
Tuesday, November 10, 2009

Thank you for your encouraging words, everyone. It's nice to know I'm not alone in this. I also have to keep reminding myself that I still have to go through the actual surgery, so I need to make peace and be content in my situation. I've burned my Superwoman suit and am praying for peace and faith. God is in control, and He hasn't failed me yet.

God bless you all,

Rebecca

The Hard Question
Wednesday, November 11, 2009

Rachel drilled her Civil Air Patrol squadron in the Veterans' Parade this morning, and I had to miss it, just like the boys' first basketball game last night. Chuck took pictures for me, but it's not quite the same as being there, cheering them on. I'm trying to concentrate on all the good times ahead and stay away from the guilt, but it isn't easy. I start to get angry at this thing in my backside, but then I remember who put it there, and that God does nothing just for the heck of it.

I've been through much pain in my life: the losses of four children, my mother, grandmother, and grandfather, other injuries and illnesses, and abuse. God has seen me through it all. But nothing has rivaled the physical or emotional pain of this, or of reading the stories of so many others—some children—who are fighting similar battles. Some who are losing.

Then my friend, Laurie, sent me this quote from David Wilkerson, author of *The Cross and the Switchblade*. Dr. Wilkerson wrote: "When God sets his heart on you, you will be tried often. But the fact is, the longer and harder your affliction, the more deeply God has set his heart on you, to show you his love and care. That is the witness of Paul's life and of Jesus' life. The enemy may come against you, but our Lord has raised up a standard against him. We find absolute rest in Jesus."

I know statements like this make those who don't know God think we're absolutely nuts, but it got me thinking—really thinking. Why would anyone in their right mind ask for this? This is not fun! This hurts like hell! Then I'm reminded of the One who was tortured to death for me, having done nothing wrong, Himself. Ever. He didn't wait for me to get my act together and start loving people and acting like a "Christian." He took me as I was, filthy rags and all, and suffered not only unbearable physical pain, but the excruciating pain of being separated from His Father for the first time in His existence—because He loved me.

Now I know God has His heart set on me. But who am I to deserve such love? Just His child. I understand now what Paul meant about being honored by trials and troubles. I don't see the big picture, but I believe God has a plan for each and every one of His own, and His plans are for our good. God's Word says this again and again (see Psalm 40:5 and Jeremiah 29:11), and God does not lie. Cannot lie.

How humbling to be chosen to be used in God's plan. If even one person accepts God's love and forgiveness because of what I'm going through, if only one person chooses to honor God with a meal for our family, a prayer for healing, a card, visit, or call, it'll be worth every minute. Because, when it comes down to it, it's not about Satan being out to get me. It's not about what I did or didn't do to deserve this. It's not about me at all.

It's all about love. God bless,

Rebecca

Chapter 8

ANSWERED PRAYER

I Wish

Friday, November 13, 2009

I wish I had that "S" on my shirt my best friend, Cathy, is always teasing me about. I've had a good day, pain-wise, and only a little nausea. But tonight, when Chuck opened the mail and handed me a letter, I broke down and cried. What he handed me was the schedule for my return to Seattle.

I know with all my heart that God is with me and in control, and I know Chuck will be there with me, but I'm still scared. I'm scared of CATs and MRIs, and I'm scared of the pain of coming out of surgery. I know this is just a tiny bit of what Jesus felt in the garden and on the cross—and He didn't have Chuck to hold His hand. Still, I wish with all my heart I didn't have to go through this again.

I feel like such a wimp. Every day I read the stories of children who are going through this and have been for years, and here I am, crying like a baby. Maybe I'm just tired. I know I'll get through this and everything will be fine. I just wish I could convince the part of me that's prone to panic attacks.

On the bright side, I have three weeks before I have to go, but that's also three weeks to sweat it out.

If I could ask anything, it would be that I could just borrow that "S" for a few days. Please pray for peace for me and a little extra courage.

Thank you all so much for the prayers, visits, and delicious meals you have blessed us with. And we are eternally grateful to those of you who take the time to care for our children when we can't get them where they need to be, and when we're out of town. I know God will bless you greatly in return.

Love and blessings,

Rebecca

Thank You
Saturday, November 14, 2009

I know you were praying for me. Today it was as if I'd stumbled into the poppy field on the road to Oz. I felt like a warm blanket of peace and comfort had covered me. When I wasn't snuggling into a movie with Gracie, I was sleeping deeply. I feel bad that I wasn't better company for my friend, Brenda R., when she came to visit, but it was such a nice feeling. No fear, no stress, just peace. That's the Holy Spirit at work, and I thank you for your prayers.

We now have a date for surgery, Thursday, December 3rd, but no time yet. We'll keep you posted.

Thank you all for your continued prayers and support, and thank those of you reading who are finding things in your homes to keep Chuck busy.

Love,

Rebecca

God Is Good
Sunday, November 15, 2009

Who could ask for a better Father? He loves me no matter how badly I screw up, or how big a tantrum I throw, or how much I doubt Him at times. He specifically chose me in spite of myself, He never lies, He keeps all His promises . . . I could go on forever. I just can't get over Him. I can be lower than low—like the other night—and feel scared, like He's a million miles away, and then, like with Elijah on the mountain, He'll whisper, reminding me He's been here the whole time.

Like the day I had yesterday, and am having today, filled with peace and rest, or a window in time, when I'm almost pain-free, or can enjoy curling up in bed or in front of the fire with my husband or the whole tribe for a movie, or just a snuggle, or a glimpse of the gorgeous fall colors out my window. It's as if He's saying, "Your journey's not over yet, child, but I Am here, and I'm not going anywhere."

I see these "love notes" most when I praise the Lord when I least feel like praising. I think God loves to hear from us that we believe in Him and His purpose even when all we see is pain and suffering. I don't know if I've mentioned this before, but a dear friend once brought to my attention that, though we often think of God as walking beside us, or even carrying us, the story of Moses, shows us there are times when He's going before us, clearing our path and dealing with our enemies, maybe arranging a few stones for our slings. It's really amazing how big God gets when you take Him out of the box. He really is bigger than life! How awesome to be loved by Him!

God bless,

Rebecca

Call Me Ginger
Monday, November 16, 2009

I have to laugh at myself. When I came home from the hospital, I was determined to really control my diet and eat healthy foods. But for some reason, I've had this incredible craving for ginger. Gingersnaps, ginger ale, anything ginger. Maybe it has something to do with my nausea; it does help. I just think it's funny how logic and instinct seem to part ways sometimes. Luckily, friends, Chuck, and the kids can send some pretty irresistible smells wafting up the stairs, so I'm eating more than ginger.

I've been thinking about 2 Corinthians 12:10. It seems a little cryptic when you first read it, but I'm beginning to see the truth in it. At least for me. When I'm scared and weak, and I make it through what I'll call the horror houses of life, I certainly can't stand up, flex my muscles, and say, "Yeah, I'm bad. I knew I could do it." Because I can't. And I didn't. God did it for me. Because He loves me, and I'm nothing without Him. And to be perfectly honest, I wouldn't want to be.

Worthy is the Lord, and worthy to be praised.

Love and blessings,

Rebecca

Giving Thanks
Tuesday, November 17, 2009

At the risk of being "punny," I'm beginning to realize what a pain in the behind this tumor is—which is exactly where my tumor is.

It was annoying when I had to miss out on Rachel's Homecoming night, and any big plans for Aaron's birthday, but now Thanksgiving is on its way.

Ever since we were married in 2003, we've made it a tradition to cook Thanksgiving dinner for the Christian Aid Center before going home to our own dinner, which I'd usually prepared the day before.

I think this is our favorite part of Thanksgiving. We've never missed a year. For weeks now, we've been trying to figure out how we're going to manage it this year. We even had the idea of taking the RV so I'd have a place to rest. But last night, after replacing the "S" on my shirt with a "W" (for "weakness"), I came to the painful conclusion that the tradition will be broken this year. Especially, with me leaving for surgery so soon after.

I'm not even sure what the family dinner will be. I know the kids are capable of cooking with some direction, and Chuck is no slouch in the kitchen. I'm just one of those people who thrives on tradition. Especially, the kind of tradition where I do things for others. I think it has something to do with that "S." So we won't have homemade pie, or rolls, or sweet potatoes. We still have a lot to be thankful for—like, I won't be in Seattle—and I know there will be someone to cook for the Christian Aid Center. I'll be with my family, and that's all that matters.

It seems I tend to get into the habit of blessing people by "doing" for them. Every once in a while, God has to stop and remind me if I'm so well-off (I'm not talking financially, here), that all I ever do is give, I'm robbing someone else of a blessing.

I first learned this when I was a single mom of four. The Good Neighbor Church reached out to me, when most of the time I didn't know where our next meal was coming from, and I saw that allowing them to help us actually blessed them. And so, I'm giving thanks for and asking blessings on all of you who walk the walk and teach me to be humble.
Love and blessings,
Rebecca

Ups and Downs
Thursday, November 19, 2009

It's been pretty rough the last three days. All I've wanted to do is sleep, and my brain doesn't seem to be playing on the same team. It's been especially rough with the colds going around, and me caring for Gracie on my own. It's been one of those sleep-with-one-eye-open things we moms get so good at.

I called Dr. Monroe today, and he said I was being over-medicated again, so we stretched out the schedule. The bad news is I feel awful, but the good news is my body is not needing as much pain relief. I'm praising God for this because if the tumor was were growing, I would expect to need more.

There is one thing to be said for being stuck in bed (aside from being forced to watch Chihuahuas dressed in tutus and booties with my princess), and that is having time to think and pray. It was in one of these sessions when I was thinking about how God was perfectly capable of healing me with a thought or a touch. I know. I've seen it.

Then my thoughts turned to my prayer life in the past year or so, and things started to come into focus. I have consistently been asking to be closer to God, to be more like Christ . . .   It never occurred to me at the time to stop and think about who He really is.

God didn't hold back a thing, including His only Son. And Jesus didn't tiptoe through the tulips for thirty-three years so I would be saved from death and hell. When Jesus said, *"Take up your cross and follow Me,"* He wasn't speaking metaphorically. Learning to trust God is scary. Submitting to God for the sake of the Gospel hurts. Holiness is not found in a church pew, or even behind the pulpit. If you really want to be closer to God, expect some slivers in your shoulders.

I've asked the question before—why would anyone in their right mind ask for this? I'm happy to say the answer hasn't changed. No one has ever loved me like my Jesus. And no matter what my life holds in store, I can never imagine my life without my Savior. And this life isn't our eternity. This is just a moment in time. Our eternity will be peace, love, rejoicing, and happiness we'll never know in this earth-age.

And that is why I say, "Take me Jesus, and do what you will with me. I am yours forever. Amen."

Love and blessings,

Rebecca

Chapter 9

THE BREAKING POINT

Praise the Lord!
Saturday, November 21, 2009

Yesterday was a hate day with my medication, but praise the Lord anyway! The nausea was really bad. I also had two kids home who were sick. It really makes me mad when I can't get up and take care of them. Thankfully, one of our angels called to take Gracie for a playdate with her daughter. What a blessing!

When Chuck got home, he changed my nausea patch and things started to improve. That evening, two more of our angels, Bruce and Helen, brought dinner and shared it with us. I absolutely love Helen's mac and cheese, but my pain and nausea kept me from enjoying it like I wanted to. It was still a blessing to have them here.

This morning I was able to eat breakfast, so I decided to keep my hair appointment, thinking it would make me feel better. But, as Grandpa used to say, "It'll feel good when it quits hurtin'." Oh well, at least I look good. That's what my husband says, anyway. And I don't care if he always says it; he's a very smart man, and I believe him.

The kids are better today, and Mr. Clock says it's medicine time, so I feel a nap coming on.

Love and blessings,
Rebecca

Family Medicine
Sunday, November 22, 2009

After the hairdresser yesterday, I slept the rest of the day, missing church, and I was still hurting when I woke up. Luckily, Chuck came home shortly after that, and for some reason, just having him with me makes me feel better.

I'm so thankful God is providing small jobs to keep us afloat. We knew it would be a lean Christmas, and with my added medical bills, it's going to be downright skinny. But God has always provided, and He always will. As long as we have each other, we have all we need.

My nausea improved last night enough for me to drink a smoothie. It was great to be able to have that to settle my stomach. If anyone has any recipes specifically for dealing with cancer, please send them along.

Evenings have become my favorite time of the day, when Chuck and I (and usually a kiddo or two or three) curl up in bed and watch a movie. That's the only time of day when I feel really good physically and emotionally. Chuck has always had that effect on me. I'm so blessed to have him.

Time is ticking down, however, and I'll soon be leaving my babies again. I know they'll be in excellent hands, but I'm still a mom. And with Gracie saying things like, "I'm scared," and, "I don't want you to go away," it's really hard. But I know who's in charge, and who "my kids" really belong to. God has a plan for every one of them, and this is part of it. Please, pray for them, though—and their mom, too.

Thank you for your continued prayers. Your messages and visits really make my day.

Love and blessings,

Rebecca

The Lesser of Two Evils
Monday, November 23, 2009

Yesterday was the worst day ever. My pain medicine didn't seem to last nearly long enough. I was hurting most of the day. If it hadn't been for Rachel watching funny movies with me, I don't know what I would have done.

When Chuck finally got home, I was beside myself, so he talked me into taking an extra pain pill. Then the real fun started. It got rid of the pain, but I started having O.D. symptoms: extreme nausea, dizziness, anxiety . . . I was clinging to God like a scared cat to a ceiling fan. It was the worst night of my life.

Chuck stayed up with me, praying and watching movies until I was finally able to sleep. Then Gracie started fussing. She's been getting over a cold, so Chuck, finally exhausted from getting up with her, brought her to bed with us where she commenced kicking the heck out of both of us. She finally settled down, and I was able to sleep until noon today and then eat a little.

I wish I could just sleep until this whole thing was over, I'm getting so tired of it. Then I read the CarePages of all the children going through so much worse, and I feel like such a wimp.

Still, I will praise the Lord for His plan in this and thank Him with all my heart that it is me going through this and not one of my children.

Thank you for your continued prayers,

Rebecca

Thankfulness
Thursday, November 25, 2009

May God bless you all abundantly this Thanksgiving and always as we remember that saying, "Yes," to God's forgiveness, and salvation is not the end of the journey, but the beginning. But God has promised us that if we keep looking forward and never look back, it will just get better and better. Even when it doesn't feel that way. I mean, listen to what He says in 1 Corinthians 2:9: *"Eye has not seen, nor ear heard, nor have entered into the heart of man the things which God has prepared for those who love Him"* (NKJV). That's so exciting to me!

God's love for you is so great, it can't be put into words. And I believe the Holy Spirit gives us only a taste of the overwhelming love we will feel when we finally meet our blessed Savior face to face! I can't wait!

Happy Thanksgiving!

Rebecca

Countdown
Saturday, November 28, 2009

Well, the clock has begun to tick down for me. One more day with my family before we hit the road.

I want to thank all you angels who blessed us with delicious treats for our Thanksgiving feast! Chuck and the kids did a great job with the rest of the dinner. But they assured me I was still needed, which was a relief. We had a wonderful dinner and then sat around the fire in the family room and watched movies. For the most part, I felt great, but I sat too long at the table and spent the evening hurting. It was worth it! I hope you all had a great Thanksgiving, too.

Yesterday was the best day ever. I almost felt like I did before I got sick. It was one of those times when it's easy to praise the Lord! It was great to have leftovers around the fire and spend time with the family. However, I seem to remember the leftovers lasting much longer when the kids were shorter. What's up with that?

I've been up some today, preparing for the big trip, so I'm a little achy. I've been dealing with nerves, too. I know God is with me and in control, but the human part of me doesn't want to leave my babies for so long, or go through those tests again, or surgery, and the pain of healing. Please be praying for peace for me, because, as Christians, we are told to fear nothing but to trust God in all things. I just wish I could convince the butterflies in my stomach. Also, please pray for safe travel.

Although I'm nervous, I'm also very much looking forward to seeing what God is going to do in all of this. The blessings and growth to come. As much as I've seen Him work in my life, He never ceases to amaze me.

Love and blessings,

Rebecca

Thanksgiving Postscript
Sunday, November 29, 2009

Some of you may remember me telling you our family has cooked Thanksgiving dinner for the Christian Aid Center for the last six years, but were unable to this year because of my illness. Apparently, no one ever calls to volunteer to cook anymore, because everyone knows we do it. However, Chuck just learned from the director, Jason, that one hour after Chuck called him to tell him the bad news, a group from AmeriCorp called to say that some of their members weren't going home and wanted to cook for them! Coincidence? I think not. Praise the Lord!

We were planning on being on the road by now, but, in true Olmstead fashion—and due to my confused state of mind—we won't be leaving until this afternoon—I hope.

Love and blessings,

Rebecca

Chapter 10

GREAT EXPECTATIONS

The Eagle Has Landed—Finally
Sunday, November 39, 2009

Did I say afternoon? What I meant was evening. We finally got on our way to Seattle around 6:30 p.m., with only one return home for something we forgot. This is a ritual with us, so we expect it.

It was a nauseating ride, with only three stops, but my pain wasn't that bad. I didn't sleep as much as I thought I would. For those of you unfamiliar with this part of the country, it's about 275 miles from Walla Walla to Seattle. The Snoqualmie Pass was clear with patches of thin fog. Chuck says it was a beautiful night.

I was ready to shoot the stinking GPS lady once we got into the city, and she kept insisting we, "Turn right, here," into concrete walls. But my husband is a very patient man. He has to be—he married me. We finally reached the hotel at 11:30 p.m. And all I can say is praise the Lord!

My tests start at 1:20 p.m. tomorrow. Please keep me in your prayers. I'm pretty calm at this point, so I know someone is praying.

We also got a call late tonight from Gracie, who is staying with friends. She was in tears and having a very hard time. This didn't happen the last two times we left her, so please say an extra prayer for her.

Thank you, and God bless you. We'll keep you posted.

Rebecca

Queen for a Day
Monday, November 30, 2009

Actually, Chuck always makes me feel like a queen, but this morning was especially appreciated. After getting to bed at 1:30 a.m., waking at 3:00, and again at 7:00 for medication, I just couldn't bring myself to go down for breakfast. So, Chuck brought me breakfast in bed. The best part was when he asked me if I wanted a shower. A shower! I've been sponge bathing for six weeks because the holes from my tubes wouldn't close. Normally, I'm a soaker, but this will do. Thank you, Jesus! Thank you, Chuck! I feel human again!

I need to send a huge thank you, also, to the families who are caring for our children. Especially, Dwayne and Angela W., who spent the night as Gracie's punching and kicking bags. I'll ask God for a special blessing for you guys as well as a more peaceful night tonight—and quick healing.

We're off to the cancer center. Praise the Lord, praise the Lord, praise the Lord . . .

4:30 p.m. – Praise the Lord! I survived the tests! God is so good! Barium on the other hand . . . not so great. In fact, I've renamed it—Bury-IT!

I had to get an IV for the contrast (always fun), and I took an extra anxiety pill to make me sleepy—which helped, but not as much as I wanted. The CAT scan went well. I took my pain pills before my MRI, but by the last twenty minutes, I was in so much pain, I barely made it. It was so hard to lie still!

I credit God's knowledge of me that got me through. First, Chuck was able to be with me and stroke my hair the whole time. Then, the MRI was built in India, Rachel's favorite place. Finally, they didn't have Christian music to listen to, so, even though I'm not a fan of country music, I chose Rachel's favorite band, Rascal Flatts to listen to. And having that image of my beautiful Rachel's smiling face made me forget my discomfort. Yes, God is very good.

Tomorrow morning, we meet with the surgical team, and later, the anesthesia team. I think Wednesday we have a day off before surgery. So in between all this, if you want me, I'll be in the shower. The nice, hot shower.

A special thanks also, to Grandma Helen for being the acting chauffeur and meals on wheels for the kids. We love you!

Thank you and bless you all for your prayers,

Rebecca

Doctor Day
Tuesday, December 1, 2009

I sure would love to sleep some more, but this handsome man brought me breakfast in bed again and promised me a shower. I couldn't resist. I'm still very tender from that MRI table, but the waiting rooms at the clinic are equipped with recliners and couches for people like me.

We see the doctors today, and I'm so grateful for your prayers and encouragement. I know what I want to hear from them, but I'm not God. Thank goodness. He created me, and not from a cookie cutter. Only He knows the purpose of my life and how to handle me on the potter's wheel.

I'm not excited about more pain, but I'm thrilled He has chosen me to do His work and someday live forever in Heaven. No pain, no sickness, no grief, no death . . . Frankly, just seeing Him face to face and being able to throw my arms around Him will be worth any pain I may have to endure here. So, whatever the doctors say, my Father knows what He's doing, and I trust Him. And I have a very large army praying for me to help me get through, so I will count it all joy.

Thank you, friends and family. I love you!

Rebecca

My mind raced as I lay on the table in the exam room. I envisioned the astonished looks on the doctors' faces as they told me the tumor was gone. The celebration we'd share with all our prayer warriors. It was perfectly logical that God would take the tumor away. Why else would He make me wait so long for surgery, if not to heal me?

I wiped my damp palms on my sweatpants when Dr. Conrad's team filed in. My heart pounded in my ears. Dr. Conrad took a seat and opened my chart. "Well," he said, "the mass has been active and growing since your last scans."

I could almost hear the helium hiss from my spirit as it sank slowly to the cold, linoleum floor. All right, so healing wasn't in the plan for me. At least there was a plan. And God promised not to give me more than I can handle . . . The question was: What did He know about me that I didn't?

Dr. Conrad's voice brought me back. "However, the mass seems to be engaged with only one nerve, now, as opposed to the mass we saw earlier." I looked at Chuck, and he smiled. God *was* moving. "That means a much greater chance of regaining your motor skills and bladder and bowel function. I'll have no problem getting it all in surgery. I'll just go in and peel it right out of there."

I sighed. Okay. I can handle that—I think.

Waiting Day
Wednesday, December 2, 2009
Good morning,

Today is supposed to be a day to lie around and relax until tomorrow's surgery. But I had to refill my pain medicine yesterday, and I took the first of the new bottle last night at 11. An hour later, I had a killer headache and was in and out of sleep. By 2 a.m. I was in a full-blown panic attack—cold sweats, shaking, anxiety, nausea, shortness of breath. It was hell.

We're waiting to hear back from the doctor on what to do about it. Chuck is such a blessing. He held me the rest of the night until I could sleep again. I will still praise the Lord. I know He's with me through it all. Please pray for a calm day and night for us. I need all the rest I can get.
Thank you, and God bless,
Rebecca

The Joys of Modern Medicine
Wednesday, December 2, 2009

I finally heard from one of the doctors, and she determined that I had a reaction to the contrast dye on Monday. I was full of it. A dose for the CAT scan, and a dose for the MRI. And that was on top of the "Bury-IT!"

It's another beautiful sunny day, but I've been sleeping most of it. Thank you so much for your prayers. I'm sure that's what made it so easy for me to sleep today.
God bless,
Rebecca

Reflections
Wednesday, December 2, 2009

We'll be checking into the surgical center at 9:30 tomorrow morning, and surgery is scheduled for 11:00 a.m.

I've sure had a lot of time to think about the whys and wherefores of this experience. If you've been reading my updates, you know I believe there's no such thing as coincidence for those who belong to God. Everything, no matter how small, has a purpose. We may not always get to know His purpose, but He created me to be a Nosey Nelly, so I look for the answers. For instance, of all the places in my body, why did He put the tumor near my tailbone? Hmmm.

Here's what came to me last night. For as long as I can remember, I've wanted to please God. I want to be more forgiving, and less self-condemning. I want the faith of a mustard seed. I want to be bolder in my faith and spend more time with Him personally—and the list goes on and on. So, what has stopped me? The answer came to me last night. One word . . . "but."

This may sound crazy to a lot of you, but God does have a sense of humor.

So, my prayer for tomorrow is that when Dr. Conrad peels away the tumor, God will be peeling away those "buts" that keep me from serving Him to my fullest potential.

I submit to You, Lord. I choose to let go of all my "buts" in my ratty, old shoebox and lay them at Your feet. Scary as it is, I'm ready to receive the gift You have waiting just for me. Amen.

D-Day
Thursday, December 3, 2009

Well, this is it. We leave for the hospital as soon as Chuck gets back from breakfast. I slept well last night, so I'm feeling pretty good. I wish I could say I wasn't nervous, but I'm no better than Peter, and, frankly, when you look over the side of the boat, waves is waves.

Help me keep my eyes on You, Lord. I praise You for this opportunity to grow closer to You.

This will be the last you hear from me for a while. Chuck will be taking over again. God bless you all and thank you so much for your prayers and support!
Love,
Rebecca

Chapter 11

THE MASTER SURGEON

Surgery Has Started
Thursday, December 3, 2009
Posted by Chuck

We got to the UW at 9:30 a.m., right on time. Rebecca went right in to the pre-op room. I was able to be with her up until she went into surgery at 10. The surgery nurse just called and said the surgery has started. It should take about three hours. She'll call me at two-hour intervals with updates.

I pray God will be guiding Dr. Conrad and his team and this will be an uneventful surgery. I'll post again when the nurse calls me.

Thank you everyone for your prayers and support.

Chuck

Rebecca Is Out of Surgery
Thursday, December 3, 2009
Posted by Chuck

Dr. Conrad just came out and told me the tumor was not in the nerve root. Praise the Lord our God! This is very good news. It was very small, and he will not be surprised if the final pathology comes back as a benign tumor. Last time this took about three weeks. The surgery was quicker than they thought it would go. Praise the Lord. No issues or surprises came up during surgery.

I think it'll be a few hours before I'm able to see Rebecca. Then I'll post a new message.

Thanks again for your prayers and support.

Chuck

Rebecca Is in Her Room!
Thursday, December 3, 2009
Posted by Chuck

Rebecca's in her room! Praise the Lord our Savior, she feels good, and the surgery pain is under control. She's not having any pain from the Foley catheter; this was very painful during her last hospital stay. She's talking about having something to eat, another very good sign. For pain management, she'll have a baseline from her pain pump for overnight. This should keep her from waking up with too much pain.

They went in from the back, like last time, so she shouldn't have any additional scars.

Rebecca told me the tumor was much smaller than the last scans three days ago!

This time, only one drain tube was used. For the most part, she's able to move around in bed with the trapeze by herself.

I have a feeling I won't be in charge of updating this CarePage for very long. That doesn't hurt my feelings. She does a lot better job than I do.

Thank you, and may God bless you all. Until tomorrow,

Chuck

Tumor, What Tumor?
Saturday, December 5, 2009
Posted by Chuck

"If it sounds like a duck, quacks like a duck, and looks like a duck, it's a duck!" The above line was from my posting, "Praise God our Lord—Update," dated October 18, 2009. I talked about the tumor Rebecca had, and how God changed it in to a blood clot.

I didn't understand something Dr. Conrad said to me after Rebecca's surgery on Thursday, but now I do. He said, "It will be interesting to see what pathology makes of this." This seemed to be a very strange comment.

This morning Dr. Conrad and his surgical team came in. It's still looking like we'll be going home on Monday. We started talking about the surgery and recovery plans, pain management, when more details of the surgery came out.

He said Rebecca didn't have a tumor; it was some kind of "mass"—what kind he didn't know. I believe it's what's left from our great and loving Lord Jesus Christ changing the tumor into a blood clot, and then into a low-grade tumor, and then into a "mass." This tumor was coming out of the nerves at the end of Rebecca's spine. I mean to say it was part of the nerves. The only (human) way to get rid of it was to remove the nerves. Yet, when they operated, it was just "near" the nerves. No nerves had to be removed!

He did say it wasn't an infection. The doctors are confused. I'm not! Rebecca's pain kept going down; it should have been going up. Tuesday, he said the mass was growing—but it was smaller on Thursday!

A lot of people won't believe this happened. As for me, I know it happened. In all things, Praise our Lord, God! I've been very blessed by God and wish and hope you'll feel His blessings as well.

It's very easy when things are going well to thank God for it, if we remember. I know I don't thank him enough during those times. Most of the time, I walk through life worried about this deadline or that appointment, how far behind I am, or why I didn't get that job, and sometimes how will I get everything done.

I know I need to do a better job praising Him in all things, even if I don't like what He's doing. Because the human side of me wants it my way, but with His grace, I'll be able to bow to His will and "praise Him in all things—period."

After Carolynn, my first wife, died, I had someone ask me if I was mad at God. At the time, this statement seemed very strange. As I look back, that was the start of my praising Him. At that time, I didn't know that was what I was doing. Now I do.

For those who don't know, Carolynn was at the end of her life, and we were on a plane to Spokane. I prayed to God (it had been a very, very, long time since I'd prayed). I was very selfish with my prayer; it was all about me. I wanted God to spare her.

The Holy Spirit convicted me of my selfishness, and I repented. Then I prayed from deep inside my soul that if He had to take Carolynn, He would do it quickly. Our Lord Jesus Christ answered my prayer before the night was over. It changed who I was.

Why would He care about me? I was living a life without Him. I believed in Him, but I didn't need Him. When that prayer was answered, I saw how much He loved me, and how He had been walking with me in spite of myself. Today, I know I can't do anything without Him.

Keep God first and praise Him in all things. May the love of our Lord Jesus Christ be inside your souls,

Chuck

Tomorrow! Tomorrow! I Love Ya, Tomorrow!
Sunday, December 6, 2009

Good morning!

Everyone keeps telling me how great I'm doing, so that works for me. I guess I don't remember much about the last time. I'll count that as a blessing.

I think the switch to oral meds is going well. Last night was very restful, even with all the interruptions to give me more medicine. Right now, I'm taking more mgs than I was when I got here, of course.

I'm still hurting, but I can get up to use the bathroom and sit in a chair for a while. I woke up with a burning stomach and nausea—not fun, but I'm doing better. Just a little dizzy and sleepy. Chuck said something about a walk today. I'd rather take a nap.

Thank you for your continued prayers and support.

Love and blessings,

Rebecca

PART II

"Your ears shall hear a word behind you, saying,
'This is the way, walk in it,' Whenever you turn to the
right and whenever you turn to the left."
Isaiah 30:21

Chapter 12

THE ROLLER COASTER RIDE

Going Home Today!
Monday, December 7, 2009
Posted by Chuck

All the doctors have been in, and we're getting ready to go home! Rebecca's doing very well. Yesterday, she went on several walks, up and down a flight of stairs, and sat up for over an hour.

The dressing was changed today, and the drain line came out. The incision looks great.

Nausea is the only thing we're worried about. Rebecca is having some today and is worried about the drive home. They've given her some more medicine; we'll know in a few minutes if it's going to help.

So, now we wait for the pharmacy to fill all of the prescriptions, and a special chair to help with pain when she is using the bathroom. She'll have her stitches out in Walla Walla on Christmas Eve, and then back to SCCA in the middle of January for a follow-up appointment. That's when we'll get the final pathology report on the "mass."

God has been with us every step of this journey, and I know He's still walking with us. I praise Him. All of the glory is His.

God bless you and your families,

Chuck

What an Awesome God We Serve!

Monday, December 7, 2009

Wow! It was a beautiful day to drive home! I know Chuck mentioned I was struggling with nausea before we left, but you guys must have really been praying. Chuck also tracked down the two prayer warriors from housekeeping who prayed over me the last time I was there. It was like God put His hand on my stomach and calmed the storm.

I felt so good, I was able to ride in the front seat and enjoy the beautiful sunshine in the mountains until we got to Cle Elum. From there, I curled up in my nest in the back seat and slept, with only one more stop.

The only bad part was I slept through my last pain dose, and, though I wasn't in pain at the time, it caught up with me really quick once I got in the house.

I can't begin to tell you how great it was to see and hold my kids again. What would have made it perfect would have been seeing our oldest son, too. He turned 19 today, and, though I sent him a card when this whole journey started, he still doesn't want any contact with me. However, I know this, too, is part of God's plan. This, too, is working for both our goods.

For now, my pain is back under control, Gracie is snoring softly beside me, and my older kids can't get enough hugs. I'm a happy mom.

I'm pretty sure we threw Dr. Conrad (and a few other people) for a loop, but to God be the glory. And now I pray for a smooth transition off pain meds. It's been so long, I can't wait to see what pain-free feels like again.

Please feel free to drop by. It will be good to see the rest of my family again, too!

Love and blessings,

Rebecca

Heavenly Sunshine!
Tuesday, December 8, 2009

I know it's very cold out there, but I'm really enjoying the sunshine coming in my windows. I'm also enjoying cuddling with Gracie.

I had a good night, aside from waking up every three hours for medicine. This morning has been really good. It would be better if pain didn't keep reminding me that I'm still healing. I was a little nauseated this morning, but my medicine helped. It's mostly a matter of finding comfortable positions. I know the perfect one, but Chuck won't let me near the bathtub! I wish I could go for a massage, but that's just a dream, too. Oh well, I'm in my own bed, and that is a big "Praise the Lord!" I'm so glad it's almost Christmas break. I missed my kids so much!

Thank you, and God bless you for your continued prayers and support.

Love,

Rebecca

Manna
Tuesday, December 8, 2009

We're standing on faith that work will continue to come in for Chuck. And Rachel is working hard to maintain her grades. Her college finals are this week, and she has her high school classes to keep up on. The great news is she passed her driver's test today, and tomorrow will be a legal, licensed driver! What a birthday gift! Actually, it's more of a gift for me, but don't tell her that.

Right now, I'm a little grumpy. I'm in quite a bit of pain and a half-hour away from meds. Gracie hasn't let me sleep at all, so that doesn't help. I'm also trying to get in some walking and stairs, but what I really need is a nap. I just have to make it to 5 o'clock, and I think I'll be all right. Maybe Gracie will let me sleep as she watches *Air Bud*—maybe.

Love and blessings,

Rebecca

Back Seat Driving
Friday, December 11, 2009

All right. I really need to learn to be a little more specific. You'd think as a writer I'd remember this. I should have made it my goal to get better each day *and* night. Though I've been feeling good in the mornings, by afternoon, I'm feeling pretty cruddy, and my outlook begins to go downhill. (Sorry I was so grumpy on the phone, Brenda.) I found this can be overcome by reading the updates of other CarePagers and realizing what a huge baby I am when so many others are in serious pain. Especially the children.

Jesus can't come back too soon for me. But, even as I say that, I hear the voice of the Lord saying, "Get behind me, Satan!" I'm reminded that I'm a kid with the board game, Operation, trying to direct the Master Surgeon, as He rewires a brain. I think I'm rambling again. I'm just writing as it comes to me.

My original thought today was how differently I see myself compared to how God sees me. I learned early on in my relationship with my Heavenly Father that walking with Him did not mean living in a state of euphoric bliss. Not in this earth-age, anyway. The path is indeed narrow—and steep, dark, and far from paved. But my desire for Him made turning around out of the question. I'm more precious to God than the finest precious metal, but even these those aren't worth much until they are refined—in fire. That's the only way to get rid of the slag keeping me from shining in all His glory. And He did promise to be my light, never leave me, and never give me more than I could handle. Piece of cake.

What I'm thinking about is the irony of the phrase, "walk with God." I've just realized that, ever since I gave God the steering wheel of my life—which didn't stop me from being a back- seat driver—there hasn't been much walking. Walking was what I did without Him. With Him, it's been more like running. I've even felt as if I were running a marathon. But I've come to the conclusion that I'm not running a marathon, now—I'm participating in the Ironman Triathlon!

At various times in my life, I've struggled with illness, and God was faithful to heal. Other times, I have struggled financially, and God was faithful to provide. Now, for the first time in my life, I'm struggling with both simultaneously. Last night, thinking about Christmas, this really hit home, and I began to despair. I lost sight of my Savior and started to sink into the waves.

I love to do holidays BIG. It's always been important to me to make great memories for my kids. Even when I was a single mom of four and poor as a church mouse, I still managed to make birthdays and holidays special and memorable. I had my health, and I could be creative and fun. We had some great times, but when I married Chuck, and we started our contracting business, I thought those days were long behind me.

Then the economy took a nosedive, and business slowed down. Still, we trusted God to provide, and He was faithful. I'd attended several writers' conferences and had some agents interested in my mystery. Things were looking up. Then the doctor told me they found a tumor in my sacral nerve root, and my narrow path took a sharp turn. God burst my self-deluded bubble.

I was wracked with guilt over not being able to give my kids great birthdays, and yet, somehow, they managed to have great birthdays. I beat myself up because I couldn't put on a great Thanksgiving, and yet, we managed to have one. Now, Christmas is coming. I bought a bunch of clearance decorations last year to make Christmas spectacular, but I can't decorate the house. I can't bake myself into a tizzy, making the house smell yummy, and, even if I could go shopping, the medical bills and slow economy have taken care of that.

Luckily, our three older kids are old enough to be happy with the gift of having Mom home and healing, as are Chuck and I. Though we won't know the results of the biopsy until January, we're all praising God for the gift of healing. But Gracie's only three, and she's been talking about Christmas since October. She's so excited about Santa coming. Daniel is a little older, but he's always been Christmas crazy. Not about gifts, necessarily, but the whole holiday spirit.

Chuck has solved the Christmas tree dilemma by taking the kids up to cut our own tree this weekend. That will make some great memories. We may be able to get a couple things for Gracie, and I've been encouraging the older kids to make some gifts for each other, but no one seems to have the time or creativity. The cloud of my illness seems to loom over everyone. They assure me everything will be fine, but I can see the strain in their faces, and I hate it. I can't make Christmas for them this year, either.

Having said that, God did pretty darn good with the birthdays and Thanksgiving without my help. So maybe I should just praise the Lord, let go of the wheel (I was getting blisters anyway), and watch God work. After all, we have the greatest gift of all—new life in Christ—and no one can take that away. It doesn't get any better than that.

Yea!!! Snow Day!!!
Tuesday, December 15, 2009

I *will* enjoy my kids being home, Charles Glen (that's Chuck), thank you very much. The only thing that could be better is if you had a snow day, too. Oh well, it's almost Christmas.

To all who shared your wonderful gifts of poetry and stories, God bless you! You make me smile!

Last night, as we sat around the dinner table (yes, I got to sit at the table again ☺) enjoying the delicious dinner Rachel R. brought us, we talked about Christmas and what a miracle gift we'd already received. A gift that far outweighs anything you could find under the tree.

After our first meeting with my surgeon (it seems so long ago now), we were making plans to sell our home, close our business, and move to Seattle. But God is so good and faithful to hear our prayers and give out of His abundance that we are still in our home, the tumor is gone, and I'm not paralyzed.

We're only here for a brief moment in time, though when we're hurting or watching our loved ones hurt, it seems like forever. But the truth—what the enemy doesn't want us to know—is that forever is what our loving Heavenly Father has promised us with Him. No, sickness, no tears, no pain, no death. Just more love and joy than we could ever imagine! Hallelujah!

And those who've left us way too soon are already basking in the glory of freedom from these weak, earthly vessels. The children of God will in nowise be forgotten, for they, through the gift of grace and salvation, are as eternal as the Father Himself. Amen!

I know I've thus far been spared from the agonizing treatments so many cancer warriors are enduring. But, "*. . . from everyone who has been given much, much will be demanded . . .*" Luke 12:48. My journey is far from over.

I just know there's a purpose behind everything—every fire God walks me through—and He doesn't just shove me in the oven and say, "There you go, kid; good luck." No! He is with me, even to the end of the age! So, let us lift one another up as we lean on the Father, knowing this is all moving us forward to that blessed day when we will walk in perfect, glorified bodies forever and ever, Amen!

I write this in the morning, when I'm feeling good, knowing that this evening I'll be sick and hurting, and I have yet to overcome my pain medicine.

I will cling to my Lord and His promise, and know I'll come out a better person than I went in.

Thank you all for your continued prayers and support.

God bless,

Rebecca

Chapter 13

A HOLE IN TIME

Check-Up Time
Wednesday, December 16, 2009

I love Dr. Monroe. He can make my worst fears seem manageable. I was shocked to hear him say that very few people were on the amount of pain medicine I am. And, compared to what I was on when I came home from my biopsy, this is just a drop in the bucket! But Dr. Monroe assured me I needn't get off of it as quickly as I'd thought, and he gave me a time frame and plan. I know it isn't going to be easy, but I don't feel as overwhelmed as I did before.

Today, my withdrawal symptoms from my last drop are nearly gone, and I feel better than I have in weeks. Part of me says it's time to step down again, but part of me wants to enjoy feeling good for a while. The boys' Christmas program at school is tomorrow night, and we still haven't decorated the tree. The boys are at their dad's until Thursday night, so we're looking at Friday or Saturday—or Sunday.

Chuck hasn't had a chance to take the kids shopping for each other's gifts, but, as long as he's doing service calls, I'm not complaining. Then there are the kids' hats to crochet. I'll finish Rachel's today, but I don't want to be going through withdrawals while I'm trying to make the others. I think I'll put off dropping my dosage as long as I can, but if I get the shakes, I'll have no choice.

I amazed Dr. Monroe and his nurse by walking (with Chuck's help), but when we got to the hospital to have my iron checked, I was in a wheelchair. That's okay. Baby steps.

The kids got their ornaments painted yesterday while Chuck and I were at the doctor's. They look really cool.

I've decided it would be best if, when I lower my dosage, Gracie has a place to go play, or one of the kids is home to watch her so I can sleep through as much of the withdrawals as possible. I really don't want to do this over Christmas break, but I may not have a choice. Please keep me in your prayers. I'm really brave when I'm feeling well, but how quickly things can change.

Well, I better get to crocheting. Thank you for your continued prayers.

Rebecca

Busy Santas
Thursday, December 17, 2009

Yesterday didn't end as great as it started, unfortunately. I started hurting pretty badly shortly after I updated. I couldn't understand it until Chuck reminded me I had done more walking at the doctor's than I had since coming home from Seattle. Funny how I don't think about consequences until they hit me.

But, several Santas made up for the pain. God bless you, Pamela M. and all the gals in my writers' group, for your generous gifts. What a surprise and a blessing. We were in shock, and we'll be eternally grateful.

I did have great news from Dr. Monroe, too. After my blood work came back, he said I didn't have to take the iron anymore! Thank you, Doc! My stomach is doing much better. I was in hog heaven with the wonderful comfort food Shelley R. and her family brought. Thank you!

I'm feeling good today. Just a little nausea and pain. But that also means it's time to take another step down from my meds. Please keep your kneepads on. I know it's one more step closer to healing, but it isn't going to be fun. And thank you, Rachel R., for taking Gracie for playdates. It's such a help.

Thank you so much for your prayers and support,

Rebecca

Ode to a Hot Bath
Friday, December 18, 2009

Thank you, Pamela M. and Brenda R., for dropping in. It really lifts my spirits to visit with my friends.

I missed the kids' program last night, but there is a video, and Chuck took pictures. Poor Daniel missed it, too, along with his school party. Sick again.

I lowered my pain dosage another 2.5mg at midnight and am now beginning to feel the effects. I'm drinking a lot of water and walking more in an effort to flush the stuff out of my system. I'm also juicing more and praying like crazy. Sometimes I just lie very still and ask the Holy Spirit to fill me completely, leaving no room for pain. It helps.

I emailed an agent who was expecting my manuscript in September to let him know what was going on. He assured me he was still interested, but to take my time healing since the market is really slow right now. That was encouraging.

Last night I was telling Chuck how much I miss taking baths, so I thought writing about it would help. Enjoy.

Ode to a Hot Bath

How heavenly to sit and dream,
amid the thick and rising steam.

To be enwrapped in soothing heat,
neck and shoulders, hands and feet.

To close my eyes and drift away
on a blissful sea to a pain-free day.

I hear no knocking, no beckoning voice,
o'er strains of Bach, as strings rejoice.

Into my bones, the heat sinks deep,
lulling my pain to gentle sleep.

Oh, to linger in this warm cocoon,
but the chill creeps in much too soon.

Why climb out with wrinkled skin?
I'll drain the tub and fill it again!

Thank you for your continued prayers, messages, and delicious food! God bless,
Rebecca

To Better Days
Monday, December 21, 2009

I'm so glad yesterday is over! If there was one word to describe yesterday, it would be "pain." We had planned to watch a movie together after supper, but I couldn't even make it through dinner. But, praise the Lord, I'm down to one pain pill! This morning, I'm dealing with nausea, but I'm no longer hurting as badly.

The only thing that's getting me through these days is the fact that God is using my pain for His purpose. It never occurred to me until last night what a miracle He truly did.

Why didn't He just take it all away? I already got my miracle, which I had no doubt the Creator of my flesh was capable of, but I believe it's His presence in my healing where He has really shown His faithfulness. He didn't just touch me with a "be healed," and go on His way. He is with me, or in me, for the long haul. As much as I'd like to be able to be a witness without the pain and suffering, His ways are not my ways. It's this time of year, when I need to remember it was Jesus who paved the way through the pain for me.

That's how I know He's with me. And He makes His presence known in the messages on CarePages, through friends and family praying, caring for our children, bringing food, visiting, calling, sending encouraging notes and gift cards, as much as in the operating room. So, to all of you who have done these things, I'd like to say thank you for being Jesus to our family. *"Give, and it will be given to you: good measure, pressed down, shaken together, and running over will be put into your bosom. For with the same measure that you use, it will be measured back to you"* (Luke 6:38 NKJV).

God bless you all. I hope you are enjoying the holidays,
Rebecca

A Great Day!
Wednesday, December 23, 2009

I'm so happy I could cry! Chuck and I just returned from a four-hour shopping trip, and I'm not dying from pain! This may not seem like a big deal to a lot of people, but last night I tried to go shopping with the family and just wheeling around the store in a motorized cart for an hour all but killed me.

I took a couple nausea pills, which helped, and some ibuprofen before we left. It wasn't pain-free, but it was tolerable. I was in the wheelchair this time and had to get up and stretch a few times.

I want to thank all of you Santas who made these shopping trips possible. You've been such a blessing!

It was so good to get out and act like a normal person. As normal as possible, pushing a shopping cart while being pushed in a wheelchair. But I didn't hit one single pedestrian. Well, none that lived to tell about it, anyway.

The kids are getting so excited. They were all able to buy each other gifts. They love watching each other open their gifts. I think they're all sleeping under the tree tonight. And I'm super-excited that my stitches are coming out tomorrow!

There's so much I want to do, but I'm going to have to pace myself so I don't spend Christmas in bed. As challenging as it's been, I can honestly say this is the richest Christmas we've ever had. It's one I'm sure we'll never forget.

Thank you all for your continued prayers and support. May the good Lord bless you all this season and in the coming New Year!

Rebecca

L *ate Christmas Eve night, I laid lay on the bed, watching Chuck wrap the last of the kids' gifts.*

"Have you read your CarePage from the beginning yet?"

His question took me aback. "I never thought about it," I said. "I mean, I lived it." I was in no hurry to relive the last four months.

"I think you should read it," he said.

I looked at him questioningly.

"I think it would be good for you."

I considered it a moment before conceding with a heavy sigh. I reached for my laptop and found his first CarePage entry. As I read and reread the passages, a cold realization crept though me. I looked to my husband, standing beside the bed, as his warning about the side effects of my medication came back to me.

He set aside the wrapping paper and tape. "What's wrong, honey?

Tears stung my eyes. "I don't remember any of this."

He came around the bed and wrapped me in his arms as I dissolved into tears. I was mortified by the gaping hole in my mind. How could I have lost such a big part of myself and not even noticed? Would I ever regain my memory? Or would I go on losing my life as I lived it? Living moment by moment?

I didn't want to read any more. It was like hearing people talk about a party I wasn't invited to. Knowing it was my party angered me. It was bad enough to endure such pain and fear, but having no memory of it? Was this a blessing or a curse?

"Keep reading," Chuck said softly. "Once you see how God has worked through it all, it'll be worth it. You'll see."

I read on.

Chapter 14

FAMILY

There Are No Strings on Me!
Thursday, December 24, 2009

My hero, Dr. Monroe, just removed nineteen stitches from my posterior. I love Dr. Monroe. Yea! I'm free! I'm pretty sure my dreams of becoming a swimsuit model are over, but praise the Lord anyway!

I thought for sure I'd be in a world of hurt today, after my shopping spree yesterday. I sure was last night, until the best husband in the world (that's Chuck, by the way) gave me some ibuprofen. But I got up this morning pain-free and didn't hurt until I started walking around and bending over to pick up wrapping paper. Back to my heating pad. I'm determined to feel better for the party and candlelight service tonight, so I'm not moving until 3.

Last night, Chuck and I stayed up late, he wrapping the kids' gifts, and I reading the first postings on my CarePage. Chuck had read them all to me before, but all of the medication has affected my memory. One more great reason for this website.

As I read, I noticed something peculiar. Some of Chuck's longer updates sounded strangely like some of my longer updates, talking about faith and praise and the goodness of our Lord and Savior. In fact, they sounded as if they had been written by the same person. Some may say Chuck and I have been married for so long that we think the same. But we know better. We know very well that it wasn't either of us writing those words, but the Holy Spirit alive within us. This was such an awesome lightbulb moment!

We've all heard the song, "We are one in the Spirit, we are one in the Lord," but until now, I'd always considered that a figure of speech. But it's not! When we surrender to God through Jesus Christ and allow the Holy Spirit to transform us, renewing our minds through His Word, He will truly make us one. The body of Christ!

May God bless you all greatly, and may you all know the forgiveness, peace, love, and joy our gracious God offers you. No requirements except that you believe and live for Him.

We thank all of our friends—new and old—and family, for your love, and wish you all the best God has to offer in the coming new year, while we offer our prayers for healing and restoration. God is bigger than it all.

Much love,

Chuck, Rebecca, Rachel, Aaron, Daniel, and Gracie

Merry Christmas!!!
Friday, December 25, 2009

Merry Christmas to one and all! May you all see blessings poured out over the coming year for the faithfulness you have shown the Lord by ministering to us.

The best laid plans of mice and me . . . at least I set goals. We did get to the family party. I put on a pair of jeans for the first time since August! And it was so great to see everyone and thank them in person for everything they've done for us and especially our children in the past months. We'd planned to attend the candlelight service at church as well, but Gracie was so thrilled to be with her cousins, some of whom she was meeting for the first time, we didn't have the heart to drag her away.

Unfortunately, I only lasted two hours before the pain and nausea became too much. I received no relief from my medication, and Chuck had to take me home to my bed and heating pad. He returned to the kids and the party, and from the sounds of it, I missed a pretty wild time.

Of course, Daniel was knocking at our door at 3 a.m. to open presents. I was due for medication anyway, so it wasn't that big of a shock, but we informed him we would not be leaving our warm, toasty bed for some time.

By 7, the whole gang was up and waiting under the tree, so we gave in. And a good time was had by all. Then Mom and Dad took a nap. The kids are all thrilled with their gifts, and Chuck and Rachel are working on dinner. I was even surprised with a box of chocolate pretzels, and Dad got a bag of dark chocolate, mint rocky road candy bars, so we are happy campers. I love Christmas!

Love, blessings, and continued prayers,

Rebecca

Bathtub Blues
Tuesday, December 29, 2009

Yesterday was pretty rough. Nausea mostly, but pain, too. I got to sleep, so that helped. Bruce and Helen brought Helen's famous mac and cheese and other goodies for dinner, and then they stayed to watch their first episode of *Rosemary and Thyme*, one of my favorite British mystery series.

It was all wonderful, but, in the end, I was in a world of hurt and welcomed my bed and heating pad. I came up with a brilliant plan, though. Since I don't own a wetsuit, I tried to convince Chuck to wrap me in Saran Wrap and put me in a nice hot tub. His baby blues sure lit up at the words "Saran Wrap," but I'm afraid his ears shut down at the word "tub." Oh well, you can't blame a gal for trying.

Last night, Gracie was fighting a fever, so we didn't get much rest. Today she seems to be feeling better, but I've been very nauseated all day, and Chuck's stomach is not happy either. So I'm not sure if my nausea is from the pain meds, or if I caught something, too. We've been napping this afternoon. I love sleep. It's the only time I'm not in pain or sick to my stomach, except for brief windows in time when I get a taste of the "well life" and I hear the "Hallelujah Chorus."

Well, my surgical pain is flaring up again, so Chuck says it's time for a walk. No Saran Wrap for him!

Thank you for your continued prayers and messages. I love you all.

God bless you!

Rebecca

Cowards, Rebels, and Wimps
Wednesday, December 30, 2009

I know God doesn't give us more than we can handle, but I'm pretty sure He's stretching me out so He can pile on a little more. Either that, or He's trying to make me drop my plate so He can take it away from me. If that's the case, *Uncle! I give up! Take it! I can't do it anymore! Consider me broken!* I'm not brave, and I'm not tough. I'm the biggest baby in the world, and if it weren't for Jesus Christ, I wouldn't be worth the dirt I'm made of!

None of my nausea medications are helping anymore, and neither is ginger; my colon is on strike, and the pain . . . don't even get me started. I just spoke with Dr. Monroe, and he said at this point it's more important for me to get active, even if it means increasing my pain meds. Those of you who've been following my withdrawal horrors know that's the last thing I want to do. I've increased my walks, stairs and all, to about once an hour, but the sciatic pain that accompanies it is enough to make me want to crawl out of my skin.

Chuck took the tape off my sutures this morning. He said it doesn't look like a bath is very far off, but it can't come too soon for me.

I have so much to be thankful for, yet this is one of those times when praising doesn't come easy. I can and will praise God, however, that there is a purpose for my pain. I know that beyond a doubt. In all the history of man, God has always chosen cowards, rebels, and wimps to accomplish His will. That said, I guess He chose the right person for this job. Praise the Lord!
Rebecca

Laughter
Thursday, December 31, 2009

Someone must have a hotline to the King. After posting yesterday, I was able to sleep for a couple of hours and felt better afterward. Thanks to all of you for your prayers and encouraging messages.

They say laughter is the best medicine. If that's true, my kids are doctors. Gracie was the last culprit. I didn't witness it, but just hearing it relayed by her big sister, who was in hysterics, cracked me up, too.

It all revolved around a bowl of soup. Now, Gracie has two brothers at home, who are all too willing to help her clean her plate, so this may have factored into it, though the boys weren't here at the time.

Anyway, according to Rachel, Gracie was really into her soup, with her face literally in the bowl. With each spoonful, she unknowingly pushed the bowl a little farther across the table. This didn't slow her down, though. Her determined little face stayed with the bowl. Rachel was laughing so hard that by the time she tried to get Gracie's attention, it was too late. Gracie had pushed the bowl off the other side of the table and was staring down at it in dismay.

Maybe it's a mom thing, but I laughed so hard, my stomach hurt. I guess if I have to recuperate from surgery, a house full of clowns is the best place to do it.

I'm feeling much better this morning. Nausea is minimal, and so is pain so far.

God has been so faithful through this journey, and so good to give me so many prayer warriors. Rachel told me yesterday that the friends she made in India on her mission trip last summer are all praying for me, too. The Lord has some network! Thank you for being a part of it.

God bless you all, and I hope you find lots of things in 2010 to make you laugh until your stomach hurts.

Love,

Rebecca

Chapter 15

A NEW YEAR

Saran Wrap Not Included
Friday, January 1, 2010

I hope everyone else's new year is starting as well as mine! I got to take a bath! (Saran Wrap not included.) I can't even remember the last time, but it felt like forever. I'm a very happy camper. I've felt so much better the last two days!

When I think of my life before I was diagnosed (my memory is slowly returning), I can't help but praise the Lord. My pain back then was so excruciating I would soak in a hot bath two or three times a night to get relief enough to sleep. Now, my back and hip pain is irritating at most, and the nausea is the same.

But it's time to step down my pain meds again, and most of you know how hard withdrawals have been for me. We're trying to go about it in a way that will have the least negative effect on me, but I have to face the fact that I'm very sensitive to drugs and pain, so I'm going to need all the prayer I can get. Thank God, I have the Holy Spirit to fall back on.

I can't tell you how much your prayers and messages mean to me. And I can't stress enough how important all of you little CarePage and CaringBridge warriors are to me. Vinny, Diego, Breana, Daniel, Lilly, Lindsey, and all the rest of you.

You are my heroes. You give me strength when I don't think I can take anymore. And you are constantly in my prayers. May God bless you all, little warriors, with healing and peace, and may 2010 be a year of miracles for us all!

Love,

Rebecca

Yet, Another Step
Saturday, January 2, 2010

I'm enjoying my new relationship with my bathtub. How could I ever have taken it for granted? Never again.

I spread my meds out another hour this morning at 5. That's the equivalent of dropping one 5mg pill. No ill effects yet, so I'm just going to believe that God is going to spare me. Even if He doesn't, the knowledge that I have my faithful bathtub to help me through makes me a little braver. I continue to increase my activity. The only problem I've had besides pain is my hip joint on the surgery side, which is very sensitive and tends to give out on me sometimes. The last two nights have been a lot of fun, watching movies with the kids in the family room with a fire going and eating stuff not fit for human consumption, like cheese in a can. But this is how we do New Years, and the kids love it.

I'm not looking forward to school starting. I will really miss the kids, and Gracie is still quite a handful on my own. It may be they won't be going back when they think they will with two of them complaining of sore throats — again! And the other one having sinus trouble. This winter has been unbelievable.

I hope you are all staying well. Thank you so much for your continued prayers and messages. You have been such a blessing to me and our family, and I thank God for you each and every day.

God bless,

Rebecca

Oh, the Irony!
Sunday, January 3, 2010

I had no more posted my update yesterday when the withdrawals hit with a vengeance.

Although the nausea wasn't unbearable, the pain was unbelievable! Of course, I headed for the sanctuary of my tub . . . only to discover that, while the hot water worked wonders on my surgical pain, it didn't touch my withdrawal pain. I was literally laughing and crying at the same time. I'd been waiting since last October to soak in a hot bath for pain relief—and now this.

So, yesterday was horrible until Chuck made me take some ibuprofen at 10 p.m. so I could get some sleep. Around 12:30, I decided to take another soak to help the surgical pain and ended up getting relief from the withdrawal pain as well! Chuck thinks the bath increased my circulation and helped my body flush the excess meds. Whatever it was, it was a gift from God. Even more incredibly, I awoke this morning with no pain. I can hardly believe it. I still have a way to go, but I can see the light at the end of the tunnel.

Also, thank you, Tim and Shelley, for dinner last night! I was wondering what you put in the burrito fixings, though. Gracie had two good-sized burritos and then shocked her siblings by climbing out of her seat, grabbing the bag of tortillas, laughing maniacally, and taking off on a dead run around the house.

When she saw her siblings pursuing her, she turned and swung the bag of tortillas at them, sending tortillas flying. Then she dropped the empty bag and continued to run, laughing the whole time. Chuck and I heard all this from upstairs, but when Rachel and the boys came up to give a report, they were laughing so hard they could barely speak. A minute later, Gracie strolled in behind them with a very satisfied look on her face. Nonetheless, the burritos were delicious. Thank you.

I'm praying for all of you—it seems there are many—who are fighting colds right now. Our kids will be going back to the doctor today.

God bless and get well!

Rebecca

Hangin' On
Monday, January 4, 2010

They can put a man on the moon, but they can't come up with a painkiller that doesn't completely screw you up? Please.

I felt so good yesterday morning I decided to go to on an as-needed basis with my pain meds. As it turned out, I didn't need them for pain at all. Unfortunately, by afternoon I was back in withdrawal hell again. I spent last night in and out of anxiety attacks and cold sweats. When I took my anxiety med, my anxiety jumped to a whole new level. To make matters worse, I also have a sore throat and congestion, which could be withdrawals or what the kids have. The older kids all got to school, but Gracie's nose is dripping all over the place.

This morning it's gray and foggy out—just about the way I feel. I haven't had any pain so far, but I'm so nauseated and anxious, and none of my medication is working. I'm waiting for Dr. Monroe to call back and tell me what to do.

Last night, as Gracie snuggled with me, she asked why I have to sleep all the time. To her, being in bed equals sleep. It got me trying to remember what my life used to be like before that stupid tumor interrupted it.

Then I got scared and started wondering if I would ever have a "normal" again. Or, would this be my new "normal"? Chuck keeps telling me we're almost there, but every time I walk past my beautiful studio, I try to picture myself back in my chair, working on my book—and I wonder.

I told Gracie I'd be better soon and we'd do all the things we used to do. As I named each part of our old routine, I was trying to convince myself as much as her, and it was hard not to cry. I know it could be so much worse, but what I decided last night between cold sweats and panic attacks is that pain is pain. Whether it's the physical pain of illness, or the emotional pain of loss, it brings fear, it makes just getting out of bed each morning seem impossible, it can make or break your faith, and it forces us to choose to persevere or give up.

Luckily, it's also temporary. And that's enough to make me persevere. Thank you, Jesus, for making a way for me to never have to hurt again.
Praying health and peace for all of you,
Rebecca

Closer to Normal
Tuesday, January 5, 2010

Well, Chuck was right . . . again. This habit could get annoying if he weren't so cute. My nausea got better last night. I did get Gracie's cold, but that's a welcome change.

Thanks so much to all of you who offered prayers and scriptures for me. And thank you, Angela, for the clothes for Gracie. She spent the whole day trying on all the new pretties. And thank you, Chris, for dinner last night. Unfortunately, I was in no shape to eat, but maybe they saved me some . . . oh, who am I kidding?

Chuck is calling to set up our return to Seattle. I have mixed feelings. First about leaving the kids again (even though it's just a day), then about the road conditions, and, finally, about my surgeon's parting words, "It'll be interesting to see what pathology makes of this." But, once again, I'll put my trust in God. He never fails.

> *"Create in me a clean heart, O God,*
> *And renew a steadfast spirit within me."*
> Psalm 51:10 NKJV

> *"The sacrifices of God are a broken spirit, a broken and a*
> *contrite heart —these, O God, You will not despise."*
> Psalm 51:17 NKJV

God bless!
Rebecca

Still Learning
Thursday, January 7, 2010

You can always tell it's cold season in our house when no matter how many boxes of tissue are in the pantry, it's never enough. I alone went through a giant box yesterday. Well, Gracie helped a little. One of the stranger symptoms of withdrawal is sudden, uncontrollable fits of sneezing. Pair this with a cold and . . . well, you can imagine. It would be funny if it weren't so painful.

I heard Joyce Meyer speak on the "Martha Syndrome" yesterday. Having a German heritage, I learned real soon that your worth was measured by how much you did. Especially how you kept your house. Fear of failure soon turned me into a perfectionist and control freak. Joyce was saying that our job as Christians is not to do everything, but to live a balanced life of peace and joy, in the Holy Spirit. This is what makes unbelievers take notice.

God has done a lot of stripping away in my life to get my eyes on Him and strengthen my faith, and I thought I'd come a long way. But I've realized that I don't know how to rest!

It sounds crazy, but it's true. I thought I was taking time to do things I enjoy, but I just realized that no matter what I do, I'm doing it for someone else. Yes, it is a noble thing to serve others, but even God took a day to Himself to rest and enjoy the fruits of His labor. Even Jesus left the crowds, climbed a mountain, and renewed Himself with His Father. Am I better than God? If you're not laughing, you don't know me.

Like so many others, I was craving approval from other people, but, when it comes right down to it, I can't give from an empty well.

When we stand before the throne, God is not going to judge us according to the cleanliness of our houses or the weeds in our gardens or how many committees we were on. Jesus came to give us life more abundantly, a life of joy and peace in the Holy Spirit. A life that will draw others into the Kingdom. So, knowing that in my brain, my prayer is that He will teach me how to put it into practice and not judge myself by the world's standards, but by His.

I wouldn't want a good tumor to go to waste. I am German, after all.

Praying 2010 will be a year of God revealing Himself to the world through the miracle of healing in us all.

Love and blessings,

Rebecca

Appointment Date Set
Friday, January 8, 2010

This cold has me pretty wiped out. I haven't been sleeping much past 2 a.m. for the last three nights because of congestion and coughing. I'm really achy this morning, and my tailbone has been very sore for the last two days.

The good news is my stomach feels better today, and Gracie's cough is a lot better.

We also have a date for Seattle. Next Tuesday. We'll leave Monday and come home after our appointment. I'm a little nervous, and Gracie is already clinging and saying she doesn't want us to go because she misses us. I'm glad we'll only be gone one night.

I'm trying to concentrate on the positives. I have faith that my report will be good. And I'll finally get to go to the Whole Foods Market with Chuck instead of listening to him describe the selections over the phone and waiting in the hotel for him to bring dinner back. Hopefully, my appetite will be better by then.

One of the blessings that has come from this journey has been that my prayer life has been refocused. I know God can make the ugliest of things beautiful, and I know He can and does use illness to reveal and glorify Himself, while growing our faith in Him.

I was recently reminded in Lamentations 3:31–33 there is no suffering on earth that can equal eternal separation from the God of our creation. So, let us persevere, trusting our good and loving Father to do His work in us and to comfort us in our pain. He has promised to never leave or forsake us (Hebrews 13:5), and I believe Him.

> *"So we fix our eyes not on what is seen, but on what is unseen,*
> *since what is seen is temporary, but what is unseen is eternal."*
> 2 Corinthians 4:18

God bless you, and thank you for remembering us in your prayers,
Rebecca

Wrench in the Works
Sunday, January 10, 2010

The Seattle trip is not looking good right now. This cold really packed a punch. I was up long enough yesterday to eat breakfast and make the bed. Then I crashed until 2. I did make it downstairs once, but it was all I could do to get back up. Between the body aches and exhaustion, I pretty much just waited for the day to be over. And Gracie still has a nasty cough. I couldn't leave her when she's sick. So, unless we get a miracle by tomorrow, it looks like we'll be postponing our appointment for a week. As with all things, I'm sure there's a reason. But your continued prayers are greatly appreciated.

Blessings,

Rebecca

Ignorance Is Bliss
Thursday, January 14, 2010

The songbirds aren't back yet, but the sunshine was a lovely surprise this morning. Fatigue, a little cough, and an achy tailbone are my only complaints this morning, so I have a lot to be thankful for. Gracie is still pretty gunky in the mornings but sounds better as the day wears on.

We meet with my oncology team in Seattle next Tuesday afternoon. We'll probably leave Monday and take Gracie with us. The butterflies are back. It's so funny, what I've learned about myself on this journey. When I was first diagnosed, as much pain as I was in, I was completely at peace with the knowledge that God was in control, and He would heal me. And even if He didn't, I would come out ahead. I still believe that, but the pain I've experienced, and the emotional and financial strain this has caused my family over the last few months has me a little nervous.

It's a little unnerving to think my endurance may be much greater than I ever realized. That smelting fire can get pretty darn hot. True, it is the only means of getting the slag to float to the top . . . but it's not exactly my idea of a good time.

I guess I'm just tired. Nerves or no, though, I doubt my own ability, God never changes; and this I know: He loves me, He will never leave me, He has already healed me, He has plans to prosper me, He will provide for me, I belong to Him, and nothing can separate me from Him.

So, I could use your prayers for our trip Monday. Yes, I would like good news, and, yes, I would like safe travel, but mostly I need my spirit to agree with my mind. Or maybe I just need to be able to yield to the peace of the Holy Spirit. Whatever I need, please keep me in your prayers.

Blessings and healing,

Rebecca

Sunday Morning
Sunday, January 17, 2010

Sorry for the delay in posting, Laurie, didn't mean to stress you out. I guess I'm in a funk. Chuck says it started when I got my new appointment for Seattle, and I know he's right. I don't want to go. For some reason, that place equals pain in my mind, and I don't want to go back. I know the trip itself is going to be painful. I'm just tired. And the sickness in the house isn't helping. I really miss church. I miss life.

Daniel has strep, and Rachel and Gracie are on antibiotics, too. I finished my antibiotics, but my lungs still aren't clear. Daniel won't be infectious by the time we leave, but the mono has certainly compromised his immune system. Rachel and I are just exhausted. And Chuck has enough on his shoulders as it is. It's pretty hard to pay bills when you can't collect from your clients.

I've no doubt that someday this will be a great story of God's faithfulness and victory, but right now, it doesn't feel so great. So, you can see where all your prayers have been going, and, boy, do I appreciate them.

Well, today's agenda includes trying to pay some bills so we have a house and utilities to come home to. As for the stack of medical bills I've added to the pile, well . . . our God is the God of miracles.

God bless,

Rebecca

Chapter 16

BIOPSY RESULTS

Travel Day
Monday, January 18, 2010

Well, we're almost packed, and we'll be hitting the road soon. I want to thank all of you for your encouraging messages and prayers. They blessed me greatly. There was a lot of truth spoken that my heart knows. I just let my head have too much reign. *"We live by faith, not by sight"* (2 Corinthians 5:7). And our God is so much bigger than our pain and bills and sickness. But that's what we're here to learn. Unfortunately (for me), it doesn't come instantly and completely. On the upside, *"When I am weak, then I am strong"* (2 Corinthians 12:10).

You remain in my prayers, and I'll post when we get to Seattle.

I love you all!

Rebecca

On the Road Again
Monday, January 18, 2010

Praise the Lord, we're here at last! Gracie is thrilled to be "at vacation," and I'm thrilled to be out of the car!

It was dark and clear when we hit the pass, and the ski slopes were lit like a huge Christmas tree. It was very exciting for Gracie, who of course wanted to join in the snow fun.

It was a long, painful drive with one stop, but I didn't take any oxycodone. The seat heater helped a lot, and I was able to walk when we got here—an unexpected surprise. We didn't bring the wheelchair because I was determined to walk into the doctor's office. We even stopped at Whole Foods Market, a block from our hotel, and I was able to walk around the store. Chuck was right—I'm in love.

Now, I hear a nice hot tub calling my name, so I'll bid you goodnight. Thank you all for your prayers. I'll post again after we meet with the doctors tomorrow at 12:45.

God bless!

Rebecca

The Results Are In!
Tuesday, January 19, 2010

I have to tell you, I'm sitting here in a state of shock. According to the pathology report, my tumor wasn't a tumor. The best they could do to explain it is some kind of hematoma caused a mass of swollen tissue—right. One of the best orthopedic surgeons in the world tells me I have a malignant tumor and will probably have to move to Seattle and have chemo and then surgery and then everything else that goes with cancer, and it turns out to be *nothing*?

Don't get me wrong, I'm praising the Lord all right, but . . . wow. I mean, I prayed, believing in a miracle, but when it actually comes, it's . . . wow.

We do have to wait for another CAT scan before we leave, and I have to come back for another in three months, but right now, I'm just trying to process all this. I can't thank you enough for all of your prayers and support. I'm not sure why God chose to bless me this way, but I do know if He did it for me, He'll do it for others as well. Don't stop asking! Don't stop believing! Don't stop praising!

I need to lie down now. God bless you all!

Rebecca

Humbled
Thursday, January 21, 2010
Okay, I'm back.

I'm still trying to process all this. All the way home from Seattle, the only words that came to mind were, "How Great Thou Art." I thought I was being humbled as I curled up in my bed, overwhelmed with pain, nausea, and cold sweats. But nothing I've ever experienced comes close to the humility I feel right now. I'm literally prostrate before my King saying, "Command me, Lord, and I will do it. I can refuse You nothing."

Part of me feels like an atom bomb was dropped on my town, and I walked away with a sliver. I know it has nothing to do with being worthy, but everything to do with grace. Still, I am dumbfounded. I think about the gift of salvation, which is the greatest gift of grace ever. I can look at a film or a picture of my Jesus hanging on the cross, knowing it was my sin He died for, and be moved to tears, but even that is a conviction on faith alone. I didn't feel the spikes being hammered into my hands and feet. I didn't feel the thorns piercing my head. I didn't feel the sword sinking into my side.

This I feel with every ounce of my being. I have the scar as a constant reminder. Who knows, I may even continue to have pain. But I know I don't see the world like I used to. I will never be the same. I still have a lot of healing to do, and I'm sure in that time, the Lord will let me know what it is He wants from me. James 1:4−8 says:

"Let perseverance finish its work so that you may be mature and complete, not lacking anything. If any of you lacks wisdom, you should ask God, who gives generously to all without finding fault, and it will be given to you. But when you ask, you must believe and not doubt, because the one who doubts is like a wave of the sea, blown and tossed by the wind. That person should not expect to receive anything from the Lord. Such a person is double-minded and unstable in all they do."

So, I'm asking. And I have plenty of time to wait for an answer because all the things I thought were so important in this world have suddenly lost their importance. I believe Kathy D. was right when she said God wanted me to meet all of you. You have touched me in ways you will never know. I believe with all my heart that we will see many more miracles on these pages.

As for whether or not the doctors can admit a miracle, I don't know. I do know that, for me, this is just the beginning.

I love you all and will never stop praying for your miracles.

Thank you for your continued prayers and words of support.

Rebecca

Singin' in the Rain
Saturday, January 23, 2010

Blessings, everyone,

It is a rainy day in Walla Walla, but I love rainy days. They remind me that God sends His rain on the righteous and unrighteous alike. But, praise the Lord, I can use Him as an umbrella!

I'm still very tender from our trip to Seattle, and the stress of it has my chest trying to entertain bronchitis again, so I've been resting as much as possible. It would be easier if I could find my stray crochet hook.

Snuggling with Gracie can be quite an adventure. Sometimes I'll wake up with crumbs on my head because she's found herself a snack. I can't believe in a few short days she'll be 4, and I'll be 29 . . . again. Chuck and the kids are having a little party for her next weekend. You can't believe how hard it is for me to stay out of it. Well, maybe some of you can, but I'm going to be good.

The doctor we met with in Seattle told us we wouldn't hear from them unless they found something on the CAT scan, so I don't plan on hearing from them until we go back in three months. I meet with Dr. Monroe here on Monday for blood work. I'm on thyroid medication, so I have to have my blood monitored while doing the Gerson diet. We started the juicing part before my last surgery. I can't wait to stop my anxiety meds and see how I do.

Well, it's movie time with my hubby now, so I will let you go for now. I am praying for you and appreciating your prayers and messages.

God bless,

Rebecca

Faith
Sunday, January 24, 2010
Blessings, Friends,

It seems I opened a hornet's nest, posting information about the Gerson healing plan, and I'm not sure that's a bad thing. While I've heard from a couple friends, I realize I may have caused some anxiety in others who don't post or email me. So, I wanted to clarify.

First of all, I didn't want to come off as a fanatic or in any way suggest this therapy is "the miracle cure." When I found out about it, I didn't know there were alternative treatments for cancer that actually worked. Apparently, there are other clinics out there as well. I do know that what is right for one may not be right for another.

That said, if you truly believe God lives inside you, you should also believe He will guide you to what is right for you. *"For God hath not given us the spirit of fear; but of power, and of love, and of a sound mind"* (2 Timothy 1:7 KJV). Follow His leading.

Secondly, I don't put my faith in medicine, or diet. I put my faith in the One Living God, the Son, who shed His blood for me, and the Holy Spirit, who reveals His truths to me. I would have that everyone be cancer-free and well, but that's not the nature of this earth-age. We won't see that age until Christ returns for us and, *"He will wipe every tear from their [our] eyes. There will be no more death or mourning or crying or pain, for the old order of things has passed away"* (Revelation 21:4). Praise the Lord!

For now, we hang on to His promises and to the pure white robe of Jesus Christ to move us through this life and closer to Him. He has a plan for every one of us. For some of us that plan does not include healing in this world, but all of His plans reveal His glory. And that's what it's all about, letting Him shine through us. It can be found right here in these pages as we encourage and pray for one another. That is God's love revealed through us. And, when He shines, we shine.

I've had many comments about my faith in these pages. Well, I'm going to tell you a secret: My faith is not the faith that God will do what I want Him to do. My faith is in surrendering to Him, and saying, "Not my will, but thine be done," and believing that no matter what that means, His grace will be sufficient to see me through. And even in this, I can't take credit, for it's not me but Christ who lives within me who makes me believe. And, if you've read any of my past updates, you know it hasn't been without anxiety, but Christ Himself sweat drops of blood as He contemplated the cup set before Him.

Yes, I believe Jesus when He says, *"Truly I tell you . . . If you believe, you will receive whatever you ask for in prayer"* (Matthew 21:21–22). Am I there yet? Obviously not, or all of you would be healed. But I believe He will get me there. He has never failed me yet, and I tell you, He will never fail you!

I am so grateful for your prayers and encouragement, and I will not stop praying for your miracles.

God bless,

Rebecca

Another Year Older
Wednesday, January 27, 2010

Blessings,

Gracie and I would like to thank everyone for the birthday blessings, music, and the gifts. Saturday, Gracie is having some friends over to help her celebrate, but yesterday morning, she was a little upset that it wasn't her birthday anymore. She didn't want it to be Mommy's birthday, because she didn't have a present for me, so Rachel helped her make a card. The kids all made beautiful cards for me and pitched in for a massage for me today! Yes!

Well, I'm another year older, and, though I didn't feel like it yesterday, I'm another year better, praise the Lord! God is good. It will be interesting to see what He has in store for my 29th (+16) year. Great. My age has become an algebraic equation.

I saw Dr. Monroe, Monday. He wasn't thrilled with my dropping 2mg of Xanax cold turkey. He used a much prettier word than "crazy," but I got the idea. So, I dropped my last medication, but it hasn't worked its way out of my system yet.

I haven't been free from all withdrawal symptoms, but it's been a cakewalk compared to dropping my pain meds. I have to say the coffee/chamomile enemas really do relieve pain and withdrawal symptoms. Dr. Monroe said my liver would work more efficiently with them, too. I strongly suggest them for anyone dealing with severe pain.

As it is, with all of the drugs leaving my system, my surgical pain has increased some, and I'm feeling the effects of so much medication on a stomach already ravaged by H. pylori. Ouch. Today, I'm doing much better. Thank You, Lord!

So, now you know why I've been slacking in sending you messages. It's amazing how much nausea can suck the joy right out of you, but we haven't heard back about my CAT scan, so I have another reason to praise.

The one good thing about Xanax is that it affects your memory, so the last four months have felt more like a dream than real life. Of course, the bad part is that it affects your memory, so the last four months have felt more like a dream than real life. (That was a joke. ☺)

I better post this and get on with the day. Please know that, even if I don't get a message sent, you are still in my prayers. Thank you all again for the great birthday! I love you guys!
God Bless,
Rebecca

Chapter 17

THE TOUGH QUESTIONS

Lay It Down
Thursday, January 28, 2010
Blessings, CarePage Family,

Though I'm feeling better physically than I have in a long time, my heart is heavy this morning. I read all the pain and suffering in CarePages, and my flesh is set against my spirit. I want to demand, *"Why?"* I want it to stop. Sometimes, I just stare at the pages, wondering what on earth I could say to make it any better. I feel guilty that I received a miracle when so many others are trying to learn how to live without their loved ones.

But I'm not of the flesh anymore. I'm of the Spirit. I live by faith, not by sight. It's not for me to know the workings of God. Rather, I am to accept that He loves us all and is doing what's best for us, even if we can't see it. Even if it hurts.

It reminds me of when I was a young mother of four. I had everything in my world in a death grip of control, from my home to my family. I knew what was best for me and my family, and I knew God would see that I was in tune with His will and bless my efforts. But I didn't know *God*. He had plans for my life I couldn't even imagine, and, when I wouldn't surrender my "safe" world to Him, He slowly began to tear things out of my death grip that were keeping me from receiving His plan for my life. My marriage came first, followed by my business, and my ability to homeschool.

Once God made all my worst nightmares come true, He was able to make my wildest dreams come true. I'd given up on my dreams and resigned myself to living with the poor choices I'd made. But God never gives up. I had to learn the hard way that my heels of fear dug into the ground wouldn't stop God from working out His will for me. I had to learn the hard way to lay it down.

This morning I received a couple updates reminding me of the beauty and freedom of being able to lay it down. One of our fellow warriors, twelve-year-old Maggie, has asked to be allowed to die. She is battle-weary and ready to fall into the arms of God. Maggie loves the Lord and knows He's capable of healing her, and though I'd love to see that miracle, I know God will do what's best for Maggie. Whether that means living here or dancing in Heaven, I will rejoice for Maggie.

I need to treat the pain on these pages like everything else I can't carry in this world and lay it down. Because I also see courage, strength, and faith on these pages—and that is good.

God bless,

Rebecca

Oh, Sunny Day!
Monday, February 1, 2010

Blessings, Friends,

Well, I started working out this morning. Nothing grand, just some gentle Pilates and 20 minutes on a slo-o-ow treadmill. I'm getting tired of being sore from the most minimal daily activities, so I decided to give my muscles something to really complain about. I can't believe how much flexibility I've lost! As painful and comical as my workout was, I have to praise God that I'm sore and walking on both legs.

Growing up, the one quoted "scripture" in our family was: "The Lord helps those who help themselves." Those of you who know scripture should be laughing with me now, because that's not in the Bible. In fact, it flies in the face of the gift of grace. But old habits die hard sometimes, and I have to stop and laugh at myself when I remember that God doesn't need my help with anything. I'm just glad He's so patient with me. I think He gets a kick out of me, too.

Gracie's party went well without my interference, and I was able to sit up for about three hours. Yesterday, I went grocery shopping with Chuck. Both activities were very painful, but my recovery time is lessening, so thank You, Lord!

The sunshine is glorious this morning, and the birds are telling me spring is on its way. God's timing is perfect. He knows I'd like to be outside, dragging myself across the yard to get to my flowerbeds. But for now, I'll try to be "content in every circumstance," like Paul. (See Philippians 4:11.). Because there's always something to praise the Lord for. And no matter how frustrating or just plain bad my life gets, it's all good in Him.

May God bless you with sunshine and birdsong,

Rebecca

Gifts from the Hand of God
Thursday, February 4, 2010

Blessings!

I'm hurting more today, but I don't care. Yesterday was one of those gifts from God I'll always be grateful for. I was relatively pain-free until evening! It was so-o-o good! I was even able to cook dinner for my family for the first time since last September. Praise the Lord! It was like He was reassuring me there are better days ahead.

When Jesus describes us as the branches in John 15, He says if we remain in Him, we will bear much fruit. Not by the importance of who we are, who our friends are, or how many hours we sacrifice, but by the Spirit. My problem is that there are windows of time in my life where I soar on the wings of faith and watch God do some awesome things . . . but then my attention gets diverted, and I plummet like a turkey! So, I've been trying to identify some things that divert my attention from the Giver of all good things. This is what I've come up with so far:

1. I fail to take myself out of the equation—When God gives me what I ask for, whether it's healing, or finding my car keys, it has nothing to do with how big my faith is, or how spiritual I am. Thinking about these things causes me to doubt. I'm just a conduit. It's all about revealing the glory of God to the world. It's all about Him. "For I can do nothing apart from Him." (See John 15:5.)

2. I take responsibility for the outcome—Again, not my place. Thinking about all of my prayers that seemed to go unanswered causes me to hesitate. I think, what if this isn't God's will? My job is to ask and believe. What God decides to do with my request is His business, not mine.

3. I worry about what people will think—Acting supernaturally isn't exactly the stuff peer approval is made of. Who wants to offend anyone, or, worse, turn them off to Jesus? But Jesus was not popular. In fact, He was *the* Rock of Offense. (See 1 Peter 2:8.) They killed Him, you know. Am I willing to die for Him? Hmmm.

4. I just get so wrapped up in the day to day I forget to spend quality time with my Father—This is a biggie. Especially for a wife and mother. But God set my priorities when He created family: God first, then family, then everything else. But God won't tug my shirt out of shape, hounding, "Mom . . . Mom . . . Mom . . ." He just waits for me to make time in my busy schedule for Him.

I'm sure there are more, but these are the main things. I don't know if it was the cancer, but I'm no longer willing to just read about God's awesome power, getting a little taste now and then. I want to bear much fruit. I don't know how many days are appointed to me, but I want to make the most of them.

The love of God is so awesome, I want to be completely saturated in it. I want it to ooze from my pores. I want to be the aroma of Christ in the world (2 Corinthians 2:15–16). This world has nothing for me; I know who I belong to. I just pray I no longer serve as my own stumbling stone. I realize not everyone is in the same place, and that's okay. When God created us each individually, He designed plans unique to each of us. He really is the best Dad ever. All He asks of us is that we believe.

Thank you so much for your continued prayers and encouragement.
God bless,
Rebecca

Grief
Thursday, February 11, 2010

I debated over whether to post this or not. After talking with God and Chuck and letting it sit overnight, I decided that when we don't share our struggles and weaknesses, we only isolate others who are struggling. Our strength and witness comes from sharing our frailties and how God is faithful to give us victory over them.

I took an emotional nosedive yesterday. Word of Maggie's passing affected me in a way I never saw coming. I'm so happy for Maggie—that she doesn't hurt anymore—but I know too well what her mother is going through. I know the hole in her heart. I know the pain of knowing you did all you could—and it wasn't enough.

As I read about Maggie and her mother, my thoughts turned to my daughter, Hannah. Grief has its own timeline. You can avoid it only for so long, and then it refuses to be ignored. The only way out of it is through it. I've never written about this before, so maybe this will help me, too.

I think of all four of my children in Heaven, but I think more so of Hannah, because I got to see her and hold her. Hannah was born five months too early. Most of the time I can shut out the images of my tiny little girl struggling for life. She couldn't even cry, but I could feel her fear. Yesterday, the pain and guilt were as fresh as if it had just happened. It's been a long time, so I guess it was overdue.

Although I know in my heart, she's happy and waiting for me in Heaven, sometimes the mother in me overrides that knowledge, and I have to forgive myself yet again for not protecting my baby. For not comforting her while she was living because the EMTs were trying to administer oxygen her tiny lungs couldn't use yet. For some insane reason, I actually thought they could keep her alive. But, an hour later, as the ambulance pulled up to the hospital, she died.

I nearly joined her from blood loss, but I had three little ones at home, and after they had watched their mother disappear in an ambulance, I wasn't about to compound their fear by not going home.

Hannah would be thirteen this April had she gone full- term. She looked just like Rachel, and she would be hot on her big sister's heels. There's a weeping cherry tree in the front yard, and a Fragrant Memory rose in the perennial bed planted in Hannah's memory. I didn't get a chance to make happy memories with her. I only had that hour. The longest hour of my life. And, of course, the memory of holding her still body tight in ER until the nurses tranquilized me to get her away from me.

Then there was saying good-bye to that tiny, white casket sitting on the cold, hard ground of the cemetery where I'd had to say good-bye to my mother and grandmother before her. I think leaving her there was even harder than watching her die. Even though I knew she wasn't there, I wanted to hold her and protect her from the cold November ground.

Luckily, we'll have an eternity to make happy memories. It's just the waiting that's so hard.

When I was in grade school, one of my younger sister's friends was killed in a tragic accident. I remember telling my mother I was jealous of the little girl because she got to be with God, and I was stuck here.

Now I just feel the pain of loss. I feel it as acutely for others as for myself. I don't know if this is a good thing. It doesn't feel good. I think it's kind of ironic because I truly believe that, for believers, to die is to live. I'm happy for those who get to go home. What could be better than to throw your arms around Jesus?

But I can't seem to escape my humanity when it comes to grief. I can take comfort in knowing my great and all-powerful God experienced the same grief, more so, as He watched His own Son die, and I know He hurts with us as well. And He didn't leave us to grieve alone; He gave us the Comforter to help us through it, and He gave us each other.

I thank God for the five healthy children I have, and for the reunion we'll have with their siblings one day. But while I'm bound in this body, I'll continue to heal as God prescribes. I'll continue to cry when others cry and rejoice when they rejoice and look forward to the day when we have nothing left to cry about.

Rachel sent me a video, "Held," by Natalie Grant, yesterday after she and Gracie baked me cookies. Of course, it started the tears flowing again, but this time she cried with me, and somehow it made it better. What a blessing Rachel is. She's always had such a tender, caring heart, and I love her for it. Live your life to the fullest, Rachel. Never miss a moment. Go to Germany, go back to England, fly fighter jets, go back to India and love all those children who fell in love with you! Just go with God, and live! I'm so proud of you, and Hannah is, too!

God bless you all and grant you His peace,

Rebecca

Apples of Gold
Friday, February 12, 2010
Blessings, Friends,

"A word fitly spoken is like apples of gold in settings of silver" (Proverbs 25:11 NKJV).

I got a bushel of golden apples yesterday, and I'm so grateful to those of you who took time to encourage me. You truly ministered to my spirit, and I love you for it. I'm filled with joy today and excited to get back to my Bible study, but I wanted to post this before I got swept away. I lose all track of time when I'm on a mission.

On the medical front, my stomach was not doing well on the Gerson diet, and Chuck reminded me I'd had an endoscopy just before my tailbone went nuts and never had my follow-up appointment for that. Funny how the word "tumor" can make you forget everything else in your life.

I went back to my stomach specialist and found out I have considerable damage to my esophagus. The good news is, my stomach showed no signs of pre-malignancy, but the bad news is the raw veggies were causing too much irritation from the amount of acid produced to break them down. I was placed on a high-fiber, low-acid diet for the next three months to give my esophagus a chance to heal. My stomach should be feeling better in a couple of weeks, so praise the Lord! Honestly, I don't know what I'd do without Chuck to remind me of these little details.

Our youngest son, Daniel, is begging to homeschool again, but there are so many things to consider. Please pray for wisdom for us to do what is best for our son.

Well, my B-i-b-l-e is calling, so I'll let you go. I count it a blessing to know you and an honor to pray for you.
God bless you all,
Rebecca

PART III

"Go therefore and make disciples of all the nations,
Baptizing them in the name of the Father and of the
Son and of the Holy Spirit, teaching them to observe
All things that I have commanded you; and lo, I am
With you always, even to the end of the age. Amen."
Matthew 28:19, 20 NKJV

Chapter 18

REFINED AS SILVER

*A*s the medication left my system, my head began to clear. My eyes were able to focus once more, and I was able to get back into the Word. As I did, a strange thing happened. It was as if a veil had been lifted. I was no longer reading black ink on a flat, white page. The words came alive, the pages fluid, plunging me into a world of light. My heart burned with God's truth—with the fullness of His glory. This fullness poured out into the posts of my CarePage. I couldn't contain it.

Jars of Clay
Tuesday, February 16, 2010
Blessings, Friends,

It was a wonderful Valentine's Day for me. Great company, great chocolate, and great movies. But the best part was that I went to church with my family! It was hard on my body, but my spirit was soaring! The phrase "clay pot" came up in the message, and it got me thinking about Jeremiah 18 and the irony of God. Of course, He's not ironic to Himself, but to us, with limited sight—not to mention the unbelieving world—He can appear that way.

Here's what I mean: As God's creation, we are literally jars of clay. Because of sin, we are born flawed, so God pounds us down on the wheel to reshape us according to His plan. To jars of clay, this looks and feels like destruction. But, in reality, it's an act of re-creation. The value of a jar is not in the outward appearance or how thick and strong the clay is, but in the empty space inside that determines the volume it can accommodate.

I believe God is reshaping me to be able to hold more of Him, thinning my clay walls as He does so. If I see a clay jar through human eyes, I think that the thicker the walls, the stronger the jar. But the jar will break just as easily as a thin-walled jar when dropped. What gives me my strength is not the condition or thickness of my flesh, but rather the Holy Spirit who fills me.

Not surprisingly, it's the Holy Spirit who gives us the faith to see it through God's eyes, but even then, it's sometimes too difficult for us to accept. But here's the crux: God only pounds the clay that's dear to Him, which is why James tells us in James 1:2–4:

"My brethren, count it all joy when you fall into various trials, knowing that the testing of your faith produces patience. But let patience have its perfect work, that you may be perfect and complete, lacking nothing" (NKJV).

I'd have to say, given the choice, I choose to be pounded by a loving God rather than live the "good life" here on earth. Even if it means losing someone I love. Because the hole left in my heart from the temporary loss of a loved one couldn't possibly compare to the emptiness of being permanently separated from my Father. I don't even want to think of life without Him. There is no life without Him.

So, when the world calls me weak and asks me how I can believe in a God who "allows" such suffering, I can stand firm and say, "Because no one could love me more."

"The word which came to Jeremiah from the Lord, saying:
'Arise and go down to the potter's house, and there I will cause you to hear My words.'
Then I went down to the potter's house, and there he was, making something at the wheel. And the vessel that he made of clay was marred in the hand of the potter; so he made it again into another vessel, as it seemed good to the potter to make."
Jeremiah 18:1–4 NKJV

Please remember little Camilla's family in your prayers. This sweet baby was taken home by the angels Sunday night.

God bless you and keep you in His peace,

Rebecca

God continued to amaze us with His faithfulness in our finances and my healing, and I continued writing whatever He put on my heart. There were days I'd have no idea what to write, but I'd put my hands on the keyboard, and the words would come. Other days, I knew exactly what I wanted to write, but the Spirit had other plans, and I'd write something completely different. It was always exhilarating and always just what I needed. I couldn't wait to get to my computer each day.

One day as I was writing, the Lord spoke to my heart.

Teach My Word.

"What? Me? Now? But I haven't even recovered from my last—adventure."

I made you a teacher. Teach My Word.

"Well, yes, I love to teach . . . and I love to study Your Word . . . but who would listen to me? No one has ever listened to me. How could I possibly teach people Your Word? I don't have a degree in theology. I'm not ordained. I'm just a housewife—a writer."

You're doing it now.

I stared at my computer screen. "But, that's different," I said. "That's not teaching."

Do you read the comments people leave?

I had read the comments on my CarePage. What had I missed? I clicked through some older postings and read:

"Once again, you've posted such an amazingly encouraging and uplifting post, Rebecca. Thank you so much!! I love to read your messages, for I can hear the Holy Spirit speaking through you . . ."

"Wow, your message is very well stated. May I pass your words on to my church congregation? Thanks so much for sharing."

"Rebecca:
You are certainly an inspiration to all of us who have the pleasure to come and read your beautiful words. No matter how hard the pain is in this life, you have for sure a place in Heaven by teaching others the Word of God and reminding us that the most important focus must always be our love for God."

"Thank you, Rebecca,
You always teach me & help lead me closer to God!"

"Amen, and I thank God for the gifts He has given you. To get His love across to others. Even a total stranger in need of the awakening of His love within me. And the realization that He is always there, loving us!"

"Wow! What a message! I was thoroughly encouraged by your update. My goodness, God is so awesome. Who would have thought I would come on a CarePage and be ministered to? I feel so blessed and encouraged. Thank you so much for being transparent and sharing your struggles. It has really helped me to realize I can do all things through Christ who strengthens me. I am so overwhelmed to the point of tears. I can hardly express how your update has blessed me. I, too, have been praying for God to just saturate me with His spirit, I want his love to ooze from me, also."

You are teaching. I'm touching people through you.

I couldn't contain my tears. All this time, I'd been wondering what God's purpose in my tumor was, and when He would reveal it to me, and it had been right there all along. It never occurred to me that I was writing for anyone but myself. I wasn't worthy of this gift He'd given me, but as I continued reading comments from people I'd never met, I knew the gift wasn't just for me. This knowledge brought the same feelings of inadequacy I'd felt sitting in my oncologist's office four months earlier.

Reconciling such an overwhelming commission with forty-five years of invisibility would take a little time—and a lot of prayer.

Purpose
Saturday, February 20, 2010
Blessings, Friends,

I wasn't going to post this weekend, but I think I need to. This week has been a difficult one, especially after doing so well the week before. I've had a searing pain in my tailbone, a tingling sensation down my right leg that makes it hard to sleep, and I nearly fell down the stairs Thursday, because my hip and knee joints weren't cooperating. Add that to the other stresses of life, and you could say my attitude hasn't been the best.

But yesterday (after watching umpteen episodes of All Dogs Go to Heaven to keep Gracie happy), I found the movie, *John*. Since John is my favorite book of the Bible, I watched it. As I listened to Jesus' words, I was reminded (again) that my whole reason for being here is not for my comfort and good fortune, but to glorify God.

When Jesus healed the man who was born blind, the disciples asked Him who had sinned to cause his blindness, and, *"Jesus answered, 'Neither this man nor his parents sinned, but that the works of God should be revealed in him'"* (John 9:3 NKJV).

A man had been born without sight for the sole purpose of being healed by Jesus that others might see and believe, or refuse to see and be blinded (verse 39). In chapter 11, Lazarus dies for the sole purpose of being raised from the dead by Jesus so that many who had seen this put their faith in Him.

Even Jesus said time and time again, it wasn't for His own glory that He walked with us, but for His Father's glory. He was doing the work of His Father. Even in the face of great fear. Take John 12:27, when He said: *"Now My soul is troubled, and what shall I say? 'Father, save Me from this hour'? But for this purpose I came to this hour"* (NKJV).

Yes, Jesus was tortured to death, but because He was faithful, God gave Him the grace to get through it. And I think we all know it worked out in Jesus' favor. Not to mention ours! So, once again, I needed to be reminded that my time for glory and the good life is yet to come. For now, Father, glorify Your name!

Go in God's peace,
Rebecca

Reasons to Praise!
Tuesday, March 2, 2010
Blessings, Friends,

We've been having incredible weather here in Walla Walla, like a beautifully wrapped gift from the Giver of All Good Things. This weekend, as I sat on the bed putting my shoes on (with my own hands), Chuck reminded me that, not too long ago, I was wondering if I'd ever be doing something so normal again. It hardly seems possible that just a few months ago, I couldn't even walk down the stairs on my own. Eating at the table with my family was a rare and painful blessing. And here I was, this weekend, putting on my grubbies to go out in my yard!

Of course, Chuck wouldn't let me get my hands on any tools, but just seeing all of my snowdrops, daffodils, hyacinths, tulips, and daylilies coming up, and the trees in bud, made my day. I'm pretty sure I heard the host of Heaven singing the "Hallelujah Chorus." God is so good!

As much as I like being mobile and pain-free, I wouldn't change the last five months for anything. The intimacy I share with the Father could have never happened if I were in the best of health, because I'm so good at keeping busy. Communion with the Lord often took a back seat to "life." How ironic, since Jesus is life.

But being pinned down by pain put my focus right where it needs to be, and I've been so richly blessed as a result. If others have been blessed in sharing my journey, then praise the Lord! That's just proof that God can use me in spite of myself.

I got to church again, and I even got to visit my brother and his wife and finally take them their Christmas present. I started an afghan for them in August. Of course, in September, I was diagnosed with the tumor. I worked on it in the hospital, in between surgeries, and post-surgery, and finally got it done.

Unfortunately, I was on massive drugs during most of that time, so it took some interesting turns, most of which I ripped out and re-did, but it came out all right, considering. My sister-in-law, Vicki, calls it my psychedelic afghan for obvious reasons. The kids weren't happy to see the afghan go because they were used to cuddling in it as I worked, so I'm making a new one for them.

I had blood work done this morning, and I see my doc, Friday, so I'll let you know how that goes.

And I'd like to ask for special prayers. God has given us yet another reason to praise Him and another opportunity to watch Him work. Because of the work Chuck missed while taking care of me, we're facing the worst financial situation of our married life. There is literally no place to go but up. We know all things (money included) are God's to give or take, and we have no doubt this will all work to our good because that's what He promised.

It's amazing to think we're facing the fire again so soon after what we've just been through, but what can I say, God loves us . . . a lot. So please pray for wisdom for us as we praise God for His fire and for His perfect plan. It is at once thrilling and terrifying to submit to God completely, but knowing Him like I do, I would never pass up a chance to watch God work.

Praise the Lord!

May God keep you in His perfect peace and grace,

Rebecca

Blood Work Results and Praise!

Friday, March 5, 2010

Happy Friday!

Just a quick update on my doctor's appointment this morning. Dr. Monroe was very happy with what he saw. I have to increase my vitamin D a little more, and I'll have to be on thyroid meds the rest of my life, but I'm doing much better than my last blood work. No sign of tissue inflammation. Yea! I do have a fairly large bit of scar tissue that may have to be removed because it is irritating my sacrum and causing abdominal pain. Not too crazy about another surgery, though it would be an outpatient procedure, but I'll find out more when we go back to Seattle next month.

I also wanted to let you know that the day after I posted my original prayer request concerning our finances, Chuck worked all day and into the evening. We're already beginning to see God's provision, and it's awesome! You guys must have some powerful connections. Thank you for your continued prayer and praise.

"I lift up my eyes to the mountains—where does my help come from?
My help comes from the Lord, the Maker of heaven and earth.
He will not let your foot slip—he who watches over you will not slumber."
Psalm 121:1-3

Amen!

I love this reminder that no matter how dark things look or how alone I feel, I am loved. And so are you!

Chapter 19

WHY?

An Answer to "Why?"
Tuesday, March 9, 2010
Blessings, Friends,

The rain has given way to sunshine again, and the songbirds are doing their best to lure me out to my flower beds. I did get my flowerpots cleaned up and ready for the porch, which really lifted my spirits, so I praise the Lord for that. I love to get my hands in the dirt!

I'm always saying God has a reason for everything He does. But when it comes to illness—or really any suffering—I think we all have a hard time picturing a purpose. We tend to think it's beyond us and say we'll find out in Heaven, and I know this is true to some extent. But there's also a very real purpose we can know here and now.

We're told in Philippians 2:12 to work out our own salvation with fear and trembling. What does that mean? We obviously can't save ourselves, or Jesus wouldn't have had to die. But, if you read all of chapter 2, Paul is talking about how we relate to each other within the family of God. And in 1 Corinthians 12, when Paul talks about spiritual gifts we all receive as members of the body of Christ, he mentions "those who can help others" (1 Corinthians 12:28 NCV). Yes, compassion, empathy, encouragement, cooking, cleaning, childcare, doctoring, nursing . . . are all gifts from God used to edify the body.

This may not be a good enough reason for some, but I tell you this, our suffering gives the saints a means of working out their own salvation just as it gives others a means of working out their own condemnation. It's not just the suffering who are blessed by these gifts. Everyone who as much as takes a moment out of their day to post an encouraging message on these pages receives a blessing from God—and those who read them receive a blessing as well—in the opportunity to pray for each other and be encouraged.

The world is watching us. Our ministry to each other is the only way they'll see Jesus until He returns. Our suffering makes that possible. I said it when I was in the hospital, and I say it again: If only one person comes to Christ or is strengthened through my suffering, then it will all be worth it.

So what's in it for the sufferers? That is the best of all!

"Blessed are the poor in spirit: for theirs is the kingdom of heaven.
Blessed are they that mourn: for they shall be comforted."
Matthew 5: 3 -4 KJV

"Blessed is the one who perseveres under trial because having stood the test, that
person will receive the crown of life that the Lord has promised
to those who love him."
James 1:12

So, take heart, beloved. Our suffering is not in vain. And, though it may seem like an eternity, our striving with this world is but a day. Eternity is yet to come. And it will be glorious!
God bless you and keep you in His peace,
Rebecca

I'm Gonna Trust God
Monday, March 15, 2010
Blessings, Friends,

It's certainly been a week of provision for us. God has met every need, no matter how big or small. The phone has been ringing, and Chuck has been working late most nights—something I wouldn't normally celebrate, but I'm praising God for it now!

Probably the most amazing gift came on Chuck's birthday. He was on his way out of town in the pump truck when he noticed the turn signal wasn't working. By an amazing "coincidence," the garage was able to take him right away, and while they were under the truck removing the signal, they just happened to notice that a couple of the rivets that keep the truck together had sheared off! The vibration and load at highway speeds could easily have caused a fatal accident. And he would have never known about the danger if the signal had been working. So, thank You, Jesus!

Chuck wasn't happy about losing work time, but, as it turned out, the pump couldn't be pulled until the next day anyway. God is good! It's funny how things we see as miracles God sees as just taking care of His children. I think He takes great joy in showing us just how much He cares about the details of our lives.

I don't know how people do it without Him. I couldn't even begin to "imagine there's no Heaven," because I know with every fiber of my being that there is. Just as I know a life without God is a life without hope or purpose. I thank God for choosing to give me "hope and a future" (Jeremiah 29:11).

My heart goes out to all of those who are suffering over the pain or loss of their loved ones, as I lift you up in prayer. Regardless of whether we receive our healing in this world or in Heaven, we all must come to terms with God's sovereignty in our own lives in order to find peace.

Survivors are plagued with whys, too. At least this one is. And every day, I must make a conscious decision to lay it down and say, *"The Lord gives, and the Lord takes away. Blessed be the name of the Lord"* (Job 1:21). Every day, I must make the choice to believe what is not seen, in someone greater than myself. And through my belief, I'm rewarded with glimpses of the Almighty. Whether it's in a few dollars in an old wallet, some sheared-off rivets, or the glorious Royal Star magnolia blooming outside my window. God is good—always.

Blessed be the name of the Lord!

Blessings and peace in our Lord, Jesus Christ,

Rebecca

Scan Date
Wednesday, March 17, 2010
Blessings, Friends, and Happy St. Patrick's Day!

I finally got my next scan and doctor's appointment—April 26th & 27th. Please be praying for good news, a safe trip, and for our kids to be safe while we're gone.

I leave you with my prayers and many thanks for all of yours.

God keep you in His grace and peace,

Rebecca

Freedom
Saturday, March 20, 2010
One of my favorite quotes comes from *Anne of Green Gables*—I may not get it word for word, because Gracie's hidden my copy—but it's when Anne asks Marilla if she could imagine being in the depths of despair, and Marilla answers her, "No, I cannot. To despair is to turn your back on God."

Not a happy camper, today. I'm dying to be out in the sunshine, pruning my roses and enjoying my family. Instead, I'm trying to elude a cold for the second time in as many weeks, and my surgery site is grossly swollen and painful. So, I'm in bed.

I was hoping a week of bed rest would calm my scar tissue down, and I'd be back on my feet this weekend, but it's only gotten worse. I'm back to taking hot baths to control pain, but it still wakes me up in the night. I won't even go into the aesthetics of a lopsided rear end. Chuck says it's hardly noticeable, but I firmly believe he may be the slightest bit biased.

My doctor at SCCA wants me in sooner than scheduled, but they haven't called with an appointment yet. I don't know what's going on, but God does, so I'm not going to worry about it. That's the beauty of accepting His sovereignty: I don't have to know it all right here and now. I know nothing happens to me that isn't by His hand, and that's enough for me. I don't have to like what He's doing, but I can rest in the knowledge that, no matter what fire He sends me into, He is not only leading me, He's carrying me. It's no coincidence that my promise verse for today was 2 Timothy 1:12: *"That is why I am suffering as I am. Yet this is no cause for shame, because I know whom I have believed, and am convinced that he is able to guard what I have entrusted to him until that day."* (An older translation of the last phrase is "entrusted to him for that day.")

So, praise the Lord! Jesus said, *"If you hold to my teaching, you are really my disciples. Then you will know the truth, and the truth will set you free"* (John 8:31–32). It's a total contradiction of the world's standards, but there's no greater freedom than total reliance on the Creator of all things. Praise God! I'm free!

Okay, I feel better now. Thank you all for your kind words and prayers.

God keep you in His grace and peace,

Rebecca

Completion
Monday, March 22, 2010

Blessings, Everyone,

Thank you for all your encouragement after my last update. It really made me feel better.

Today's promise is 1 John 2:17: *"The world and its desires [its cancer, sickness, suffering . . .] pass away, but whoever does the will of God lives forever."* Amen!

My new appointments at SCCA are next Tuesday, March 30th. I'll get an MRI and meet with Dr. Conrad on the same day, so we'll only be away from the kids one night, unless they decide to do surgery. We'll drive to Seattle on Monday. I also meet with Dr. Monroe tomorrow to see what I need to do until then. Although the pain increased over the weekend, I'm confident it's not serious. Just a feeling. But then, really, what is too difficult for God? He's carried me this far, and He'll take me the rest of the way. Please pray for His will to be done regarding the care of our children while we are gone, as well as my appointments.

Some "good news" is that I'll only be getting an MRI. Not a CAT scan. I put that in quotes because they are Chuck's words. I have to have happy pills to get through an MRI, but the last time I had both tests, the contrast for the CAT scan made me so sick, I woke up in the middle of the night thinking I was dying. So praise God it'll only be one test. And praise God for Xanax!

I'm reading a book called *Yes, Lord,* by Dona Hoffman about her journey through cancer. I don't know where I got it; (the past months are still pretty foggy), but I read a line today about God that I loved: "who regards our Completion as great an act of His glory as our Creation."

What a wonderful Father, who doesn't merely give us life but stays with us to our completion. Molding us, shaping us, correcting us, blessing us, comforting us . . . all the while keeping us in His gentle but mighty hands. What a privilege to be made complete by the One who laid the foundations of the world!

A privilege indeed, when I consider it was He who made the way for me. I would have never been able to reach Him, but He willingly came down to my level so I could crawl over His crucified body spanning the great chasm. Back to my Father's arms. Never to be separated again. The Beginning.

God keep you in His grace and peace,

Rebecca

Chapter 20

MIRACLES

I *tried to imagine what "teaching" would look like for me. I felt completely unqualified for this commission. What I'd been doing came as easily as breathing, but now, somehow, the stakes had been raised. I knew God judges teachers of His Word by a much higher standard, and I would sooner die than fail Him. But, if I was already teaching on my CarePage, maybe God just wanted me to keep doing that. That would be easy enough—as long as His Spirit didn't leave me. What a relief that would be.*

But God was quick to remind me that CarePages was limited in its scope. What He had in mind was bigger. He wanted me to create another blog. One that would challenge believers to take Him out of the box and discover who He really is.

"Wow. How exciting that would be—but, what about the Great Commission? I thought You wanted us to share salvation with the lost," I questioned.

And He replied: *My church has backslidden into darkness. They have forgotten their first love. They no longer serve Me, but their own selfish desires. Because of this, I have withdrawn My Spirit, and they are lost. Bring My people back to Me.*

"Oh—is that all? No problem."

Reaching out to the lost was one thing—but, confronting the Church? I remembered all too well the fate of God's prophets. With the exception of Elijah, who was taken to Heaven in a cloud, it was not a position I would have asked for. But I also remembered Jonah. How could I refuse God? I couldn't. I'm not that fond of fish.

I knew the Holy Spirit would be doing all the work. But when I ruffled feathers—and I knew I would—I would be the target of the arrows. Paul had written much about suffering for the sake of the Gospel, but—actually doing it? Somehow, cancer didn't look so scary anymore.

Miracles
Wednesday, March 24, 2010
Blessings, Friends,

Today's promise is Job 11:18–19: *"You will be secure, because there is hope; you will look about you and take your rest in safety. You will lie down, with no one to make you afraid, and many will court your favor."* Amen.

Another young sister has joined the Heavenly Host. I've followed Lindsey's journey since my own began and am just as amazed by her mother's love as Lindsey's strength. What a powerful testimony. So reflective of God's determination to go as far as it takes to save His children. Our prayers are with Lindsey's family.

Many warriors, mostly children, have gone to be with the Lord since I first signed on. By comparison, only a few have been given a new lease on life on earth. When I began my journey, I tended to be disheartened by the disparaging inequity. But, as God has ministered to me in my own pain, I've come to think I've been viewing life upside-down, from the perspective of the creation instead of the Creator. I've been laboring under the impression that the ultimate miracle is when God heals a person of their illness. These are miracles to be sure, and they serve to make some people believe who wouldn't believe otherwise. And that gives people hope.

But I've come to understand there is a miracle far more powerful than healing. That is the grace to endure unimaginable pain and suffering— sometimes for years—and not only trust in God through it all, but to love and glorify Him even in the face of death. The grace to shout above the roar of pain and fear, "Even so, Lord, I love You, and I will praise You!" That is not human.

That is superhuman. That is the living God. That is where my faith belongs, not in what He does for me, but in who He is.

A Poem by Dona Hoffman

To wrest from every savage moment
the infinite peace of God
to cling to His promises
even when my heart would be a scoffer
to live abundantly and with joy
centering my thoughts upon Him
this is the challenge
the goal and the prize.

The Lord keep you in His grace and peace,
Rebecca

New Lab Results—Finally
Friday, March 26, 2010
Blessings, Friends,

Today's promise is Matthew 6:31–33 (from Jesus' mouth to my ears): *"So do not worry, saying, 'What shall we eat?' or 'What shall we drink?' or 'What shall we wear?' For the pagans run after all these things, and your heavenly Father knows that you need them. But seek first his kingdom and his righteousness, and all these things will be given to you as well."* Amen!

Boy, don't I know it. Chuck has been swamped with work. Praise God! But I feel bad for him because he's so tired, and still has to deal with me and the kids. But, just like me, he's learning to let go and let God.

On Tuesday, Dr. Monroe had more labs done, and they found an infection. Unfortunately, it took them until today to identify it so they could give me the right antibiotic. Don't ask me to spell it. Hopefully, the antibiotics will kick in and make my trip to Seattle on Monday a little more bearable. Doc thinks the pain from this infection is unrelated to the pain and inflammation of my scar tissue, but any relief will be welcome. I don't relish the idea of dipping into my vast narcotic supply to make the trip, but I'm thankful it's there if needed.

Got a call from SCCA this morning, reminding me of my 8:00 a.m. MRI on Tuesday. Yea! What a way to start the day!

The kids are all set for when we leave, thank you, Mom, Dad, Shawna, Vicki, and Rachel R. What a blessing you are!

Chuck and I always said we would take time for romantic getaways, but I never thought we'd have to go to such extremes. Maybe next time we can plan something that doesn't include needles, scalpels, or torpedo tubes. How about a nice, warm beach?

Thank you all for your continued prayer and uplifting messages. They mean more than you can know. I'm going to practice my visualization now. God's grace and peace be with you,

Rebecca

Back to Seattle
Monday, March 29, 2010
Blessings, Everyone,

Today's promise is Philippians 2:13 (fittingly enough): *"For it is God who works in you to will and to act in order to fulfill his good purpose."*

Of course, that's preceded by verse 12, which tells us to continue to work out our salvation with fear and trembling!

Thank you all for your wonderful posts. It was so nice to share a laugh with you.

Your messages were all comforting and a nice distraction, but it's still taking every ounce of my will to focus on any task. I hate feeling this way, trying to move through the thick muck in my head and breathe through the crushing weight on my chest. And it makes me angry because it's totally irrational! I mean, it's not like I'm facing a den of hungry lions, or a fiery furnace. It's not even opening night—I don't have any lines to forget.

Chuck and the kids have been so good, trying to keep me preoccupied, and I love them for it. I just wish it was were over so I could laugh at myself again for being so silly. But even Paul had his thorns to contend with, and I guess this is just one of mine.

I think the antibiotics are starting to work, but my tailbone hurts so bad I'm not sure I'll make the whole 275 miles in the front seat. But God is bigger than my pain (or fear), so I'll keep praising Him, and He will get me through.

We're almost packed, and Gracie is ready to drive herself to Shawna's because we aren't moving fast enough. But Chuck has to make a couple service calls first. So, I guess I'd better get back to it. I can't believe I was able get this much written! More from Seattle.

God keep you in His grace and peace,

Rebecca

Out of Control . . . Again
Tuesday, March 30, 2010

Blessings, Friends,

Today's promise is 1 Corinthians 15:58: *"Therefore, my dear brothers and sisters, stand firm. Let nothing move you. Always give yourselves fully to the work of the Lord, because you know that your labor in the Lord is not in vain."*

We made it! The drive over went much better than I expected. Only Tylenol (and caffeine). I know it was your prayers. I'm not hurting nearly as bad as I was the last trip. We got snowed on in Snoqualmie Pass, but the snow soon turned to sheets of rain. It was a beautiful drive, though, with all of the little waterfalls pouring down the rocks on the roadside.

We listened to a message on walking in the Spirit on the way. A great reminder that I'm not in control of any of this, and though that's one of the hardest things for me to learn, it's vital to my spiritual growth. Learning to trust only the Holy Spirit. Not my eyes, or ears, perceptions, or knowledge. Just Him.

As Chuck and I talked about it, I started thinking about the old hymn I used to sing in church, "I Surrender All," and I got this picture of me at various times in my life singing my heart out," "I surrender all . . .", all the while desperately cramming possessions into my pockets. It went something like this:

I surrender all . . . (except my children, 'cause you might take them away)

I surrender all . . . (except my marriage, 'cause I don't want to get hurt)

All to Thee my Blessed Savior . . . (except my money, ''cause if I give You that, I may not have enough left over to feed my kids)

I surrender all . . . (oh yeah, and my business, 'cause I need security)

I had to laugh. In reality, none of those things I stuffed in my pockets were mine anyway. They all belong to God and always will. What a relief to be able to empty my pockets and praise Him for choosing to bless me with them. So here I am, out of control again, and learning. Always learning. Have Your way with me, Lord. I surrender all. Really.

I'll let you know how the appointments go!

God's grace and peace be with us all!

Rebecca

Clear Scan!!!
Tuesday, March 30, 2010
Praise the Lord!

Yes, I survived another MRI! Of course, I took my happy pill in the hotel, so by the time we got to SCCA, I didn't care what they did to me. And, in spite of the needles and the torpedo tube, my wonderful husband managed to make it a romantic getaway complete with a date at Whole Foods Market and holding my hand for the "ride on the Magnetic Resonant Imaging machine." Gotta love him.

The scan showed no signs of tumor activity, but although Dr. Conrad told me earlier, I'd be free if this scan was clear, now he says I'll have to go back in six months. If that scan is clear, I'll be going back once a year. Oh well, praise the Lord, anyway. More romantic getaways.

As for the scar tissue, Doc said that after surgery, sometimes nerves go numb and take a while to wake up, and that may be what's going on with me. I'll be taking a new medicine to calm those nerves down and starting physical therapy. Apparently, he wasn't too impressed with my tread-milling and Pilates.

He told me I was going to have to learn to live with chronic pain. But that's unacceptable, so I'm just going to act like I didn't hear it. Besides, he also told me once that I'd be paralyzed, and we all know how that turned out.

Well, it's time to lay some big hugs on my babies, so to all of you who are praying for me and encouraging me, thank you, thank you, thank you!

God bless you all!

Rebecca

Chapter 21

RAISED FROM THE DEAD

Thank You for the Cross
Friday, April 2, 2010
Blessings on Good Friday!

Today's promise, Isaiah 30:20–21: *"Although the Lord gives you the bread of adversity and the water of affliction, your teachers will be hidden no more; with your own eyes you will see them. Whether you turn to the right or to the left, your ears will hear a voice behind you, saying, 'This is the way; walk in it.'"*

Hallelujah!

Lord, it never ceases to amaze and humble me that, even before You laid the foundations of the world, You knew me. My rebellion, my bullheadedness, my temper, my selfishness, my fear, my stupidity . . . everything I would do and fail to do. You knew I would constantly be falling short. And even then, You didn't look on me with condemnation. You saw me as your child. You saw my desperate need for You, and You decided even then that You would rather die than see me perish. Because You are love.

How could I ever repay such a debt to the only Father I've ever known, except to offer up that which You have saved? A living sacrifice. It isn't much, but it's all I have, and I'm all Yours. You alone can bring forth beauty from desolation. You make the barren desert blossom with color. You make the frigid arctic teem with life. Have Your way with me, oh Lord, and make me shine for You.

Thank You for loving me. Thank You for Your beautiful gift. Thank You for the cross.

Blessed Resurrection Sunday!
Sunday, April 4, 2010

Blessings on this beautiful day!

Today's promise is Ephesians 2:4–5: *"But because of his great love for us, God, who is rich in mercy, made us alive with Christ even when we were dead in transgressions—it is by grace you have been saved."* Amen!

I woke up in excruciating pain this morning, but the sound of happy kids and the knowledge of who I am in Christ makes the pain of no significance.

Last night, I was reminded again (it's so easy to get caught up in the world and forget) that the true miracle of Christ's resurrection wasn't a dead man coming back to life. Jesus brought several dead people back to life, probably more than we know. And I'm talking about physical death here.

The true miracle is mentioned in the above scripture. He raised me from the dead as well (spiritual death). From the moment I believed, I was seated in the Heavenly realms in Christ Jesus. I may be in the world, but I'm not of the world.

To deny this is to deny Christ and His great gift. To accept and live it is to glorify God as He says to the world, "Look! See what I have done!"

This is the truth that breaks me, brings me to my knees. And, only when I accept this awesome truth, knowing it was all His doing—not because I earned it, but because He loves me—am I capable of fulfilling the command of Colossians 3:12–17.

Pride and self-delusion are stripped from me in the light of His grace, just as it was when He turned my cancer into "a lump of inflamed tissue." This is what makes me so eager and willing to be a servant. And it's all by His hand. He makes it possible for me to live in the Spirit, so contrary to the world. What a God!

My prayer is that God will show you the incomparable riches of His grace, expressed in His kindness to you in Christ Jesus. My prayer is that you will all know His peace. Jesus is with us. He hears us. He cares for us. And He alone can get us through. Don't trust your eyes, or ears . . . or tailbone. Trust in the Giver of Life and receive His Life.

May the peace of Christ rule in your hearts,

Rebecca

Physical Therapy Begins
Tuesday, April 6, 2010

Blessings,

Today's promise is Romans 8:17: *"Now if we are children, then we are heirs—heirs of God and co-heirs with Christ, if indeed we share in his sufferings in order that we may also share in his glory"* (NIV).

It doesn't get any better than that!

I had my first physical therapy session yesterday, and Chuck was right . . . again, praise God. My therapist said the swelling causing the pain most likely came from my fall on the stairs. I just didn't connect it because the pain came so long afterward. Apparently, it takes time for tissue to swell, and it will take time for it to "unswell." The good news is that there is a solution! Yea!

I guess when I fell, I also knocked my pelvis out of alignment, and my right leg was almost two inches longer than my left! No wonder I was having problems walking! But she had me do some exercises that helped realign me, so I am walking much better today. She also said I was really "wobbly" because my body isn't sure where it is in relation to anything else. I hadn't really noticed, but I guess this is a normal post-surgery thing. She said that would improve as I rebuild my muscle. She gave me some mild (but potent) exercises with Pilates balls and is allowing me 5 minutes of walking at a time, on the treadmill or elsewhere. But that will increase after this week. She is also using some special tape that Olympic athletes use to give support and reduce swelling. Once we get the swelling down, I'll get to move on to the pool to work on my range of motion.

I'm really excited about getting rid of this pain and getting on with my life, but the best news was when she told me that I was already way ahead of most patients who have had similar surgeries. That fall set me back some, but I'll regain that ground. And that is another huge praise the Lord! Thank you all so much for your prayers and support!

I hope you are all enjoying spring. Easter was beautiful here, and we had a wonderful day, as I hope you did, too. You're ever in my prayers.

In God's grace and peace,

Rebecca

From the Mouths of Babes
Monday, April 12, 2010

Blessings, Friends,

Today's promise is Psalm 71:20–21: *"Though you have made me see troubles, many and bitter, you will restore my life again; from the depths of the earth you will again bring me up. You will increase my honor and comfort me once more [again]."*

What a wonderful promise. No matter how low He takes us, God will always lift us up again. Better than ever!

What a beautiful weekend! Though a few of us were fighting colds, I was able to get out and enjoy the sunshine with Chuck when he took me for a drive date.

Rachel was off to Wenatchee for the Civil Air Patrol's Spring Conference, where she was awarded the Billy Mitchell Award for achieving the rank of second lieutenant, as well as the Outstanding Cadet Award. That's our girl!

I had my third PT session today. Though the pain hasn't been affected much, the swelling is greatly reduced. I can now feel what's left of my tailbone, which is strange, to say the least. My therapist (or "terrorist," as Kathy D. puts it ☺), thinks the pain is just the bone in the process of healing. Apparently, when you chop off a bone and remove the tissue or fat that pads it, the bone isn't very happy. I told the surgeon to feel free to take a little fat off, but I was hoping they would take it off my hips! Oh, well.

The therapist told me the body can rebuild the padding, but it can take two or more years! So I'll have a pain in the rear to remind me of God's love for some time. I guess I'd rather have one than be one. Although, I must say, sometimes they go hand-in-hand . . . or cheek-in-cheek in my case. I just praise the Lord the therapy is working, and my exercises are gradually increasing. I don't mind carrying a seat cushion around as long as I'm moving forward.

We have a bumper crop of dandelions this year. Chuck says if we spray them, we won't have a lawn. Since I'm on restriction, I spend a lot of time gazing out the window and sighing in discouragement as nature reclaims all of my hard work. Friday, as I was at the window, wallowing in self-pity, Gracie nudged in beside me for a look. I heard her gasp.

"Oh, Mommy!" she said. "Look at all the beautiful yellow flowers! Can we go out and pick some?"

I had to smile. No wonder Jesus said, *"Let the little children come to me, and do not hinder them, for the kingdom of heaven belongs to such as these"* (Matthew 19:14). The same innocent mind that has no problem understanding God can be everywhere in the world and in her heart at the same time, found joy looking out the same window that gave me grief. I was so focused on the negative, I had missed the beauty.

I began to wonder how many other times I'd missed it. Missed God's smile, assuring me of His love and faithfulness. It certainly would have been easy to do in the past six months.

Gracie made me determined to stop (no matter what circumstances surround me), find the beauty, and thank God for taking the time to send me a love letter. Thank you, Gracie.

Thank you so much for your love letters from God. May He bless you richly for your faithfulness!

May God's grace and peace reign in your hearts,

Rebecca

Chapter 22

NOT MY WILL, BUT
YOURS, LORD

*T*he more I thought about the new website, the more I questioned what I thought I'd heard God telling me. Maybe it wasn't God's voice at all. Maybe all that medication had affected my mind . . .

I'd nearly convinced myself it was all my imagination when God kicked it up a notch.

A dear friend and fellow author, Helen Heavirland (the Helen H. in my posts), stopped in with some goodies—and a well-timed word.

"You know, Rebecca," she said, "I've been following your CarePage from the beginning, and you have written a book."

"I feel like I've written a book," I joked, but she just smiled.

"I'm serious," she said. "There are people out there who need this."

Her words stunned me into silence. Who would possibly want to read my ramblings? I knew Helen was not given to drink, and I knew of only one other source that would bring her the fifteen miles to my doorstep with such a declaration. The Holy Spirit wasn't opening the door of the furnace to let me out—He was adding wood to the fire!

"You really think so?"

Her expression was firm. "Yes. I do."

I shook my head, as if that could calm my racing mind. "Turn a blog into a book? But—how? What would that look like?"

"Pray about it," she said. "I have a book I think might help. I'll bring it by. But do pray about it. God will show you."

We said our good-byes, and I walked numbly back upstairs to my heating pad.

A blog *and* a book? I trusted Helen. She was a godly woman and an accomplished author. She'd been my friend and mentor for many years, and I knew if anyone could help me do this, she and our critique group, Walla Walla Christian Writers, could.

Meanwhile, the Spirit overlooked my weak and quavering flesh, and continued to minister to my receptive heart.

One God, One Body
Friday, April 16, 2010
Blessings, Friends,

Today's promise is John 8:31–32: *"If you hold to my teaching, you are really my disciples. Then you will know the truth, and the truth will set you free."*

You

Though confusion blackens my world,
I will hold fast to Your hand
You are my eyes

Though a sea of lies roars around me,
I will know the truth
You are my ears

Though my heart is pierced with sorrow,
my body wracked with pain,
I will sing Your praise
You are my tongue

Though the world bares its sharp, yellow teeth,
I will reach out
You are my hands

Though fear holds me fast,
I will boldly forge on
You are my feet

Though the grave claims my flesh,
I will live forever
You are my life

—by me

What is it in our nature that makes us think we should be privy to understanding? Is it some remnant of the forbidden fruit? That grievous lie that led mankind to believe they could be equal to God by their own volition? As those who have been reborn, who have supposedly died to our old delusions of divinity, we are commanded to abandon the ways of the world, including our old ways of thinking, and surrender completely to the Spirit, letting Him live through us. Yet, when we face the trials that are intrinsic to our new life (God didn't say we *might* have trials; He said we *would*), we demand to know why, confounded, and even angered when we don't get all the answers.

Some take solace in the fact that they may find out "someday." Even though we were given Job to show us how it is, we still seem to think we are entitled to know the mind of God. Are we better than Job? More obedient? Humble? Righteous? Has anyone suffered more than Job? Is anyone more deserving of understanding? I know I'm not. And what was God's answer to Job in Job 38:2–5?

"Who is this who darkens counsel
By words without knowledge?
Now prepare yourself like a man;
I will question you, and you shall answer Me.
Where were you when I laid the foundations of the earth?
Tell Me, if you have understanding.
Who determined its measurements?
Surely you know!
Or who stretched the line upon it?" (NKJV)

And that was just the beginning! He goes on for four chapters!

Is God some pompous, power-mongering egomaniac? No. God is God. In His own words:

"The Lord, the Lord God, merciful and gracious, longsuffering, and abundant in goodness and truth, keeping mercy for thousands [of generations], forgiving iniquity and transgression and sin, and that will by no means clear the guilty; visiting the iniquity of the fathers upon the children, and upon the children's children, unto the third and to the fourth generation."
Exodus 34:6–7 KJV

God knows exactly who He is and what His place is. It's His desire that we know ours. So, what is that? Given that we were created by Him for His glory, apart from Him, we have no place or purpose. That's why it's so vital for us to relinquish our own desire to know the mind of God, and instead, seek to know His *heart*.

If indeed we have died with Christ, then we are dead. If indeed we have been resurrected with Christ, it is not we who live, but Christ who lives within us. It is no longer what we want, but what He wants. It is no longer our will, but His will. Likewise, it is no longer our skills, or power, or responsibility to accomplish any of it, but His. Who we are as children of God are extensions of Him. Parts of His body.

When your mind tells your arm to reach out and catch a falling child, does your arm say, "Why? I don't understand. What's the point?" Does it instead reach out and slap the child? Some of us know the grief and chaos that results when parts of our bodies forsake unity under the guidance of our minds and decide to act on their own will. Peace no longer reigns, and the whole body feels the effects. In a healthy body, the arm does what it's told, and every member of the body is at peace and filled with joy.

God's Word tells us over and over that what the world calls a curse, the body of Christ calls a blessing. Peter says, *"Dear friends, do not be surprised at the fiery ordeal that has come on you to test you, as though something strange were happening to you. But rejoice inasmuch as you participate in the sufferings of Christ, so that you may be overjoyed when his glory is revealed"* (1 Peter 4:12–13).

And, again, James 1:2–4 tells us to, *"Consider it pure joy, my brothers and sisters, whenever you face trials of many kinds, because you know that the testing of your faith produces perseverance. Let perseverance finish its work so that you may be mature and complete, not lacking anything."*

Just as Christ's suffering glorified God, so too does ours. It's His way of showing the world that He alone can save us. He alone provides the faith, courage, and strength to persevere. And as part of His body, when He is glorified, we all share in that: *"And we know that all things work together for good to them who love God, to them who are the called according to his purpose"* (Romans 8:28 KJV). The fact that He loves us and has a purpose for everything should be enough.

When we see another believer suffering, our first instinct is to say, "I'm so sorry you have to go through this." That's what the world says. But the world doesn't know God. I feel the pain of others very deeply. My family can testify to the tears I shed for you. But who am I to apologize for God? Who am I to devalue the great work He's doing in His body?

God tells Job, *"Will the one who contends with the Almighty correct him? Let him who accuses God answer him! . . . Would you discredit my justice? Would you condemn me to justify yourself?"* (Job 40:1, 8).

I'm certainly not saying we should stop fighting, stop seeking a cure, or stop comforting one another, but if we believe God doesn't lie, should we not say, "Though my heart hurts for you, I praise God for showing you His favor and making provision for you. What can I do to help you through this?"

These words may sound harsh to some. You may say, "That's easy for you to say; you've obviously never watched your child or loved one die. You were healed of cancer, what would you know about suffering?" But those of you who have followed my story from the beginning know I have been spared nothing. Nor do I expect to be spared. I'm no better than Christ; why should I be spared?

But this is in no way a criticism or judgment. I tell you these things that your joy may be made complete in Him. That you would know the peace that passes understanding. *Truly* know it. This is what God has laid on my heart, and I must be faithful to it. *"His word is in my heart like a fire, a fire shut up in my bones. I am weary of holding it in; indeed, I cannot"* (Jeremiah 20:9).

Jesus came that we might have life and have it more abundantly. Not just those in perfect health with perfect marriages, and families, and finances, but all who believe. But we cannot be partial partakers in the Kingdom. We cannot be both of the world and of the Spirit. If we truly believe in God, we must believe His Word in its entirety, no matter how incredulous it sounds to the world. Worldly knowledge impedes faith. And the only thing God commands us to understand is His Word, His heart.

When we turn our eyes from the world and earnestly seek His heart, He will give us all the faith we need to receive His will, His blessings. And we will finally know true peace and unbounded joy. We will finally be free.

God's grace and peace be yours,

Rebecca

You Are God!
Wednesday, April 21, 2010

Blessings, Friends,

Today's promise is John 16:33: *"I have told you these things, so that in me you may have peace. In this world you will have trouble. But take heart! I have overcome the world."*

What a beautiful promise Jesus made just before He went to the cross. And He claimed the victory before He was even crucified and resurrected! If I know that Jesus has overcome the world—has won—then it doesn't matter what happens to me here. He has overcome it. And if He has overcome it, I have overcome it. I'm free to dance, as the song goes. I can have perfect peace. Praise the Lord!

It was another beautiful weekend! It's hard for me to stay out of the garden when it's so nice out, but God made it easier for me by giving me another cold. I did lay out in the sun for a little while on Saturday, and it was heavenly!

We have so much to praise God for, not the least of which are all of the calls the business is getting. Ask, and you will receive! Chuck hasn't had much time to stop and think, and he's loving it! God is so good!

We asked God if He wanted us to let go of the business, or part of it (heating/air- conditioning, pumps, or electrical), and Chuck has had steady work in all areas, so I guess we got our answer! Certainly, it will take time to recover fully, just like my body, but with God as our CEO, we have no doubt we will.

PT is going well, in spite of the fact that my scar tissue swelled up a little again after sitting too much. The good news is the pain is changing, and I'm starting to itch! The cold laser treatments and taping are making a difference. For some reason, my pelvis keeps going out of alignment, but the PT therapist taught Chuck how to fix that at home, and that helps with the pain. They're also looking into a TENS unit for me, which fakes the nerves out with mild electrical stimulation. I guess that would give me an electric personality, ha ha. (Yeah, I know, that was bad. But that's what you get on decongestants. I'm here all week, folks.)

Thank you for your prayers and messages. It means so much to me to know I have that support!

God's grace and peace be with you,

Rebecca

Chapter 23

JOY AND GRIEF

Snapshots
Monday, May 3, 2010
Blessings, Friends,

Today's promise is Acts 1:8: *"But you will receive power when the Holy Spirit comes on you; and you will be my witnesses in Jerusalem, and in all Judea and Samaria, and to the ends of the earth."* Let it be, Lord. Just as You said.

God is so good! What a great weekend! After a great day with Chuck on Saturday, I felt well enough to go to church.

Sunday, Chuck and I took Gracie to the park to play, and even with all the walking and sitting on hard park benches, I felt great! We returned to a house that smelled heavenly. Rachel got a craving for potstickers, and Daniel got a craving for chocolate chip cookies, so between the two of them, they cooked and baked up quite a feast.

I just can't tell you how good it was to feel so normal again! I don't know if the pain medicine is finally kicking in, or what, but I really feel blessed. It seems like God has just blocked all the nasty side effects of the Neurontin, to give me a little sunshine. Praise the Lord! My physical therapist said recovery goes in waves and I should take mental snapshots of my good days so when I hit the valleys, I can look back at them and know I'll get there again. And, boy, have I been snapping!

As always, thank you for your treasured prayers and messages!
God's grace and peace be yours,
Rebecca

Mother's Day Blessings
Monday, May 10, 2010
Blessings, Friends,

Today's promise is 1 John 2:10: *"Anyone who loves their brother and sister lives in the light, and there is nothing in them to make them stumble."*

I sure hope all of you moms had a great a Mother's Day! Mine was fantastic! Midweek, I was praising God I had taken snapshots the weekend before, since Gracie got a fever on Monday and, being the cuddle bug, she is, promptly gave it to me. I thought it was going to be another Mother's Day in bed with the flu, but God is good, and I was feeling much better in a couple days. I was even able to get out and enjoy the Balloon Stampede on Saturday.

The kids surprised me with breakfast in bed. It reminded me of the first time our oldest did that with peanut butter toast. That was a l-o-n-g time ago. They've been doing it ever since, but their culinary skills have increased dramatically over the years: blueberry crepes, bacon, and fresh-squeezed orange juice.

And I love all their handmade cards! Gracie made about twelve. She thought it was my birthday again. Of course, the dozen roses and chocolates were wonderful, too, but the poem Rachel wrote me, and the boys' and Gracie's artwork will be framed. Chuck says they did it all on their own, though he did contribute a card and a letter cataloging the number of days, hours, minutes, etc., we've been together, which was just too many numbers first thing in the morning! But I love it.

I began to suspect they may have been trying to do me in when Chuck started whipping up one of his killer coffee cakes for lunch, but he put me at ease when he took me out to finally get some plants for my pots. I love nurseries! I did pretty well, pain-wise. I think the walking was good for my back muscles. It made me sore, but it was a good sore.

It was such a beautiful day, Rachel and I soaked up a few rays when I got back with my plants, and, boy, that felt good. But, when I found out they were making Monte Cristos for dinner, I knew the end was near. My body isn't very happy with me today, but I survived (miraculously) and am back on my healthy diet—until the next holiday.

Bless you, for your continued prayers and encouragement.

God's grace and peace be yours,

Rebecca

Though I was warned about the physical roller coaster of healing, nothing could have prepared me for the emotional roller coaster of surviving. One moment, I'd be soaring on wings of praise, and the next, an update on another warrior's CarePage would send me plummeting into an abyss of heartache and guilt. My faith in God's plan didn't protect my heart from the pain of others. If anything, it heightened my sensitivity. A Mother's Day post from just one of the many grieving mothers on CarePages and CaringBridge led me to write the following poem.

The Walk
Wednesday, May 12, 2010

The Walk

Walking with the Lord
stomach churning, fists clenching, heart aching
I turn on Him.

Why?
Why did You take my child
so young, so innocent, so beautiful?

His warm gaze draws me in

167

Yes, too beautiful for this world
He belongs in My Kingdom

Tears sting my eyes. I push back
But why the suffering
so much, so long?

This world is cold, selfish
People must learn to love

Tears roll down my cheeks
But why *my* child?

Remember?
When you carried him?
You asked Me to make you
the best parent you could be

I did that for you

I hurl myself into Him
angry fists hammering His chest

What now?
What do I do with this pain?
This hole?

His arms close around me
I soak His robe with my tears

He anoints my head with His

—by me

In the Hands of God
Monday, May 17, 2010
Blessings, Friends,

Today's promise is Colossians 1:27: "*To them [the saints] God has chosen to make known among the Gentiles the glorious riches of this mystery, which is Christ in you, the hope of glory.*" Amen.

Tough week. Physically and emotionally. I know I was warned that healing would be a roller coaster, but nothing quite prepares you for the lows. Even so, I take comfort in the fact that no matter where I am on this roller coaster, God remains constant. Yesterday, today, and forever, He will always be my Rock.

God's grace and peace be yours,

Rebecca

Standing Firm
Monday, May 24, 2010

Blessings, friends,

Today's promise is 2 Corinthians 1:21–22: *"Now it is God who makes both us and you stand firm in Christ. He anointed us, set his seal of ownership on us, and put his Spirit in our hearts as a deposit, guaranteeing what is to come."* Amen!

I had two snapshot days last week. It was wonderful. Unfortunately, another virus cut my celebration short. But, for this too, I must praise the Lord. I'd rather be in pain with Him than in perfect health without Him.

I was reminded last weekend that when Jesus said, *"I have come that they may have life, and that they may have it more abundantly"* (John 10:10 NKJV), He wasn't talking about abundant life as the world defines it—success, wealth, or even good health. Our abundant life comes from the Holy Spirit, who swallows up our fears and infirmities, lifting us high above them, where we can soar on wings like eagles and sing God's praises forever!

So although I haven't broken out the oxycodone yet—though I've been tempted—I do have a tub and hot running water. Another "Praise the Lord!" But I've been warned by Gracie that I can't spend all day in the tub, or my fingers and toes will get all "broccoli." What would I do without her? Will the blessings ever cease? Oh, that's right. No!

You're all in my prayers. And I truly value your prayers and messages.

God's grace and peace be yours,

Rebecca

Looking Forward
Wednesday, June 2, 2010
Blessings, Friends,

Today's promise is Matthew 5:4: *"Blessed are those who mourn, for they will be comforted."* Amen.

It was a different Memorial Day for me this year. We decorated the graves of our little girl, Hannah, and my mom, grandma, grandpa, and aunt, as usual, but the mood was much different.

Normally, I cry myself out, reliving the losses, overwhelmed with the pain of missing them. But there were no tears this year—only stories and laughter. And peace. Even Chuck noticed the difference in me.

I was closer to my grandma than I'd ever been to anyone on earth. She was my safe harbor in the tumult of my childhood, my only constant in a world of uncertainty. I'd always believed that when she died, I would die with her. I couldn't possibly imagine my life without her. But it didn't work out that way. I was grown and married and had lots of other family, but when I held Grandma's hand as she took her last breath, I was utterly alone. For weeks, the only prayer I could manage was, "God, help me."

One night as I prayed, He answered with a deep abiding assurance that everything was going to be all right. That was when I realized that God Himself meant to fill the void left by my grandma. Though this was comforting, I still missed her terribly. I would be so thrilled to see her in my dreams, busy in her kitchen, so real and alive. Then I'd remember I was dreaming, that she couldn't stay, and I would lose her all over again. It was crushing.

Then, I had a different dream. I dreamed Grandma called me from Heaven. Yes, on the phone. I'll bet you didn't know AT&T could do that! Anyway, I cried my eyes out, telling her how I missed her, how miserable I was without her, couldn't she please come back . . . I don't know how long I'd gone on pouring my heart out when I realized I was the only one crying! Not that she spoke. I could just feel she wasn't sharing my pain. In fact, she didn't miss me at all! Well! I don't have to tell you, I was pretty incensed in my dream. I thought she loved me!

But, when I woke up, I knew the truth. I'd felt a sense of complete joy and peace coming from my grandma I knew she'd never experienced on earth. And why would she miss me? Nothing is hidden from her now. Like God, the past, present, and future are all one to her. She knows God is in control, that I'm well cared for, and that we'll be together again. After seventy-five years of striving and carrying the weight of the world on her shoulders, she is free. She hasn't stopped loving me, she just knows there's nothing to be miserable about.

I had no problem accepting this . . . in my head. But my heart was so focused on me—my loss, my pain, my fear—I couldn't really own the truth. Until now. Don't get me wrong: I still feel the absence of my loved ones. But as I sat with Chuck and the kids in the cemetery, I felt something so much stronger than loss. Something bigger than myself. I knew in my heart it wouldn't be long until I was with them again.

And this isn't coming from any scripture I've been reading, or sermons I've been hearing. I can only describe it as a quickening in my spirit. A sensing of my Lord's nearness. Kind of like the spaceship in *Independence Day* that lit up when the mother ship entered the atmosphere. And it lingers still. It probably sounds nutty to some of you, but I know I'm not alone, so if you've felt it, too, give a shout-out. I'm not saying Jesus is coming for us a week from Thursday—just that I know it will be soon. And for the first time in my life, I'm looking forward instead of back.

God's grace and peace be yours,

Rebecca

Chapter 24

MAKING WAVES

The Power of Prayer
Monday, June 14, 2010
Blessings, Friends,

Today's promise is 1 Corinthians 15:58: *"Therefore, my dear brothers and sisters, stand firm. Let nothing move you. Always give yourselves fully to the work of the Lord, because you know that your labor in the Lord is not in vain."*

Wow! What a perfect verse for today. Just before I read that, I was praying for you all, the persecuted church, and a little boy who was recently kidnapped in Oregon, and I was overwhelmed by the conviction of the importance of prayer. I've always known it, I just didn't *know* it. Second Thessalonians 2:7 says: *"For the mystery of lawlessness (that hidden principle of rebellion against constituted authority) is already at work in the world, [but it is] restrained only until he who restrains is taken out of the way"* (AMP).

He who restrains evil is the Holy Spirit, and He is not just floating around doing His own thing; He is in us. That's right. It is we, the church, who are restraining evil by the power of the Holy Spirit! If we are to truly have an impact on this world, we must be praying fervently—in the Spirit. Not repeating the same words each day as we rush through our busy lives (as I have a tendency to do), but spending quality time enjoying relationship with the Spirit and letting Him heal us, minister to us, and guide us. There truly is no better feeling in the world.

Then, letting the Spirit guide us through our requests, exercising His power in the name of Jesus Christ. Jesus said in Matthew 16:19: *"I will give you the keys of the kingdom of heaven, and whatever you bind on earth will be bound in heaven, and whatever you loose on earth will be loosed in heaven"* (NKJV).

And in Matthew 18:19:, *"Again, truly I tell you that if two of you on earth agree about anything they ask for, it will be done for them by my Father in heaven."* How great is that?

Our communion with the Holy Spirit should set the tone for our day, empowering us throughout it.

I'm convinced the world would be a much different place if Christians understood the power we've been given through Jesus Christ.

Well, this update didn't go at all as I intended. Further proof that I'm not the author, but merely the scribe.

This morning, as I was making the bed and stacking all of my pillows, it occurred to me it wasn't that long ago the bed wasn't getting made because I was always in it. When I think of how far God has brought me from the physical and emotional agony I went through just eight months ago, I can't help but be humbled by God's grace and faithfulness. I can gladly praise Him for the pain I feel now because I know even this is part of His wonderful plan for me, and He is carrying me through this as well. Who could help but love a God like that?

Thank you so much for your wonderful messages and prayers! And I pray God will bless you all richly. Now, I must go and make potato salad for my kiddos. I've got to spoil them just a little bit. It's a mother's privilege, you know.

God's grace and peace be yours,

Rebecca

Working on the new blog quickly overwhelmed me. I could picture it in my mind, but getting it from my head to the page—that was another matter. I was a writer, not a computer programmer! I needed a professional. Unfortunately, I couldn't find one who would work for *brownies. I was about to learn that the mechanics and finances of this assignment were the least of my worries. The very gates of hell were about to unleash their fury. They would be bent on obscuring the path God had set before me and robbing me of my faith. I never saw it coming.*

Our youngest son, Daniel, had had a difficult time when I was in the hospital, and his stress crossed over to school. Though I'd convinced him to finish the year at the small Christian school he and his brother, Aaron, attended, he was determined to homeschool again in the fall.

Chuck insisted I wasn't strong enough, but we could no longer afford private school, and, frankly, my need to help my son far outweighed my need to help myself. Against Chuck's better judgment, I gave in.

Unfortunately, my ex-husband was just as determined that Daniel attend public school. As was usually the case in all decisions concerning our kids, a nasty court battle ensued, adding to my emotional and financial strain. Statements rolled in from my ex-husband and his family cataloging my failures as a teacher and as a mother. Even our oldest son, who hadn't spoken to me in five years, joined the attack.

The enemy's arrows hit their mark. Instinctually, my hands went from the work God had given me to shielding myself from the razor-sharp points.

What the enemy didn't know was that my Father was using him for a purpose all His own. It was time in my training to get to know my enemy, to learn to fight spirit in the Spirit. It was time to take my faith to a whole new level.

I Will Praise You in the Storm
Monday, July 19, 2010
Blessings, Friends,

Today's promise is John 6:35: *"I am the bread of life. Whoever comes to me will never go hungry, and whoever believes in me will never be thirsty."* Amen!

One of those weeks. I really got both barrels, but I guess it's my turn. Sometimes it feels as if I'm hanging on to Jesus by my fingernails. When the pain seems to own me, and people I thought would love me as Christ does, instead become my judges, and the evil accuser of this world attacks with his hordes, I just want to curl up in my Father's arms and cry. I'm tired. And I sometimes wonder if people are really praying for me or just paying me lip service. But I know the truth, and the truth is that even if no one on earth is praying for me, Jesus is.

"Therefore, he is able to save completely those who come to God through him, because he always lives to intercede for them" (Hebrews 7:25).

And, the truth is that even if there's not a soul on earth who will stand beside me, Jesus will.

"Be strong and of a good courage, fear not, nor be afraid of them: for the Lord thy God, he it is that doth go with thee; he will not fail thee, nor forsake thee" (Deuteronomy 31:6 KJV).

And, the truth is, I am not hanging on to Him by my fingernails—He is holding me.

"Fear thou not; for I am with thee: be not dismayed; for I am thy God: I will strengthen thee; yea, I will help thee; yea, I will uphold thee with the right hand of my righteousness" (Isaiah 41:10 KJV).

So, I will praise Him in the storm. And I will bask in the love He has given me in my family and praise Him for the healing He is doing—in my body and my spirit, ever drawing me closer to Him.

God's grace and peace be with you,

Rebecca

Cultivating
Wednesday, July 21, 2010

Blessings, Friends,

Today's promise is Psalm 91:4: *"He will cover you with his feathers, and under his wings you will find refuge; his faithfulness will be your shield and rampart."* What a beautiful picture!

The funny thing about God is that when you ask Him to give you the qualities mentioned in 2 Peter, chapter 1, He doesn't come down with a silver platter and say, "Here you are." Instead, He gives us opportunities to cultivate those qualities. They aren't earned as much as learned, but they're still gifts in the fact that He gives us everything we need to cultivate them. Still, the cultivating is a choice and an effort we each must make.

I, dear friends, am cultivating cheerful endurance at the moment—again. Obviously, this patch in my garden has been found wanting. Thank you so much for your encouraging words. You just can't know what a difference you made. You've made the cheerful part of the endurance possible.

I saw Dr. Monroe because my surgery site is swollen and badly bruised, though I haven't had any falls or bumps. I was running a low-grade temp, so they checked my white count. Of course, as I was waiting for the results, my scratchy throat became sore. The cold I thought I'd finally gotten rid of was back, yet again. Thankfully, my counts were fine, and the doctor doesn't think there's infection at the site, so it must be the cold.

The physical and emotional challenges I'm facing haven't disappeared, but thanks to your faithfulness to God, I'm facing them with—well, with joy. There's just no other way to put it. Matthew 18:19 says, *"Again I say unto you, that if two of you shall agree on earth as touching anything that they shall ask, it shall be done for them of my Father which is in heaven"* (KJV).

So, you've got me more than covered! Thank you, and God bless you!

God's grace and peace be yours,

Rebecca

It's All Good—It's All God
Sunday, July 25, 2010

Blessings, Friends,

Today's promise is Psalm 34:15: *"The eyes of the Lord are on the righteous, and his ears are attentive to their cry."* Amen!

Saturday, I felt that sting again as I read of my dear friend Daniel going to be with Jesus. I would have preferred that he live to tell of God's healing, but my ways are not God's ways, so I bow to His wisdom and praise Him for it. I also praise Him for the example of faith Daniel and his mother, Mari, set. They've been such an inspiration to me. I love Daniel so much, maybe because I have a Daniel of my own, but I'm so happy he's finally free of that hospital bed and pain. I can't wait to give him a big hug in Heaven. Please keep his family in your prayers.

I hope you're making lots of good memories this summer. And bless you for your continued prayers and encouraging words.

God's grace and peace be yours,

Rebecca

Chapter 25

THE BALANCING ACT

Our Divine Direction-Finder
Monday, August 9, 2010
Blessings, Friends,

Today's promise is John 17:19: *"For them I sanctify myself, that they too may be truly sanctified."*

This, of course, is part of Jesus' prayer for His disciples and ultimately us. The Father knew very well why His Son was sanctifying Himself and going to the cross. It is we who need reminding of the ramifications of His actions. And still, we are so slow to believe.

Last week, I went to battle—again. Those of you who are divorced with children may be familiar with this battle. Inevitably I come under personal attack, and even though I know God is in control and has already won the war, it's hard not to be nervous going in. Some would give Satan credit for the attack. But I know, like my ex-tumor, the only evil that touches me, a child of the living God, is by God's permission and for His good purpose in me. Just like Job before me.

So, like my ever-present healing pain, this battle is nothing more than a thorn in my flesh to remind me to daily rely on God's grace—not only for my spiritual growth, but for the blessing of others as well. This is what Christ's prayer is all about, as He prays earlier:

"My prayer is not that you take them out of the world but that you protect them from the evil one. They are not of the world, even as I am not of it. Sanctify them by the truth; your word is truth. As you sent me into the world, I have sent them into the world. For them I sanctify myself, that they too may be truly sanctified" (John 17:15–19).

Because Christ sanctified Himself, I'm off-limits to the evil one. It's in this knowledge that the full measure of Christ's joy resides. But this truth can slip away so easily in this busy world when I don't take the time to allow God to "sanctify me by the truth." It's only through daily seeking God in His Word and prayer that I truly learn who He is, and my spiritual roots can grow deeper into that rich soil, holding fast so the strongest winds can't topple me.

There's great power in God's Word. His Word is alive! But it doesn't live in me by proxy. I have to make the choice to make my relationship with Him my top priority. Because, in the end, it's only Him and me, face-to-face. All else will pass away. And I want to know Him.

We're gearing up to go to the Oregon Coast next weekend. One last fling for the summer. Please pray for safe travel and that pain won't prevent me from enjoying this time with my family.

Until next time, know you are in my thoughts and prayers, and take some time to get into the Word. You won't regret it!

God's grace and peace be yours,

Rebecca

Contentment
Wednesday, August 18, 2010

Blessings, Friends,

Today's promise is Isaiah 40:31: *"But those who wait on the LORD shall renew their strength; they shall mount up with wings like eagles, they shall run and not be weary, they shall walk and not faint"* (NKJV). Amen!

Boy, did I need that one! This vacation was a continual lesson in contentment for me. There were times when the pain and swelling confined me to quarters, keeping me from really enjoying my time with my family. Disappointment and depression lurked at my door, and I was forced on many occasions to stop and rebuke my thoughts and praise God for His goodness. If He hadn't shrunk my tumor, not to mention making it benign, I wouldn't even be walking on my own, let alone going on rides with my kids and walking arm-in-arm on the beach with my favorite guy.

There's nothing like being at the sea, watching the waves crash on the shore, to remind you how small you are and how big God is. It's a constant struggle for me, learning like Paul to be content in all my circumstances, especially where "doing" is concerned. But, luckily, I'm not too stubborn to be reminded again that it's not about what I do or don't do. It's about what God has done. So, when I found a coffee mug in Lincoln City, Oregon, with the above verse on it, it was just the reminder I needed that my Father is holding me in His arms—and all is right with the world. God is good. Always.

I have to say this trip was a blessing all around. We spent an entire day at one of our favorite places, Enchanted Forest, a storybook land amusement park built into the side of a hill. Can you say buns of steel? As I mentioned already, I was able to go on some of the rides with the kids. I avoided the haunted house this time around but was actually dumb enough to go on the log ride—twice! (I say "dumb" because I hate the sensation of falling more than anything!) Gracie, the Energizer Bunny, shut the place down, of course, but what else is new?

We had a nice stay at Depoe Bay. Gracie made friends with everyone and their dogs. Literally. You haven't lived until you've watched a four-year-old share the love of Jesus with strangers old enough to be her grandparents. We checked the weather forecasts before heading to the coast—one said warm and sunny, one said cold and cloudy. Turns out, they were both correct. On the same day, no less. That's the Oregon Coast for you. It's a very strange feeling to be surrounded by cold fog in August. At least in our part of the country. But nothing keeps our kids from the beach. Gracie would be there building castles, and the boys digging holes still, if they could. So seeing everyone having fun—and the added bonus of getting all our school clothes shopping done—was well worth the pain.

We ended our vacation with a visit to the University of Portland campus. I can't believe Rachel has reached this pinnacle so soon, but it had to come. I'm so proud of her. I was packing tissue around the whole time. I didn't make a scene, though, so I'm proud of myself, too. She is so excited about college and the Air Force ROTC. I can't blame her. I'd apply myself, if I could—except for the Air Force stuff. I love school. For me. Not too excited that the kids are going back any day now. Aaron is off to high school—AAAHHH! Summer was too short! Well, at least Daniel and Gracie will be homeschooling, so I'll have them at home. Call me crazy, but I love having my kids around.

I spent most of the trip home on the bed with my heating pad, one of the great things about R.V.s, and we got home around 10 p.m.. We unpacked the necessities and snuggled gratefully into our own beds, only to be awakened by an emergency service call at 1:30 a.m.! Chuck sailed off to a neighboring town with no power to keep one of our client's basement from flooding. Boy, am I glad we didn't stay at the coast an extra day! He got back home around 3 and was finally able to get some sleep. A few hours anyway.

Well, I have things to get ready for the fair, so I'd better get crackin'. Thank you all so much for your prayers and messages. Next month is scan time again, so please be praying for God's provision—for my nerves as well as care for the kids. I hate the idea of leaving them just when school is starting, but God already has it all worked out.

God's grace and peace be yours,

Rebecca

Promise
Tuesday, August 24, 2010

Blessings, Friends,

Today's promise is Matthew 28:20: *"And surely I am with you always, to the very end of the age."*

What a beautiful promise from our Lord and Savior before He went to be with the Father. When I'm really down and discouraged, that verse can bring me to tears. Just knowing that no matter how tough things get down here, how cruel people are, or how painful life can be, my Jesus is right here with me. In me. Giving me all the strength I need to get through anything. He promised. And He didn't say, "Cross my heart and hope to die." He *did* die. I need only remember to rest in Him and let Him be my strength.

Why is that so easy to write and so hard to do? Everything in me wants to live in the peace of knowing God is in control. My mind believes it beyond a doubt, but my body defies logic. Fear grips the back of my neck and churns my stomach. Guilt and sadness press down on my chest until I feel I can't breathe. The pain tries to steal any memory of goodness.

And then I turn back to the Word—read that verse again and cry tears of thankfulness and humility that the Creator of all things actually wants to be with me, to comfort me and lift me up, to love me. And I realize that, no matter what my body is doing, my heart has no choice but to go on believing and trusting in Him. He is my life, and I love Him.

Yes, it's been a week of practicing cheerful enduring. As best I can. But it isn't the pain that bothers me as much as the feeling of disappointing Chuck and the kids. Not being able to do much with them beyond the walls of my bedroom. Especially with school starting and all the activities involved.

And with the continuously mounting medical bills that come with a tumor diagnosis, the refrigerator and dishwasher dying, two sinks leaking, and business lagging again, I should be helping Chuck with the business. Other people work full time while going through chemo. What is wrong with me? Of course, the stress is probably contributing to the pain, not to mention the stress of upcoming scans, so there you have it. I simply have no choice but to trust God's plan.

But, if I have to be between a rock and a hard place, I'd rather be between *the* Rock and a hard place. God will provide.

In all my complaining, I do have reason to praise. I finished Grandpa's book! Praise the Lord! That's something I can do in bed—write. The book is called *Them Were the Days: Stories My Grandpa Told Me*. It's my grandpa's biography in the form of short stories and anecdotes he used to tell, complete with photos. Probably not something people outside the family would be interested in, but it's been a five-year journey, so finishing it feels so good!

Before I was diagnosed, I was working on the "final" rewrite of the first in my mystery series. Now, it's time to get back to that.

It already feels like autumn here. Mainly because my senior (Rachel) and freshman (Aaron) have hit the campus running. I just can't figure out where the summer went. Oh well, it'll come to me sooner or later. Right? Daniel and Gracie's homeschool curricula haven't arrived, so we're not going full speed, yet. Still a little time to breathe.

We continue to remember you in our prayers, and we treasure your prayers and kind words. I hope you all have memories of summer that bring smiles. God's grace and peace be yours,
Rebecca

Precious

Monday, August 30, 2010

Blessings, Friends,

Today's promise is Psalm 91:15: *"He will call on me, and I will answer him; I will be with him in trouble, I will deliver him and honor him."* Thank you, Lord!

I want to thank all of you who left such awesome messages of encouragement on my last update! You have no idea what you did for my spirit. Thank you!

And, before I forget again, thank you so much to our friends for the gifts from your gardens and pantries. It's such a wonderful surprise to be reminded that we're being thought of. I know people are praying, and I deeply appreciate it. But, when people actually make contact, it's like a healing balm, whether it's a message, email, card, food, or, best of all, a visit! So thank you again, and God bless you greatly as you have blessed me.

"The King will reply, 'Truly I tell you, whatever you did for one of the least of these brothers and sisters of mine, you did for me'" (Matthew 25:40).

I saw Dr. Monroe this morning. He also thinks my healing process is not progressing as it should. He increased my Gabapentin, and you know how much I love my meds! (That was sarcasm.) I was hoping to be decreasing by this time. Oh well. Praise the Lord! He also referred me to a rehab specialist. I told him I still haven't paid for all the PT, but I guess if he can get me in working condition again, the bills will get paid even sooner. I know they will anyway, I just hate being in debt. Like I'm in control. Let go, Rebecca, let go! Praise the Lord! Anyway, I can't get in to see the specialist until October, after my scans, so I'll keep you posted.

I said good-bye to a very special man on Saturday. An adopted grandpa. Lloyd was 92, and the most vibrant man I've ever met. He was like the Energizer Bunny with the Holy Spirit. He really knew how to show Jesus' love to people, and I really miss him. A verse was shared at his service that blew me away, so I had to look into it for myself. Have you ever wondered how God feels when one of His kids dies? I have. And now I know.

"Precious in the sight of the Lord is the death of his faithful servants" Psalm 116:15.

Wow! The word "precious" here is the Hebrew word *yakar*, meaning "heavy in price." To put it into perspective, there are only five things in the Old

Testament described as yakar. They are, in order: the Word of God, redemption, the death of His saints, the lips of knowledge, and the thoughts of God.

Precious. As in precious metal or precious stones—diamonds, rubies, emeralds. But those things have a price that people can pay. What makes the deaths of His saints so much more precious is that the price was the blood of His one and only Son. We who are left behind feel the pain of separation and loss. But our Father is finally taking possession of His most valued treasure, for which He paid the ultimate price—His precious Son. They are finally safe in their Father's arms, out of reach of the enemy, of pain, of cancer and disease—of death. Forever!

Fortunately, we are precious to Him in the flesh, too, which is why I know He cries with us, as Jesus did at the tomb of Lazarus. Not for the end of a life—because for we who believe, to die is to live—but He cries for the tender hearts He created in us—in His likeness. How awesome is our God? His love is immeasurable, unfathomable, and best of all, absolutely free. How precious to the Lord are His saints who trust in His love in the face of adversity, pain, and fear.

You are precious to the Lord! Believe it! Trust it! Live it!

God's grace and peace be yours,

Rebecca

Chapter 26

A CLOSER WALK WITH THEE

Draw Near to Me . . .
Sunday, Sep 19, 2010
Blessings, Friends,

Today's promise is 1 Corinthians 6:9–11: *"Do you not know that wrongdoers will not inherit the kingdom of God? Do not be deceived: Neither the sexually immoral nor idolaters nor men who have sex with men nor thieves nor the greedy nor drunkards nor slanderers nor swindlers will inherit the kingdom of God. And that is what some of you were. But you were washed, you were sanctified, you were justified in the name of the Lord Jesus Christ and by the Spirit of our God."* Praise God!

Like the Israelites, we were under bondage—the bondage of sin. But our Savior led us out of bondage, washed us white as snow, and gave us the keys to freedom. The keys to the Kingdom of God. So, why are so many Christians still living in bondage? Maybe the better question is: Why are so many Christians *choosing* to live in bondage?

Here's what I think: Moses kept his focus and therefore his faith because he was in constant communion with God—one-on-One. While the Israelites were whining, and doing whatever else they did in the wilderness, Moses was talking and listening to the Lord. So much so that he glowed! It was this communion that empowered him not only to trust and obey God, but also to have compassion with on those who wronged him (Numbers 12:1–16).

Jesus' power to love, serve, and forgive came from the same source as Moses' power. While the disciples concerned themselves with practicalities, Jesus climbed the mountain alone to talk with His Father.

The grace of God is transforming. But it's not a one-time shot. Second Peter 3:18 tells us we need to keep growing in the grace and knowledge of Jesus. There's only one way to do that. Not in church, not listening to Christian music, not watching televangelists, but spending time alone with God. With the Bible, and in prayer, yes, but more than anything, *listening.* It is this personal relationship with Jesus Christ that sustains us when people fail us and everything around us seems to be falling apart.

Like all of my updates, I wrote this for myself. Not that my faith is failing, but my attitude could certainly use a little adjusting. The last two weeks have been mind-bending, trying to settle into a new curriculum and having to fight a legal battle to be able to do so, among other things. I've been so exhausted I haven't made the effort to get out of bed to spend time with God before I start the day, and I'm feeling it. The length of time since my last post bears witness.

I can't help but think my medication change isn't helping matters, but I really need to do better. Why is it that when life gets busy, I decide it's God who can wait? I feel like the workaholic parent whose sad-eyed child is standing in front of me, holding out a book for me to read with him, and I keep promising, "Just as soon as I get this done." Is that backward, or what? How glad I am that God isn't a workaholic parent!

God did give me a couple special gifts, though, to encourage me. I taught a writing class for the homeschool co-op five years ago (wow, has it been that long?), and I ran into two of my former students. One is now majoring in journalism, and the other thanked me for teaching him how to write because it's making college a lot easier. That made my day. Onward and upward!

I finally got my appointment scheduled for my scans—October 1st. Perhaps I won't have to go back for a whole year? Hey, never would be even better! Please, Lord!

Please keep us in your prayers for safe travel, for people to take care of the kids while we're gone, and most of all for clear scans. I don't know if I'll ever understand my scaniphobia. Chuck explains it so well, how that place is full of memories of pain, so I'm fearful of it—not to mention my claustrophobia. Unfortunately, understanding this doesn't make the jitters go away. Luckily, God is bigger than my fears.

Thank you for your continued prayers and encouraging words. And please know that even when I can't keep up with every one of your updates, you are in my thoughts and prayers.

God's grace and peace be with you,

Rebecca

In the Garden
Thursday, Sep 24, 2010

Blessings, Friends,

Today's promise is Isaiah 40:8: *"The grass withers and the flowers fall, but the word of our God endures forever."* Amen!

Well, my visit with the rehab specialist didn't exactly yield the results I was hoping for. I guess short of an instantaneous healing from God, the best a body can do is the best a body can do. I did receive one of those healings, but God has decided to let me heal from my surgery at a more leisurely pace. As I wait for my body to heal, the therapist had other drugs to offer for the pain; however, my refusal to take narcotics greatly limited the selection. But I'm okay with it. I know people are praying for me, because before I even saw this therapist, I received a peace in my heart I haven't known since my diagnosis. I've just felt the Lord's reassurance that I'm right where He wants me right now, so I can back up off myself. I know some of you have been telling me this all along, but feeling it in my heart really made it okay. Then, yesterday, I received an awesome gift.

I often dream of planting gardens. In these dreams as in real life, there is such joy and anticipation in the planting as I envision the lush, green growth filling the plot and the harvest of beautiful, flavorful fruits and vegetables.

However, in these dreams, what usually happens is that life intervenes. I get sick or other circumstances keep me from watering, weeding, and nurturing my garden like I should. The dreams end sadly when I remember what I started, and I am grief-stricken at my failure. In some dreams, the plants have managed to grow somehow and even set fruit but have all died down when I find them. And always, I vow to do better next spring.

I had a different garden dream yesterday. In this dream, Chuck was walking me out to the backyard to show me the garden. I resisted because I knew I'd failed the garden once more, and I didn't want to be reminded of it.

But, when I looked where he pointed, I saw the biggest garden I'd ever seen. It was more like a field. And it was thriving with every kind of fruit and vegetable imaginable! Even as I looked, green was breaking through the earth and growing, literally taking over every inch of bare ground it could find! It was so amazing, all I could say was, "Chuck, look!"

And this was the really amazing part: The Lord God spoke to me! (And no, this doesn't happen every day.) He told me we would have all we needed to get us through the coming storm. In my dream, this was symbolized by the Revolutionary War, and I knew we would be under siege, but I'm not sure exactly what it was referring to in my time.

But then He told me that all the seeds I've been planting will not be wasted, but they will, instead, grow and thrive and produce fruit, even though I think I've failed to nurture them. That's what the garden represented—and why it was so much bigger than what I remembered planting!

I'm telling you that I was so humbled by His loving encouragement I cried. Those of you who know me, or have been following me for some time, know how I struggle with being of service to God when I'm so restricted by my pain and seemingly constant illnesses. But I don't have to struggle anymore. And neither do you. Keep seeking Him. He loves you and wants to bless you. No matter how bad things get, there's always something to praise Him about— the harder you look, the more you find. Don't be discouraged. God is using you right where you are when you share His amazing love with others. I know that now—without a doubt. And I rejoice even more in my infirmities! Thank You, Jesus, for letting me plant Your garden!

Until next time, thank you for your prayers and encouragement. And go forth and be fruitful!

God's grace and peace be yours,

Rebecca

Clear Scan! Praise the Lord!
Monday, October 4, 2010

Blessings, Friends,

Today's promise is James 1:3–4: *"Because you know that the testing of your faith produces perseverance. Let perseverance finish its work so that you may be mature and complete, not lacking anything."* Lord, please give me the strength to persevere. Amen.

What a trip! You know, a five-hour drive with a sore tailbone to take a ride in an MRI torpedo tube wouldn't seem like the ideal way to celebrate your seventh anniversary, but it was. Last year, I spent our anniversary in bed, unable to walk on my own. Chuck had to cancel reservations he'd been looking forward to surprising me with, and that was even worse than the pain. God has brought me so far in a year; I'm extremely humbled.

Gracie had a great time with her cousins again, and Chuck's dad came to keep the older kids out of trouble—or the other way around. I'm not sure which. Thank you, Dad and Shawna! Even so, I was anxious leaving.

We had a beautiful drive through the Cascades—gorgeous fall colors. The first trip, a year ago, I spent laying in the back seat, shaking in pain and trying not to vomit from the morphine, so I enjoyed every minute of this drive.

The morning of my scan, I took my happy pill as usual. Unfortunately—and you know this never happens—they called me in before I got settled in the waiting room! Chuck had gone back to the car to get my music, and my happy pill hadn't even begun to kick in, so I was on the verge of panic! You know how it is when your brain is so preoccupied with fear you can't even remember how to pray? I was there.

I know you were praying for me because I actually managed to get through the beginning with God, Chuck, and my classical music. About halfway through, the Xanax started to kick in, but I was doing all right, so it was just an added bonus.

My appointment with the doctor went just as quickly. I was called back before my mocha had a chance to cool; forget about doing any crocheting. The news was awesome, as you know.

I got to see my before and after MRIs for the first time, which was amazing. I still have a pocket in my tailbone. Dr. Conrad cleaned it out during the surgery, and though it looks like it may be smaller, it has filled with fluid again. I learned my tumor was also filled with fluid, but they still don't know why it developed or what the tissue was. But God does. The big "praise the Lord" is that I don't have to go back for another year! Yea!

So we'll have another anniversary in Seattle next year, but that's all right with me. We stayed an extra night, and the Xanax didn't knock me out, so we had a great time exploring, shopping, and researching restaurants for my mystery. I had so much fun with Chuck I could have stayed another night—or two. Even the drive home was beautiful. You never know what weather will greet you as you go through Snoqualmie Pass.

Thank you for all your prayers. We were truly blessed by this trip!

God's grace and peace be yours,

Rebecca

Chapter 27

HOLIDAY FEASTING

Feast

Monday, November 29, 2010

Blessings, Friends,

Today's promise is Hebrews 9:14: *"How much more, then, will the blood of Christ, who through the eternal Spirit offered himself unblemished to God, cleanse our consciences from acts that lead to death, so that we may serve the living God!"* Hallelujah!

The precious blood of our great High Priest does more than make us pretty on the outside. When He cleanses us, we are clean through and through! So claim it, believe it, live it! It doesn't get better than that.

What an amazing Thanksgiving! With news of two of our dear friends getting much- needed jobs and God's miraculous provision for our family as well, we can only say that our God answers prayers. It may not be in the way we want, or when we want, but it is always to our greatest blessing—and His greatest glory!

It was good to get back into the kitchen at the Christian Aid Center! We had so much fun cooking four thirty-pound turkeys with all the trimmings, for more than 100 people.

Rachel, Gracie, and I had a lot of fun in our kitchen on Wednesday, while Chuck took care of the turkeys at the Center and made service calls. I won't say I wasn't hurting by the end, but my recovery time was much shorter than

I anticipated. I just can't thank God enough when I think of how I spent last Thanksgiving!

There's a saying that life is either feast or famine. But it occurs to me that we who live in Christ are the only ones who feast even in the midst of famine. So, there is no famine for those who eat of the Bread of Life.

No matter how bad circumstances seem, we know He is moving in all things—for all things are His—to pour out His blessings and show us how He cares for the smallest details of our lives. There is always reason to praise Him as He grows our faith through adversity, makes provision for us, and, most importantly, intercedes on our behalf, cleansing us from all unrighteousness and preparing a place for us in our Father's house. That alone is worthy of our praise.

My prayers continue for you that you will be filled with a burning desire to know our Savior more and seek Him daily, that you may rise above the confines of the physical world and know the joy and peace of supernatural living in the power of the Holy Spirit. That is living!

God's grace and peace be yours,

Rebecca

The Gift
Monday, December 6, 2010

Blessings, Friends,

Today's promise is John 14:14: *"You may ask me for anything in my name, and I will do it."* I'll claim that with a big Amen!

Better than Santa Claus! Jesus says in verse 12 of that chapter: *"Very truly I tell you, whoever believes in me will do the works I have been doing, and they will do even greater things than these, because I am going to the Father."* Just think of the things Christ could accomplish through us if we would just let go of what we *think* God should be, and embrace Him as He is! This is what I ask.

This time of year, thoughts begin turning to gift-giving—hopefully to the most precious gift ever given, Jesus Christ, our Savior. Like so many other families, ours will be a very skinny Christmas, but I have a gift beyond measure to offer my King. Worth more (to Him) than gold, or frankincense, or myrrh. It is, of course, myself. Christ gave His all to me, some 2,000 years ago, so I can hardly give Him less. Besides, what do you give the guy who has everything? The only thing He wants. The ironic thing is that this gift isn't worth much of anything *until* I give it to Him. No one else. Just Him.

So, happy birthday, Jesus! May you get much good use and pleasure from my humble gift.

You remain in my thoughts and prayers.

God's grace and peace be yours,

Rebecca

Blessed Art Thou
Monday, December 20, 2010

Blessings, Friends,

Today's promise is Luke 2:10–11: *"But the angel said to them, 'Do not be afraid. I bring you good news that will cause great joy for all the people. Today in the town of David a Savior has been born to you; he is the Messiah, the Lord.'"*

Yahoooo!

The Christmas pageant was wonderful! Rachel and Aaron played Mary and Joseph, and, although Joseph was minus some facial hair, they were wonderful. Of course, Daniel was a great wise man, and Gracie, the littlest angel, played her part to the hilt, looking as angelic as she could and dutifully taking a bow each time the audience applauded one of the singers.

This season, I've felt the story of our Savior's birth more deeply than I remember in past years. Perhaps, it's because of the miracle He worked in my life over the last year—though, I'd have to say the miracle He's working in my heart by far outshines the healing He's doing in my body.

Perhaps it's because our time here is so short, and, like Gracie with the Advent calendar, the closer I get to seeing Jesus face-to-face, the more excited I get. Gracie, at least, has a date to look forward to. I only have a growing sense of anticipation. I also feel a sense of urgency from the Spirit that people know and accept God as He really is—and not what we want Him to be. And this brings me to Mary (Jesus' mom).

Here, we have a young girl. A good girl, by all accounts, espoused to a good man, and coming closer to the day she will finally be married. Blessed with the comfort of a husband's arms. Finally, to be able to experience love's first kiss, make a home of her own, and start a family. What more could a girl want? She'd probably been dreaming of this since she was a little girl. Stealing glances at Joseph in the marketplace or at various festivals. Feeling a rush of heat in her cheeks when he looked back at her. It wouldn't be long now.

Enter Gabriel.

"Hail, thou that art highly favoured, the Lord is with thee: blessed art thou among women" (Luke 1:28 KJV). And Mary responds logically.

"What???"

Then Gabriel explains, and though some of his explanation is just plain weird, the bottom line is that Mary has received unwarranted favor from God! She has been blessed! What must this have looked like to Mary? Parades in her honor? Gifts? Riches? Respect? It would sure put in their place those girls who looked down their noses at her! But, what did God's blessing look like in reality?

First of all, she'd never known the touch of a man, and here she was to be with child? Pardon my frankness, but most of us tend to look forward to our wedding night, don't we? That part of married life kind of makes up for the nine months of discomfort and pain—not to mention all the years that follow. But that was all right. She would have a loving, supportive husband to get her through and share her joy, right?

Wrong. The man she'd dreamed about all those years did not take the news at all well. In fact, he wanted nothing to do with her. After all, if he married her, he would appear just as guilty of sin as she obviously was. It may be commonplace in the world, but fornication is a stoning offense to God, which was why Joseph wanted to *"...put her away secretly..."* (Matthew 1:19 NKJV).

Even after an angelic visitation convinced him to go ahead with the marriage, he didn't cohabit with Mary until after Jesus' birth. Any moms out there who have had to go through a pregnancy alone?

And Joseph was very much human. His reputation was shot. I can imagine he had a hard time looking at Mary, and when he did, I'm sure Mary saw a look that said, "My wife is carrying someone else's child, and I haven't even been with her yet." Or maybe, "I know the prophets foretold a virgin birth, but did it have to be *my* virgin?" I don't know how many of you have experienced rejection like that, but this must have been horrible for Mary.

Even now, some people have a very hard time sharing their spouses with God. And for all Joseph knew, his dream could have been just that—a dream. And, don't forget the looks and whispers among the villagers —"Good little

Mary. Boy, she had us fooled!" Mary had to go live with her cousin, Elizabeth, for three months, probably wondering when the "blessing" would begin. Elizabeth got it—she understood. What was with everyone else?

But, it just went downhill from there. With the census came a nice vacation—not.

When I was four months pregnant with my first child, my husband and I drove from Northern Oregon to Southern California in the summer to visit family. Now, we had a new car—with AC—but even so, it was the most miserable trip I have ever taken! Stopping every thirty minutes to throw up, trying to no avail to get comfortable. It was horrible!

But here was Mary, very near her due date, having to make this journey from Nazareth to Bethlehem—at least sixty miles—either walking or riding a donkey! (It was probably a four- or five-day journey.) Tears come just thinking about that poor child!

But it gets better! When they arrive, there are no rooms left!

I don't know how Mary handled all this, but I know how I would have:

"Are you serious, Joseph? You couldn't make reservations? Don't these people know who I am? I—am—blessed—among—women! And you'd better do something fast 'cause my water just broke!"

The mother of our Savior then proceeded to bed down and give birth in a barn. I personally like the smell of horses, but cow, sheep, and donkey doo? Yuck.

There was no golden bassinette or soft receiving blankets for this King. Only bandage-like strips of cloth, much like He would be wrapped in at His burial, and a dirty feed trough that countless animals had slobbered in and chewed on. I'm sure Mary thought things were finally looking up when the visitors and gifts began to arrive—some two years later—and Joseph's attitude probably took a turn for the better.

But it wasn't long before the little family was on the run to save their child's life. (See Matthew 1:13–15.) Perhaps it was then Mary finally realized the gravity of being blessed of God, even though old Simeon in the temple warned that even her own soul would be pierced through by a sword. (See Luke 2:21–35.) *Silly old man, I am blessed among women. Pierced through my own soul? I don't think so.*

My point is that our idea of blessing is sometimes vastly different from God's sometimes because our vision is limited. God sees the big picture— beginning, middle, and end. I'm sure Mary wondered at God's interpretation as she raised this "king" in poverty, this kid who was so different from everyone else's kids, right up until the time she watched her child hanging on that cross and being pierced with a sword. The sword that pierced her own soul through and through. Even then, she had no idea how she had been blessed. She just had to take God at His Word. Thank God she did! Her blind faith blessed us all!

It was not just Mary who was to be blessed by this great event, but the whole of Israel. Ironically, they missed it, for the most part, simply because they refused to give up their preconceived notions of who God was and just take Him at His Word, as Mary had done. And that, my friends, is still the choice before us. Accept the blessing as is, or lose it altogether. I'll take it. No amount of pain and suffering in this life will extinguish the Light of my life. The Light of the world.

May God bless you richly this Christmas and in the coming New Year!

Rebecca

Chapter 28

I WILL GIVE YOU REST

People, Get Ready

Monday, January 3, 2011

Blessings, Friends, and Happy 2011!

Today's promise is 2 Corinthians 3:16–18: "*But whenever anyone turns to the Lord, the veil is taken away. Now the Lord is the Spirit, and where the Spirit of the Lord is, there is freedom. And we all, who with unveiled faces contemplate the Lord's glory, are being transformed into his image with ever-increasing glory, which comes from the Lord, who is the Spirit.*"

Hallelujah!

What a promise to start a new year with! Praise God! That is certainly my new year's resolution: to reflect Him more and more in thought, word, and deed! And, to tell the truth, the older I get, the more overrated stress and worry become!

It was a Christmas of loaves and fishes at our house! We were content with our homemade Christmas, but some very generous, earthly angels saw to it that our baskets overflowed. It was very humbling, and as I got caught up on my friends' CarePages and CaringBridge, I realized many other families were blessed by the generosity of others as well.

I don't think some people realize just how much this means. I know everyone is feeling the effects of the economy, but for families who are dealing with catastrophic illness, it's been devastating. Two-income families have to become one-income, or even no-income, families in order to be twenty-four-hour caregivers while medical bills mount higher and higher. Mortgage and utility companies don't say, "Oh, you have a sick child or spouse? Well, don't worry about your bills; we've got you covered."

To me, a new year means we're all the closer to Jesus' return, and that's so exciting! My prayer for the new year is that God will open the floodgates of Heaven and pour out His blessings of faith, healing, wisdom, joy, and peace. That the true Gospel will sweep our nation and the world, that millions will come to salvation through Jesus Christ, and that they would look not to the world for proof of His working, but to their own hearts. To God be the glory forever and ever, Amen!

Matthew 7:7: *"Ask, and it shall be given you; seek, and ye shall find; knock, and it shall be opened unto you"* (KJV).

God's richest blessings be yours in 2011!

Rebecca

Peace, Be Still
Monday, January 10, 2011

Blessings, Friends!

Today's promise is Philippians 1:6: *"Being confident in this, that he who began a good work in you will carry it on to completion until the day of Christ Jesus."* Thank you, Lord!

I've decided the minimal pain I occasionally experience is not worth the side effects of Neurontin, so Dr. Monroe is weaning me off! Yea! This may take a while, as I was on 900mgs a day, and I can only decrease by 100mgs a week, but hopefully my vision will clear and my anxiety level will drop before I'm completely off it.

I've also had my thyroid medication cut in half—not by choice, but by necessity. From what I understood, this isn't supposed to be possible, but with God, all things are possible. So, you can see how today's promise is very timely. For the good work, He began in me is not just in my spirit, but in my flesh as well. Praise His name!

Has it ever occurred to you that the story of Jesus calming the sea was more than just a day in the life of Jesus and His disciples? It didn't occur to me until last night when I realized for the first time (I love it when this happens) that this "day in the life" was an incredible metaphor for our journey with Christ.

Mark 4:35–36: *"That day when evening came, he said to his disciples, 'Let us go over to the other side.' Leaving the crowd behind, they took him along, just as he was, in the boat. There were also other boats with him."*

When we decide to follow Christ, we get into the boat with Him and leave the multitude behind (*"For many are invited, but few are chosen"* Matthew 22:14)—and we begin our journey to the other side.

Mark 4:37: *"And a great windstorm arose, and the waves beat into the boat, so that it was already filling."*

Nowhere in the Word does He say this journey will be smooth sailing. But many, believing this, lose faith.

Mark 4:38: *"But He was in the stern, asleep on a pillow. And they awoke Him and said to Him, 'Teacher, do You not care that we are perishing?'"* (NKJV).

Another faith killer. We focus on the storm raging around us and are overcome by fear, thinking God doesn't care about our struggles, pain, and suffering.

Mark 4:39–40: *"Then He arose and rebuked the wind, and said to the sea, 'Peace, be still!' And the wind ceased and there was a great calm. But He said to them, 'Why are you so fearful? How is it that you have no faith?'"* (NKJV).

But He is there with us the entire time. He is in full control. And yes, He does care!

I used to think the wind and waves obeying the command of Jesus was the highlight of this story, but I was wrong. Like the disciples, my focus was on the storm. The truly amazing thing is what happens next.

Mark 4:41: *"And they feared exceedingly, and said to one another, 'Who can this be, that even the wind and the sea obey Him!'"* (NKJV).

Suddenly, it wasn't their circumstances they feared, but Jesus.

When we learn who is truly worthy of our attention, fear, and reverence—then and only then—will we have peace in the journey to the other side. God is so much bigger than our circumstances, and He has promised to never leave us. He is in control. What an awesome place to be, where I can lay back in the boat on my pillow and actually enjoy the storms, trusting with all my being in the One who calms the storm, knowing the true meaning of those words, "Peace, be still."

Please remember me in your prayers as I continue to lift you up.

God's grace and peace be yours,

Rebecca

Joy in the Lord!
Monday, January 17, 2011

Blessings, Friends,

Today's promise is Joshua 1:9: *"Have I not commanded you? Be strong and of good courage; do not be afraid, nor be dismayed, for the LORD your God is with you wherever you go"* (NKJV). Thank you, Lord!

Not feeling so great, today. Rachel has been very sick for days, Aaron is trying to catch it, and, of course, Gracie is still fighting that respiratory bug. It seems like everyone is just sick and tired of being sick and tired. I'm not sure if I'm trying to come down with a cold, myself, or if it's my medication adjustment, but I've definitely had better days. Of course, I've had worse days, too—much worse. So I can't complain. Usually, it's when you feel like praising God the least that you need to do it the most. I know it is when I am physically weak and run down that the enemy comes to steal my joy, and my faith:

"For our struggle is not against flesh and blood, but against the rulers, against the authorities, against the powers of this dark world and against the spiritual forces of evil in the heavenly realms" (Ephesians 6:12 NIV).

Well, I refuse to let him take it! There is power in praise!

"But thou art holy, O thou that inhabits the praises of Israel" (Psalm 22:3).

The last thing the enemy wants me to do is to praise the Lord right now, so that is exactly what I will do!

"For though we live in the world, we do not wage war as the world does. The weapons we fight with are not the weapons of the world. On the contrary, they have divine power to demolish strongholds. We demolish arguments and every pretension that sets itself up against the knowledge of God, and we take captive every thought to make it obedient to Christ" (2 Corinthians 10:3–5 NIV).

I will be praising the Lord for you, too!

Rebecca

I Will Give You Rest
Monday, January 24, 2011

Blessings, Friends,

Today's promise is Matthew 11:28: *"Come to me, all you who are weary and burdened, and I will give you rest"* (NIV). Thank you, Lord!

Some of you may think that I pick these promises myself, and sometimes I do. But usually, I get them from the Promise Calendar I receive from Jack Van Impe Ministries each year. I just mention that because some days, like today, it's just the promise I need on that day. Like a special hug from the Father. Some days I have no idea what I will update on, but once I read that promise, the Holy Spirit lets me know exactly what to write. I never know who I'm writing for, though sometimes one of you will let me know, which I thoroughly enjoy. It lets me know how to pray for you. But, I am always blessed by this discourse, too.

Take today's promise. A few days ago I was so overwhelmed by all the things I "needed" to do, I found myself thinking, "I wish I could just lie in bed and relax for a day." I had no more completed the thought when I realized just a year ago I was in bed wishing I could get up and do something! Being a chronic over-achiever, I'm having difficulty finding a happy medium. Being a wife and mother of busy kids, there are things I "have" to do, but there are also things that I "want" to do. Things that revitalize me and refill my emotional well that so many are drawing from constantly.

Jesus was a prime example of "mom-itis." Constantly serving. Constantly teaching. Constantly giving. But He knew His limits. He knew when to set boundaries—to get in the boat and go to the other side. I need to learn from Him. I may want to do it all, but it would be foolish to think that I can. So, I need to set realistic goals for myself and learn to forgive myself for being human—and to reject the guilt (real or imagined) that others try to lay on me. If I accomplish even one goal in a day, I need to thank God for helping me do that and enjoy the satisfaction of that accomplishment. Then, I need to make time to do something I love—to feed myself. (While some may take this literally, and I am a huge fan of chocolate, I strongly suggest a low-cal activity.)

Most importantly, Jesus knew where—or from Whom—His strength came. From the Father. Many times we read in the Word that Jesus went off alone to plug in to His power source and recharge. This is where today's verse comes in. And this is probably why I find myself counting the days to Wednesday and Sunday. No matter how much "me time" I spend, nothing recharges me like coming together with family to praise God, and to dig into the Word. Even that pales in comparison to spending one-on-one time with God, but, being much in demand at home, that doesn't happen often enough unless I'm kneeling at the altar in church. Only He can give me the rest I need and can help me put it all in perspective.

Everything in nature speaks to God's perfect balance. There is joy in balance, and I know if I acknowledge Him in all my ways, He will direct my path—(Proverbs 3:6). He will show me what really needs to get done, and what will wait. I just need to remember to ask Him. Ironically, trying to be everything to everyone is incredibly selfish when it comes right down to it. Idolatry. Trying to be God. We were made to work in unison with God and each other, not to do it all ourselves. And the result of this behavior is not pretty, either.

If any of you are fasters, you know that, at a certain point in the day, when your body realizes it's not getting fed, it starts to rebel. You don't feel well, and you can get short-tempered—sometimes, downright mean. Well, our spirits and minds are the same. When I begin to get rebellious, and snappy, if I have the presence of mind to stop and question my behavior, I always find I am neglecting one of the three areas of my life required to maintain balance: spirit, mind, or flesh. And I can't fill one area in with more of another, either. If I haven't been in the Word all week, crocheting or writing won't fill the gap, and vice-versa. In God's image, we are three-in-one, and all three must be nurtured to achieve balance and joy.

This is a busy week for me. Gracie turns 5 five tomorrow, and Wednesday is my birthday—I haven't decided how old I'm going to be this year. I have homeschool things to be done, and I'm teaching Sunday School and singing for Singspiration next Sunday. So that is where I will focus my energy this week. Of course, there are a million other things that need to get done— eventually—but they can keep for now. Luckily, teaching enables me to be in the Word, too, so the only thing left is my creative time, and I have plenty of projects to keep me busy there. The trick is to not dive into the to-do list, thinking if I just get it all done, I'll have more time to relax later. 'Cause, guess what? Later never comes.

Well, there's my self-motivational pep-talk for the week. Now, Lord, please give me the grace to turn words into action!

Thank you for your prayers and words of encouragement. Everyone here is on the mend, and finals week went very well! I will be praying for you this week.

God's grace and peace be yours,

Rebecca

Reason to Praise!
Monday, January 31, 2011

Blessings, Friends,

Today's promise is 1 John 2:12: *"I am writing to you, dear children, because your sins have been forgiven on account of His name"* (NIV). Thank you, Jesus!

I survived the week! And what a week it was! Wednesday night, my sneaky husband surprised me with a birthday party at Bible Study. I honestly didn't suspect a thing, even when our three oldest kids came in with cards. Not until I saw the flaming cake back in the kitchen, did I realize I'd been got! I finally decided on 32 this year. Twenty-nine was getting old, and, besides, the 20s are so overrated. I discovered that Chuck had been scheming for 2 two weeks! Boy, you think you know someone . . . Thank you, honey!

Thursday was Aaron's last home wrestling match, and I have to say, I'm glad the season is almost over. If I had high blood pressure, I'd probably be in the hospital! No matter how good he is, it is very stressful watching my "baby" fight his own battles! I'm very proud of him, though.

Friday, Chuck took me out for my first birthday dinner in three years! He has had to cancel more reservations because of my illness than I care to mention, so this was a wonderful blessing! And the meal won't soon be forgotten, either! Don't ask me to recount everything we had, but it was six courses of yum! While we were at dinner, the kids were enjoying a movie/pizza night at the church.

Saturday, Gracie had her fifth princess party. I think it is safe to say she has enough princess and fairy stuff to keep her busy for the year! Right now, her favorite is the Royal Bath Set. Her favorite movie is *Last Holiday*, so she is totally getting into her "spa days." Though she is a little put out that she hasn't been able to get in for a massage! I made her a "super tutu", so when she isn't "spa-ing," she's dancing. After that big day, I was ready to collapse—but my week wasn't over yet!

Yesterday, I taught the adult Sunday School class, and it went really well. I shared with the class that I gave a sermon on the same subject (love) seven years ago, and by the end of that day, Chuck was on his knees proposing to me, so I couldn't wait to see what the end of this day would bring! I love to teach—of course, you wouldn't know that.

The end of the day brought Singspiration and a potluck! I finally sang a solo, which went as well as could be expected for having not done it in 20 years and having a last-minute song change, and then I sang "Jesus and Me" with the ladies' trio. That was fun! I would say it felt good to get up and sing a solo again, but being that nervous never feels good. But we are not called to be comfortable, are we? We are called to use the gifts God has given us to be a blessing to others and to give glory to Him. And I certainly have plenty to sing about! I couldn't believe how many people sang, played instruments, and read poetry last night. It was amazing! None of us are "stars," but we sure know how to make a joyful noise unto the Lord, and we sure love to praise Him! Everyone was blessed last night.

The week was not without pain, especially after cutting my pain meds, but I plan on lying low this week. Emphasis on plan. With the pain I'm having, after reducing just 100mg, I'm not sure being drug-free is in the cards for me just yet. And I was not happy to learn that Neurontin has its own withdrawal issues, too. But, you know, I really feel that it won't be long before I get my new upgraded model and won't have to deal with pain or meds again. Ever! Praise God!

In this world, where sin isn't even considered sin, we are truly a "peculiar people." But I thank God that no matter what the world is doing around me, I can always enter into the Holy of Holies and find Him there waiting for me. Waiting to receive my worship, waiting to lift my burden, waiting to comfort me. Even when I feel He's not listening, He's there. He promised. And my Dad never lies. Never.

I have been lifting you all up in prayer. I may not know what your needs are, but God does, and I pray you feel His presence and love in your lives each day.

God's grace and peace be yours,

Rebecca

Chapter 29

PERFECT LOVE

Keep Standing in the Gap
Tuesday, February 8, 2011
Blessings, Friends,

Today's promise is John 15:15: *"I no longer call you servants, because a servant does not know his master's business. Instead, I have called you friends, for everything that I learned from my Father I have made known to you"* (NKJV). And, what a friend we have in Jesus!

I don't even know where to begin today. I have been reading some really awesome testimonies on CarePages and CaringBridge. Some in awe of God's healing here on earth, and some in the grief of learning to live (temporarily) without a loved one who received their healing in Heaven.

I didn't really understand Jesus' invitation to, *"Take up the cross, and follow me"* (Mark 10:21 NKJV) until God turned up the refining furnace. I think, for some reason, I thought that, because Jesus was already crucified on that cross, the way would be easier for me. But the hard truth is, that Jesus came not to eliminate our pain and grief, but to show us how to be overcomers. Yes, He did take the penalty of sin for us, but He did not take away the effects of sin on the world. This He uses to teach us to trust and obey Him. It's also what He uses to let us know just how much He loves us and wants to bless us. That is why it is so very important to praise Him in all things—because He loves us and has a plan to bless us and prosper us. Though, sometimes it sure doesn't feel like it.

We may feel at times like lashing out at Him in anger, and He can handle that. But, you know, I've learned—sometimes the hard way—that in the long run, it is much easier to praise Him from the beginning. There is supernatural power in praise. It's like saying, "I don't know what you're doing, Lord, but I choose to trust you anyway." I love it when I read updates like that! I know that God is about to move mightily in that person's life. But some of us have a hard time with that, which is why it is so important to stand in the gap for each other.

A wonderful friend and fellow author, Shirley Pope Waite, has given me permission to use a poem of hers, which was published in her own book, *Delight in the Day*, as well as the *Women's Devotional Bible #2*. She wrote it for her son, but its message is not limited to a certain situation or time. I have included it at the end of my update. I know it will continue to touch lives and give hope for many more years to come.

At home on the range, I have a sick little girl—again. So we spent yesterday in bed writing thank you cards—lots of thank you cards! Now that Gracie is five, she insists on signing her own name on top of her usual artwork. Today, we'll concentrate on Valentine cards.

My pain finally settled down, so I reduced my Neurontin another 100mg. Please, pray for me. The last adjustment was not easy. Praise the Lord!

Standing in the Gap
by Shirley Pope Waite

I'll stand in the gap for my son,
I'll stand 'til the victory's won.
This one thing I know
That You love him so,
And Your work with my child is not done.

I'll stand in the gap every day,
And there I will fervently pray.
And, Lord, just one favor,
Don't let me waver
If things get quite rough...which they may.

I'll never give up on that boy.
Nor will You, for You promised him joy.
For I know it was true
When he said "yes" to You.
Though the enemy seeks to destroy.

I'll not quit as I intercede.
For You are his Savior, indeed.
Though it may take years,
I give You my fears,
As I trust every moment I plead.

And so in the gap I will stand,
Heeding Your every command.
With help from above,
I unconditionally love,
And soon he will reach for Your hand.

God's grace and peace be yours,
Rebecca

You Are Loved!
Monday, February 14, 2011

Valentine Blessings, Friends,

Today's promise is Romans 8:38-39: *"For I am persuaded that neither death nor life, nor angels nor principalities nor powers, nor things present nor things to come, nor height nor depth, nor any other created thing, shall be able to separate us from the love of God which is in Christ Jesus our Lord"*(NKJV). How's that for a Valentine?

My week was spent in bed with a very sick little girl. Gracie had a fever of 103 for several days and was drowning in mucus, poor thing. I did get a few things done, but for the most part, was not allowed to leave the room. She is finally up and around, but still coughing and sneezing. I received some words of wisdom from our friends at church, though, that I will pass on. Onion juice. You read right, onion juice. Apparently, drinking a little juice from a boiled onion breaks up mucus and sends it out the other end. Gross, I know, but I wish I'd known this sooner! Of course, we have to put it in some broth or something, but so far it's working. Praise the Lord! So, Gracie missed all of the Valentine festivities at church and Missionettes, but her beloved teachers brought crafts and goodies for her, so she felt a little better.

I have gained a new respect for moms who are caring for children with cancer and other chronic conditions. After just a week of hearing my baby crying and struggling to breathe and sleep, I was physically and emotionally spent! I was blessed to get some relief on Saturday at our church's craft day at Chuck's insistence. I wish I had the means to provide more support for the moms out there dealing with more than bronchitis, but I have determined to seriously pray that God will speak to the hearts of people around them who can provide much-needed breaks. I know God has some pretty sweet hookups. If you know an overtaxed mom, please pray that God will show you how you can help. Sometimes we spend so much time in "overdrive" we can no longer recognize our own exhaustion. But, even a half-hour to recharge can mean so much to our physical and emotional health. How much more so for those who provide care 24/7!

I know that Valentine's Day can be difficult for some people who either never felt loved or are trying to live without a loved one. So, I thought I would focus this update on the greatest Valentine of all and remind everyone reading this that you are indeed loved beyond measure.

Of course, everyone should know John 3:16 (paraphrased): *"God loved you so much, that He sacrificed His one and only Son, so that if you believe in Him, you will live forever!"*

And Romans 5:8 (paraphrased): *"This is how God showed His love for you, Christ didn't require you to be perfect before He died for you."*

Galatians 2:20: *"I have been crucified with Christ; it is no longer I who live, but Christ lives in me; and the life which I now live in the flesh I live by faith in the Son of God, who loved me and gave Himself for me"* (NKJV).

Ephesians 2:4-5 (paraphrased): *"But God, who is so rich in mercy, had such great love for you that, even when you were dead in your sin, He brought you back to life in Christ—and not to guilt and shame, but as joint heirs with Christ!"*

Ephesians 5:1-2 (paraphrased): *"So, follow God, as His dear child; and walk in love, as Christ also has loved you. So much so, that He gave Himself as a sacrifice to God in your place as a sweet-smelling savor."*

2 Thessalonians 2:16-17 (paraphrased): *"Now your Lord, Jesus Christ, Himself, and even God, your Father, who have loved you and given you everlasting consolation and good hope through grace, comfort your heart and make you strong in every good word and work."*

1 John 3:1 (paraphrased): *"Wow! How God must love you! He calls you His child!"*

1 John 1:9 (paraphrased): *"This is how God showed His love for you, that He sent His one and only Son to you, that you might live through Him."*

1 John 4:10 (paraphrased): *"This is real love—not that you love God, but that He loved you, before you were even born, and sent His Son to be a payment for your sins!"*

So, Happy Valentine's Day, beloved of God and Christ our Savior. You are loved, cherished, and held! And, if you have any favorite love letters from God, please share! I hope that, no matter what your situation, you will find a smile on your lips today as you feel His arms around you!

God's grace and peace be yours,

Rebecca

Delighted!
Monday, February 21, 2011

Blessings, Friends,

Today's promise is Joshua 1:9: *"Have I not commanded you? Be strong and courageous! Do not be terrified or dismayed (intimidated), for the Lord your God is with you wherever you go"* (AMP). Lord, help me in my unbelief.

Why is it that God's words are so easy to believe when I read them? They seem perfectly doable in the moment. But then life steps in and all at once I'm at a loss as to how to turn those words into action. It reminds me of my son in his English class. He does the exercises and understands the concepts all right. But there comes a point in each lesson where he has to do a project that requires him to put those concepts to work. In my son's case, he does not want to do the projects. He says, "I know what it means, why do I have to do it?" He doesn't understand yet that understanding is only part of the equation. Application completes the equation.

So I ask myself, how can I learn to apply what I learn in scriptures to my life? If I take a lesson from my son's schooling, I would have to say that learning application comes from *doing* application. Logically, I know that practice improves any skill. (I'm too far at the other end of the scale to think about perfection at this point.) We learn by doing. But . . . if I do before I've perfected the skill, I might screw up—actually, you can bet I'll screw up. I hate screwing up. I want to do it right the first time. Now you know where my son gets it. My grandpa used to say that if you aren't making mistakes, you aren't learning. I wish I had my grandpa's temperament. We Christians tend to screw up more than others, or are more aware of it than others, simply because the Holy Spirit's job is to remind us of our imperfections, and that the only thing good in us is Jesus. Apart from Him, we can do nothing right.

Honestly, if you're looking at Christianity expecting to see perfection, you're going to be sorely disappointed—until Christ returns. Which is the very theme of Christianity. This is why Paul instructs us, *"Brethren, if a man is overtaken in any trespass, you who are spiritual restore such a one in a spirit of gentleness, considering yourself lest you also be tempted. Bear one another's burdens, and so fulfill the law of Christ"*(Galatians 6:1-2 NKJV).

Oops. I was just convicted. Am I supposed to give myself a break, too? "Physician, heal thyself?" I just get so frustrated with myself sometimes. I wish my heart knew what my head knows. But, when I'm under attack, my mind is hard-pressed to even keep up with my emotions, never mind, override them. It's so hard not to want justice *now*. It's hard not to cry out like David, "Why, Lord, do you let my enemies prevail over me?" Even though I know very well they won't. It only seems that way at the moment. I just get battle-weary, wondering if a little peace is too much to ask. I find myself asking, "How far does loving your enemy go? Should I defend myself and my family, or just take the harassment and abuse (even when it involves felonious behavior) and let God handle it?" But I don't seem to get an answer.

I know I'm not to repay evil for evil, that's easy enough to understand. But, does turning the other cheek mean volunteering for whipping post duty? I would really like to know—what would Jesus do? I guess until I learn the answer to that burning question, I'll just follow Him through my "projects" to the best of my ability, knowing that His grace is sufficient to cover my screw-ups.

Your prayers are very much appreciated. I have been fighting illness all week as I try to get Gracie well, and that just adds to the fun. Oh well, as Paul said in 2 Corinthians 12:10: *"That is why, for Christ's sake, I delight in weaknesses, in insults, in hardships, in persecutions, in difficulties. For when I am weak, then I am strong"* (NIV). Here's to being delighted!

God's grace and peace be yours,

Rebecca

Letting Go
Monday, February 28, 2011

Blessings, Friends,

Today's promise is Galatians 1:3-5: *"Grace and peace to you from God our Father and the Lord Jesus Christ, who gave himself for our sins to rescue us from the present evil age, according to the will of our God and Father, to whom be glory for ever and ever. Amen"* (NIV). I'll just add my own "Amen" to that.

I am so happy this morning to be at home with Gracie (still sick) instead of in court, where I thought I'd be. God is so good—and good for His Word! You know, in my last posting, I was so consumed with having to make choices, hoping they were the right ones, and trusting God's grace to cover me if they weren't. I didn't even stop to consider the possibility of God not even giving me the option of screwing up! I had completely forgotten Isaiah 22:22:

"I will place on his [Jesus'] shoulder the key to the house of David; what he opens no one can shut, and what he shuts no one can open" (NIV).

So, regardless of my choice, God's will *will* be done as long as I am seeking it. And that's exactly what He did. What a relief!

As far as my enemies prevailing over me, well, I was reminded again in church yesterday in Psalm 2:1-5 what David said about that problem. Verses 4-5: *"He that sits in the heavens shall laugh: the Lord shall have them in derision. Then He shall speak to them in His wrath, and distress them in His deep displeasure"* (NKJV).

I think my biggest struggle in my Christian walk is giving up my will. I just know that I know what needs to be done and when it needs to be done, and that's that. It's purely emotional, of course. In my mind, I know that God's way of doing things is far superior to mine; I just can't convince my heart. I guess it comes down to faith. I haven't had much luck controlling my emotions, but I am so thankful that, once God has spoken on the matter, the peace that follows is almost immediate. I can remember a time when I would have let anger and self-pity eat me up for weeks, but that doesn't seem to be the case anymore.

So, while I'd just as soon not have my stomach churning or lose any sleep at all, I will take this small change as evidence that the Holy Spirit is alive and at work in me. The more of me I let go of, the more of Him I'll have room for. Praise the Lord! Praise Him for the peace only He can give. It makes no sense at all to fuss and fret when I am in the hands of a loving, all-powerful Father. I look forward to the day when every fiber of my being rests in that truth.

A couple days ago, I was trying to get a much-needed nap with Gracie, and I heard a racket outside. It sounded like someone was walking around in my flower bed and yard, rustling leaves like crazy. I got up to see who it could be and was amazed to see my yard filled with the biggest robins I'd ever seen, hopping around, digging up goodies. It was such a beautiful sight! I think that sometimes God sends us gifts like that to let us know He loves us and that everything will be okay. I sure took it that way.

I will be in prayer for you, friends. I may not know your every need, but God knows, and He is faithful to provide. Above all, I pray that His peace will reign in your hearts, no matter what your circumstances. Jesus gave up everything so we would no longer have to carry the burden of stress, worry, fear, guilt . . . But *"that we might have life, and have it more abundantly"* (John 10:10). Who wouldn't want that? If we continually seek Him, He is faithful to replace our stress, fear, and guilt with His perfect peace as He grows our faith. It may not be overnight, but it will happen. I'm so thankful for that.

God's grace and peace be yours,

Rebecca

Chapter 30

ALL OR NOTHING

Overcoming

Monday, March 7, 2011

Blessings, Friends,

Today's promise is James 4:6: *"But He gives us more grace. That is why Scripture says: 'God opposes the proud but gives grace to the humble'"*(NIV).

That seems very appropriate. The lesson I taught yesterday was on overcoming temptation as Christ did in Luke 4:1-13. This verse passage may not seem to have much to do with overcoming temptation, but it really does.

Hebrews 4:15 tells us, *"For we do not have a high priest who is unable to sympathize with our weaknesses, but we have one who has been tempted in every way, just as we are—yet was without sin"*(NIV). A great promise in itself.

The word "tempted" here is *peirazo* (pi-rad'-zo), meaning to test, i.e.: endeavor, scrutinize, entice, discipline.

Why so many seemingly different meanings? All these meanings have the same result. We know that God tests us to grow our faith and purify us— Malachi 3:3: *"He will sit as a refiner and a purifier of silver"* (NKJV). But, we are also enticed to sin. James 1:13-14 makes it clear that God cannot be tempted to sin, nor does He tempt any man to sin. He also makes it clear that temptation is within us, not all around us, trying to take us down. Fortunately, 1 Corinthians 10:13 promises that God will not allow us to be tempted beyond what we can bear, and that with the temptation, He also will also provide an escape, that we might endure it. So, He is in control.

Whether we are in the midst of a trial or facing a moment of weakness, temptation all boils down to one thing—one choice: do I take my own path or trust in God's plan? This is the same question Jesus faced each time Satan made Him an offer. He could have had everything God offered Him instantly and pain-free, had He accepted. God's path included much pain and difficulty, so why wouldn't He take the easy way out? Because His Father's will was more important to Him than His own physical well-being, wealth, or social standing.

It's obvious to see the importance of knowing God's Word in overcoming temptation, as Satan loves to use it to lead people astray. But, Jesus' willingness to humble Himself before God was just as powerful a weapon. Jesus didn't come to serve Himself, but His Father—for us. Because of this, Jesus achieved the ultimate victory and empowered us to do the same.

No matter what we are facing, we can draw strength from that; just as Jesus, we are not alone, because the Holy Spirit is with us all the way. If we follow Jesus' example, we will do three things. 1) Above all else, stop and ask ourselves what is more important to us: our Father's will, or our personal well-being, comfort, or pride. 2) Learn to recognize when we are vulnerable and get into the Word, prayer, worship, and calling on our faith family to stand in the gap for us. 3) Know God's Word, so we can use it effectively, and it can't be used against us. Ephesian 6:17 calls the Word "*the Sword of the Spirit.*" And Hebrews 4:12 says the Word is "*living and powerful, and sharper than any two-edged sword, piercing even to the division of soul and spirit, and of joints and marrow, and is a discerner of the thoughts and intents of the heart*" (NKJV). Wow! How's that for power?

Best of all is how temptation or trials end when we follow God's plan. In Matthew 4:11 we read that when Jesus had been victorious, "*. . . the devil left Him, and behold, angels came and ministered to Him.*" What a comfort!

God's way may not be the easy way—in fact, it can seem unbearable at times. But that is the way that led to my salvation. That's the way for me.
God's grace and peace be yours,
Rebecca

Real Power
Monday, March 14, 2011
Blessings, Friends,

Today's promise is Luke 21:15: *"For I will give you words and wisdom that none of your adversaries will be able to resist or contradict"* (NIV).

Thank you, Jesus! This is such an important promise to Christians in light of the Great Commission to spread the Gospel to all the ends of the earth. Most of us freeze up just thinking about sharing our testimony with someone. We worry we'll make fools of ourselves, or that we don't know the Word well enough to be convincing or to answer any questions which that might come up or to defend our faith.

After Jesus defeated Satan in the wilderness, Luke 4:14 tells us that He *"returned to Galilee in the power of the Holy Spirit, and news about Him spread through the whole countryside"* (NIV). The key phrase here is "in the power of the Holy Spirit." Jesus was in the power of the Holy Spirit because of His willingness to give up His will for the will of His Father. This power not only gave Him wisdom and words that went to the hearts of His listeners, it also protected Him when His words turned some listeners into murderous mobs. Not to mention all of the healings and casting out of demons. If only all Christians had that power.

But, wait . . . in Luke 24:49, Jesus tells His disciples, *"I am going to send you what my Father has promised; but stay in the city until you have been clothed with power from on high"* (NIV).

Was Jesus' promise for the disciples only? Nope. Luke 11:10–13: *"For everyone who asks receives; the one who seeks finds; and to the one who knocks, the door will be opened. Which of you fathers, if your son asks for a fish, will give him a snake instead? Or if he asks for an egg, will give him a scorpion? If you then, though you are evil, know how to give good gifts to your children, how much more will your Father in heaven give the Holy Spirit to those who ask him!"* (NIV).

Today's promise verse, among others, tells us that it is not we who testify, but the Holy Spirit. How much harm has been done by people doing it their way (the Crusades being an extreme example)? Does this mean that people won't ever be offended by our message if it is from the Holy Spirit? No. Jesus said the world hates Him, so they will hate us. But, as with Jesus, the Holy Spirit will protect and sustain us. And the God-given seeds that fall from our lips will find fertile soil in the hearts God has prepared. They will take root, and grow, and, in turn, produce seed that testify to the glory of God.

God makes even witnessing a no-brainer. He does it all for us, leaving us once again with only the choice of obedience over self-will. Something not even Satan or his demons have; see Matthew 8:28-34, Mark 1:21-28, and Luke 9:37-43 for a start. I find it hard to believe that something demons won't even dare to do comes so easily to me. Maybe that is what Paul meant when he talked about the thorn in his flesh. We may not wrestle against flesh and blood, but my will is a force to be reckoned with. Thank the good Lord, He never gives up on me. *Lord, help me to abide in You. Help me die to you—every day—every hour—every minute. Amen.*

Where did the week go? Oh, that's right, Aaron home with the flu all week, Gracie with a sinus infection and on another antibiotic, and Rachel and I fighting sore throats and sinus colds. My, how time flies! But, we are all on the mend—again. I had a follow-up for my blood work, and it seems my thyroid meds were adjusted too low. I can't reduce my Neurontin again until that is sorted out, but that's okay; my pain level has increased some since I began reducing, but I don't know how much of that is from the cold. But, signs of spring are everywhere, and if that isn't reason to praise God, I don't know what is! The forsythia is blooming, and songbirds wake me every morning. They sound suspiciously close (like under the eaves), but they sing so beautifully, I'll cut them some slack if they want to raise a family in our house.

You remain in my prayers.

God's grace and peace be yours,

Rebecca

Ask, Seek, Knock!
Monday, March 21, 2011

Blessings, Friends,

Today's promise is Luke 11:9: *"So I say to you: Ask and it will be given to you; seek and you will find; knock and the door will be opened"* (NIV).

What a wonderful promise! But, I wonder how many people go back and read the beginning of this chapter. Jesus prefaces this promise with a blueprint, or step-by-step instructions on how to ask, seek, and knock—what has come to be known as the Lord's Prayer. Afterward, He goes on to give a very important admonition about asking. I'm going to use Matthew 6:9-13 for the prayer, since it's what most of us are familiar with.

Matthew 6:9-13:

"Our Father in heaven, hallowed be your name . . ."

Sometimes, in the heat of the moment, or in the rush of daily life, it's tempting to just rattle off a laundry list of wants and needs to God, without a thought that we are speaking to a person—a person with an incredibly big heart. A person who gave up everything to save us. Wow! I know how it feels to have my kids walk up to me and just start making demands. I just want to walk away without even acknowledging them. It makes me feel like a servant, not a mother. Well, we have been created in God's likeness. Yes, God loves to answer our prayers, but He also loves to know we know how blessed we are to be loved by Him, and how awesome He is—He really is, you know. So, we should come to God, acknowledging that He is our Father and that there is no one above Him in our lives—and I hope that is true.

"Your Kingdom come . . ."

Do we love Him? Do we miss His physical presence? Do we want Him to return and set up His Kingdom on earth? We should *tell* Him. And until He does return, we want His Kingdom firmly established in our hearts. More on this later.

"Your will be done, on earth as it is in heaven . . ."

Next is a part that's vital to any healthy relationship. We laugh at comic sketches where one person rattles on to another, asks them a question, and then cuts them off before they can answer, over and over again. Maybe you've been in such a "conversation" yourself? People like to know they're a part of the conversation and that their opinion is valued. But, when we petition the Creator, we take it a step further. We are not just to ask His opinion, but, in all humility, to acknowledge and submit to His sovereign authority. This is absolutely essential for answered prayer. Why? First of all, He deserves it; secondly, He knows what is best for us better than we ever will. Even Jesus prayed, *"Not My will, but Yours be done."* So, what is the point of asking for anything? The point is that what God wants is not to stand over us with a clenched fist like an over-bearing parent. He wants a relationship with us—communion. He wants to give us the desires of our hearts, because it pleases Him; but He also wants to be recognized and appreciated for who He is.

"Give us today our daily bread . . ."

Have you ever had one of your kids thank you for a meal you prepared or some clothing you bought them? Doesn't that feel good? This is not so much a request, as recognition and a "thank you" for providing all of our needs, for it is God who gives us all we need—not just bread.

"And, forgive us our debts, as we also have forgiven our debtors . . ."

Have you ever had someone stomp all over your feelings, and then come to you later for a favor as if everything were hunky-dory? It's very insulting. We are sinners. We hurt God every time we choose our way over His. We need to acknowledge this and ask His forgiveness. Not just because we want something from Him, but because it should hurt us when we hurt Him. That's love.

But notice, Jesus doesn't say we will forgive those who hurt us, but that we have forgiven them before we ask for our own forgiveness. It's that whole "do unto others" thing. God makes it very clear in His Word that He will not forgive the unforgiving (Matthew 6:14-15). And really, how can we hold grudges, when we have been forgiven so much?

"And, lead us not into temptation, but deliver us from the evil one."

I'm a *Biggest Loser* fan, and I'm always amazed when the contestants get to go home, and all of their friends and family take them out and start chowing down on foods that the contestants can no longer have. God doesn't do that, but He does try us to show us where we need change. And, as I've written about before, we all have weaknesses that make us vulnerable to sin. This is actually a prayer we need to be saying throughout our day, especially when we are feeling vulnerable. How do we triumph over trials, overcome temptation, and remain safe from the evil one? By abiding in God, communing with Him. Which is what we ask for when we say, *"Your Kingdom come"*: establish *Your* Kingdom in my heart, Lord; I give you full reign.

It takes time and effort to establish and nurture a meaningful relationship with someone. We make time for them. We talk, but we listen, too. We work to know more about that person, who they are, what they love, and what they don't. We find ourselves thinking of them often, if not always. We think of ways to make their lives easier or more enjoyable, and we try to avoid doing things we know will hurt them. We think of them when we see something we know they like. Little things remind us of them and bring a smile to our lips.

We miss them when we're apart and long for the next time we can be with them.

We were created for communion with the Father. Yes, this takes time and effort, but, I guarantee you, this relationship will be the most rewarding one you will ever have.

Jesus follows this example of prayer in Luke, with an illustration of the importance of persistence. We are to keep asking, keep seeking, and keep knocking. My favorite part of this lesson comes in verses 11–13. I quoted it in my last update. Jesus simply says that if we, who are sinful, know how to give good gifts to our children, how much more will our Father in Heaven give the Holy Spirit to those who ask Him! The Holy Spirit, in this case, is without the article "the" in the Greek, meaning spiritual gifts as opposed to the person of the Holy Spirit.

So we are to ask for spiritual gifts before anything else? Absolutely! For we are to *"seek first His kingdom [Thy kingdom come] and His righteousness—and all these things will be given to you as well"* (Matthew 6:33 NIV).

See? Simple! Ha, ha. But seriously, if you feel your prayers are going unheard, make time each day to commune with the Father. Let Him know you love and appreciate Him. Use the example Christ gave us for establishing the lines of communication. Not because of what He can do for you, but because of who He is. Amen!

Thank you so much for your continued prayers. We are all well on the road to recovery. Gracie and I spent a beautiful Saturday in the yard, and I'm sore all over and loving it! Thank You, Jesus, for Your healing power! And thank you to those of you who take time to encourage me with messages. I so appreciate you!

Please be praying for wisdom and guidance for me as well. I have felt led for some time to pursue an education in ministry, and an opportunity has recently presented itself. I'm very excited about it, but I want God's will in this. Thank you.

God's grace and peace be yours,

Rebecca

All or Nothing
Monday, March 28, 2011
Blessings, Friends,

Today's promise is Philippians 2:12–13: *"Continue to work out your salvation with fear and trembling, for it is God who works in you to will and to act in order to fulfill his good purpose."* Amen!

What a relief to know that the only effort required on my part is to trust and obey! Praise God we have the power of the Holy Spirit to help us do just that!

Our church was visited yesterday by Randy and Colleen Martin, our missionaries to Indonesia, which has the largest Muslim population per capita in the world. I knew Muslims have one thing in common with Christians in that we are monotheistic—we believe in one God, or god, as the case may be—but I thought that's where the similarities stopped. I was wrong. We also share something that—while it is good for the Muslims because it makes them reachable for Christ—is deadly for Christians.

It was a new term for me, though I always knew it existed; I just didn't have a label for it until now. The label is "nominal Christian" or "nominal Muslim."

These are people who profess a faith, but the only outward proof of their faith is the fact that they attend a church or mosque (and, for Muslims, the clothes they wear). They go through the motions, doing as little as possible, and don't think about living their "faith" outside of their prospective houses of worship.

This accounts for the largest part of the Muslim population, and, as I mentioned before, these are the ones most reachable for Christ. They are not committed in their hearts and are therefore open to other options. (Please pray they receive the Truth.)

I'm afraid, however, that this also accounts for the largest part of the Christian population. These Christians are missing out on the relationship of a lifetime, with all the blessings, peace, and joy that comes with it!

Even more importantly, the same apathy that makes Muslims open to the truth makes Christians susceptible to lies—false doctrine. They labor under the false assumption that they are covered—that they are safe. They couldn't be more wrong. God tells us in Revelation 3:15–16: *"I know your deeds, that you are neither cold nor hot. I wish you were either one or the other! So, because you are lukewarm—neither hot nor cold—I am about to spit [vomit] you out of my mouth."* I encourage you to read the rest of that chapter as well.

I think what amazes me most is that the cost of giving your all to Christ is so much greater in Indonesia and other countries as well. Even Christians in "nominal Muslim" homes are disowned by their families, and in other countries, they are imprisoned and killed—yet, they are bold in their faith.

Here, where we have so much and so much reason to want to please God and share the wealth of the Gospel, we are so reluctant to give our all for Christ. Is it because we have become so preoccupied with our blessings that we have forgotten the Giver? Maybe we think we are responsible for our own prosperity? I don't know; maybe we're just too comfortable. It wouldn't be the first time in the history of God's people.

The point is, I don't want to be a "nominal Christian." I want everyone I come in contact with to see that I have something worth having. Our missionaries said that when Muslims see "nominal Christians," their reaction is, "Why would I want to convert to Christianity? They are no different than I am."

I don't want that. That is not why Jesus came to die for me. So I'll keep my eyes on the cross and pray God will make me His walking, talking billboard for what the blood of Christ can do.

God's grace and peace be yours,

Rebecca

Chapter 31

REBIRTH

Counting the Cost
Tuesday, April 5, 2011
Blessings, Friends,

Today's promise is Titus 3:4-6: "*But when the kindness and love of God our Savior appeared, He saved us, not because of righteous things we had done, but because of His mercy. He saved us through the washing of rebirth and renewal by the Holy Spirit, whom He poured out on us generously through Jesus Christ our Savior*" (NIV). Thank You, Lord!

What an appropriate promise for a beautiful spring day—in Walla Walla, anyway. I'm so glad the Lord is my strength, because I'm just about tapped out. Last Tuesday, Gracie, Rachel, and I succumbed to yet another bug, and we are still in the thick of it.

But I can look out my bedroom window and see the Royal Star magnolia and weeping cherries bursting in bloom, and who can complain when they see the bright pinks, purples, reds, and yellows of all the bulbs in their spring finest? What a beautiful reminder of what the Lord has done for us—rebirth and renewal at its best! True, I would love to be out there, but it's church that I really miss.

With Easter so near, my thoughts turn to Jesus; not only to the awesome sacrifice He made for me, but also to His admonition to all who wanted to follow Him. I think so many believe that accepting Christ as their Savior is all it takes. And, really, to think beyond that can be inconvenient at best, and downright terrifying at worst. That's why Jesus actually discouraged some from following Him:

Matthew 16:24-26: *"Then Jesus said to His disciples, 'If anyone desires to come after Me, let him deny himself, and take up his cross, and follow Me. For whoever desires to save his life will lose it, but whoever loses his life for My sake will find it. For what profit is it to a man if he gains the whole world, and loses his own soul? Or what will a man give in exchange for his soul?'"* (NKJV).

Mark 8:34-36 and Luke 9:23-25 repeat this message.

Luke 14:25-33: *"Now great multitudes went with Him. And He turned and said to them, 'If anyone comes to Me and does not hate his father and mother, wife and children, brothers and sisters, yes, and his own life also, he cannot be My disciple. And whoever does not bear his cross and come after Me cannot be My disciple.*

"'For which of you, intending to build a tower, does not sit down first and count the cost, whether he has enough to finish it— lest, after he has laid the foundation, and is not able to finish, all who see it begin to mock him, saying, this man began to build and was not able to finish?

"'Or what king, going to make war against another king, does not sit down first and consider whether he is able with ten thousand to meet him who comes against him with twenty thousand? Or else, while the other is still a great way off, he sends a delegation and asks conditions of peace. So likewise, whoever of you does not forsake all that he has cannot be My disciple'" (NKJV).

I suppose some would say, "Well, I'm not called to be a disciple. I'm just a believer." But Jesus never made any distinction between the two.

Luke 18:18-25: *"Now a certain ruler asked Him, saying, 'Good Teacher, what shall I do to inherit eternal life?'*

"So Jesus said to him, 'Why do you call Me good? No one is good but One, that is, God. You know the commandments: 'Do not commit adultery, Do not murder, Do not steal, Do not bear false witness, 'Honor your father and your mother.' And he said, 'All these things I have kept from my youth.' So when Jesus heard these things, He said to him, 'You still lack one thing. Sell all that you have and distribute to the poor, and you will have treasure in heaven; and come, follow Me.'

"But when he heard this, he became very sorrowful, for he was very rich. And when Jesus saw that he became very sorrowful, He said, 'How hard it is for those who have

riches to enter the kingdom of God! For it is easier for a camel to go through the eye of a needle than for a rich man to enter the kingdom of God'" (NKJV).

Jesus wasn't saying that we should literally "hate" our families, or abandon them, or that we shouldn't have any belongings or money. What He was saying is that if we are to be called children of God, then God must have first place in our lives. Over pride, money, home, family, even children. We must be willing to give it all up if He asks it of us. After all, it all belongs to Him, anyway. The rich ruler was willing to follow all the rules, but his riches were precious to him. That's exactly why Jesus asked for it.

What is Jesus asking you to surrender today? Unforgiveness? Anger? Resentment? Material things? An addiction? An addicted spouse? Your child? For me (at the moment), it's my dependence on sugar for comfort. The good news is that we are able through Christ Jesus, and the rewards are so great.

Our story picks up . . .

Luke 18:26-30: *"And those who heard it said, 'Who then can be saved?'*

"But He said, 'The things which are impossible with men are possible with God.'

"Then Peter said, 'See, we have left all and followed You.'

"So He said to them, 'Assuredly, I say to you, there is no one who has left house or parents or brothers or wife or children, for the sake of the kingdom of God, who shall not receive many times more in this present time, and in the age to come eternal life'" (NKJV).

So much more than a handful of cookies, don't you think? And when it comes to my children, knowing they, too, will share in this reward is reason enough to let them go—into the capable hands of the Father.

Yes, our God is "a consuming fire, a jealous God" (Deuteronomy. 4:24), but He has every right to be, in my book. He gave His all for me when I least deserved it. Can I give Him any less?

God's grace and peace be yours,

Rebecca

God's Way
Monday, April 11, 2011
Blessings, Friends,

Today's promise is Psalm 65:3: *"When we were overwhelmed by sins, you forgave our transgressions"* (NIV). Thank you, Lord!

It's been a trying week. I've been praying for grace for myself. I seem to be able to cut others slack so much easier than I can myself. I get so frustrated with being sick so much, that I start wondering what's wrong with me—isn't my faith strong enough?

My tumor is gone, so I should be up and running, not up and down, and up and down. But this week, the Lord has shown me a flaw in my reasoning. In my fervent self-debasement, I had completely forgotten God's ultimate design. I have been striving to rebuild my depleted immune system, forgetting that the way the body creates antibodies is by exposure to harmful viruses and bacteria. You get sick, your body creates a defense, you become stronger.

Sometimes, I have to laugh at myself. God is the same, always, in all things. Why would I think He would deviate from His methods for my little circumstance? It's really kind of amazing when you think about it. Our physiology bears witness to His purpose and order just as our spiritual development does. When your immune system needs strengthening, He provides opportunities for your immune system to be strengthened. Just like when you need patience, or faith, or love. I'm sure you've heard someone say, "Never pray for patience." God wants to strengthen us, and He does this not by removing all obstacles from our path, but by teaching us to trust Him to empower us to overcome all obstacles. Even in sickness. *"Therefore I take pleasure in infirmities, in reproaches, in needs, in persecutions, in distresses, for Christ's sake. For when I am weak, then I am strong"* (2 Corinthians 12:10 NKJV).

No one understood this better than Jesus. His path to eternal glory was far from easy, but Hebrews 12:2 tells us He patiently endured the most humiliating and excruciating death of the time, for our sakes. And He did it because it was His Father's will. Yes, we have places to go, and things to do, but we are not here to serve ourselves. We are here to do the will of our Father—even when we don't understand it. The important thing is that He understands it, and that should be good enough for us. If we do not trust him in our infirmities, what good are miracles?

I'm so humbled that, out of all the millions of people that have walked the earth, God chose to love me—in all my weakness and failings, He believes in me and will never let me go. I pray, this Easter season, that you take time to bask in His love for you. Let it fill you to overflowing, and know that, no matter what you may think of yourself, God thinks you are worth giving up everything for.

God's grace and peace be yours,

Rebecca

My Redeemer Lives!
Tuesday, April 19, 2011

Blessings, Friends,

Today's promise is Job 19:25–26: *"I know that my redeemer lives, and that in the end he will stand on the earth. And after my skin has been destroyed, yet in my flesh I will see God."*

Hallelujah!

This brings me such hope at times like these when sickness seems to linger. I also stepped down my Neurontin, which seemed like a really good idea at the time, but I'm questioning my timing now. I wish they'd told me before I started taking it that I'd go through withdrawals when I tried to get off of it. I just heard "not a narcotic" and went, "Yea!"

Now my head is filled with sludge, and the rest of me is just wanting my bed and heating pad. But yesterday I couldn't even remember how to tie my shoes, so I'm making progress. This is going to be a long road, but God has brought me this far—and He'll get me to the finish line.

If you are in the midst of a trial today, be of good faith. You are in the best company. Take the authors of the New Testament, who left all they had to carry on Christ's work. Tradition and fact say many of them suffered greatly, many meeting dreadful deaths:

Matthew—died from the wounds of a halberd (an ax blade and pick with a spearhead on top, mounted on a long handle)

Mark—dragged to death by a team of wild horses

Luke—hanged

John—thrown into boiling oil and survived only to be imprisoned on an island.

Peter—crucified upside down

Jude—killed with arrows

James—clubbed to death after surviving a 100-foot fall from the temple pinnacle

Paul—received thirty-nine lashes five different times, beaten with clubs three times, had his skull crushed once, and he was left for dead in the garbage dump (Acts 14:19), stoned, shipwrecked three times—and the list goes on (2 Corinthians 11:23–28)—eventually tortured and beheaded.

And don't forget Christ Himself. Apparently, no one shared the "health and wealth" message with these men. So, where's the good news in all this?

In 2 Timothy 3:10–11: *"But you have carefully followed my doctrine, manner of life, purpose, faith, longsuffering, love, perseverance, persecutions, afflictions, which happened to me at Antioch, at Iconium, at Lystra—what persecutions I endured. And out of them all the Lord delivered me"* (NKJV).

Yes, we are being watched, and if we stand fast in Christ, He will deliver us, and those who are watching will see He is faithful. They will see that Paul's words are true in Romans 8:37–39: *"Yet in all these things we are more than conquerors through Him who loved us. For I am persuaded that neither death nor life, nor angels nor principalities nor powers, nor things present nor things to come, nor height nor depth, nor any other created thing, shall be able to separate us from the love of God which is in Christ Jesus our Lord"* (NKJV).

If you are enduring a trial right now, know you are at the center of God's will. Don't worry that your body is ailing or that your pockets are empty. Rather, serve the Lord with all your heart where you are, and *"store up for yourselves treasures in heaven"* (Matthew 6:20) *"that when he appears we may be confident and unashamed before him at his coming"* (1 John 2:28).

Rejoice! Rejoice, oh, Christian! God has not forsaken you! He is with you, holding you, loving you, bringing you through. Stand firm on His promises, for He has been proven time and time again, and He will never fail.

You may be hurting now, but keep your eyes on your Salvation and give Him praise, *"that the genuineness of your faith, being much more precious than gold that perishes, though it is tested by fire, may be found to praise, honor, and glory at the revelation of Jesus Christ"* (1 Peter 1:7 NKJV).

James 1:12: *"Blessed is the man who endures temptation [testing]; for when he has been approved, he will receive the crown of life which the Lord has promised to those who love Him"* (NKJV).

Our Redeemer lives! He is interceding for us, strengthening us, building in us a house that will withstand the test of fire (1 Corinthians 3:12–15), and He's coming back soon, bringing with Him our everlasting reward. Praise the Lord!

Have a blessed Easter!

God's grace and peace be yours,

Rebecca

Because He Lives
Monday, April 25, 2011

Blessings, Friends,

Today's promise is Psalm 86:13: *"For great is your love toward me; you have delivered me from the depths, from the realm of the dead"* (NIV). Praise the Lord!

What a mighty God we serve! I just read the wonderful words of encouragement from Frank D. on my page (thank you, Frank) and then this Psalm. It was just God reinforcing that message to me. I never thought of it before, but I do believe that, through the cursing and mocking that was hurled at Jesus on His way to Golgotha, He saw us, our love for Him, and our immeasurable gratitude for His sacrifice, and was strengthened to complete His journey. And it is His very faithfulness unto death that strengthens me to stay the course—no matter how much it hurts.

I was so grateful to be able to attend church yesterday. Though I wasn't able to get to Sunday School or the evening service, it was such a blessing to worship as I was able. As I stood with my family, singing "Because He Lives," my body wracked with pain, I was overcome by the words of the last verse and the knowledge that, because of what Jesus did for me, all the pain I'm going through now is only temporary; that the day is coming when I'll never feel pain, or sickness, or grief, or sadness again.

Some people think that death is just the end of life. How wrong they are! We are created in the likeness of God: eternal. Just as death for the children of God means eternity with our Father, death to those who reject Him means eternal separation from Him. No pain on earth could equal this, as Christ himself experienced on the cross when He echoed David's words, *"My God, My God, why have you forsaken Me?"* I truly believe that the pain of the beatings, mocking, betrayal, denial, and even the crucifixion, paled in comparison to the

233

pain Jesus experienced when His Father left Him because of the sin He bore—my sin.

Words can't express how grateful I am that Jesus loves me so much He willingly took on that pain, to spare me having to know it. How could I not love Him? How could I not want to give Him my all? It is that love that makes me praise Him in my pain. Great is my God, and great is His love for me!

I didn't let my pain spoil our Easter festivities completely. And, I have to take my share of responsibility for the pain as I insisted on making Gracie's Easter dress. My best friend accused me of trying to wear my "supermom" cape, but I figured an Easter dress wasn't too much to ask of myself. I so want to be a mom to my kids. Who knows when my pain will be gone, but kids don't remain kids for long. Our egg hunt was epic. The older kids wanted a challenge, and they certainly got one! After an hour and a half, we had to start giving them clues. Rachel was the finder of the coveted golden egg this year, but there was booty for all, and everyone had fun. We then enjoyed a laid-back dinner (what a blessing to have kids who are great in the kitchen) and the movie, *Matthew*. Then I crashed, sleeping for several hours. I will probably be recovering for the rest of the week, but I think the memories we made are well worth it, and I am so thankful I was able to do as much as I did.

Thank you so much for your continued prayers and words of encouragement. There is nothing like pain and sickness to make you not want to do anything, but I am determined that, no matter how bad I feel, I will not let it interfere with my prayers for you. If anything, it makes me more determined. I pray for your healing, comfort, and peace, but mostly I pray that the joy of our Lord Jesus Christ overshadows your circumstances and that you will draw ever closer to Him, living in His victory each day.

God's grace and peace be yours,

Rebecca

Chapter 32

A SHELTER IN THE TIME
OF STORM

*A*fter wrestling with several blog templates, I came to the conclusion that I hated technology. I was a creative person; why couldn't I make these programs understand that?! My frustration and discouragement brought me to tears. I was certain I was letting God down.

"Honey," Chuck finally said, "what was the name of that blog designer you met at your first conference?"

"We can't afford a professional," I told him with a heavy sigh.

"Well, God told you to do this, didn't He?"

"I'm beginning to wonder."

"You know He did. Maybe we should trust Him to provide the money."

I stared at him a moment. "What are you saying?"

"Give that lady a call and find out what it'll cost."

Reluctantly, I called Laura Christianson at Blogging Bistro and explained my situation. Hope dawned with the news that an affordable deposit would set my vision on the road toward publication. Chuck was quick to agree to this. We stood on faith that God would provide the rest of the money when it came due.

While Laura's team went to work on my new design, Chuck convinced me to publish what I had on the template. This would give me a chance to get familiar with the process and find out what I wanted to change. It wouldn't be pretty, but it would be a start. I kept working at it, praising God that I was able to take this step of obedience.

My joy was cut off at the knees when the enemy launched his next attack.

My Solid Rock
Monday, May 16, 2011

Blessings, Friends,

Today's promise is Job 1:10: *"Have you not put a hedge around him and his household and everything he has? You have blessed the work of his hands, so that his flocks and herds are spread throughout the land."*

Today finds me standing in the gap for yet another son, so I'm claiming that promise big time. Thursday night, our youngest son, 13, ran away to live with his dad. After a court battle to be able to homeschool him, he decided he no longer wanted to homeschool or to live by our rules.

We went through this five years ago with our oldest son, but the shock and pain are no less overwhelming now. We would certainly appreciate your prayers as we seek God's will and peace. I've often written that God's will seldom resembles our own, and even though I'm hurting, I'll praise my awesome God. He's so much greater than our anger, rebellion, fear, or pain. I trust this is God's will for Daniel at this time and pray for the grace to let go of my child and let his Heavenly Father do His good work in him.

I've also written many times that if you're facing trials in your life, you're at the center of God's will, so I must be doing something right. But, I must not let my pain and grief, which can be debilitating, rob me of my power in Christ Jesus. I will continue to bind and rebuke the enemy, I will continue to study and teach the Word, I will continue to encourage and pray for others, and to do anything else God asks of me.

This is not my world, and the circumstances of this world hold no power over me. My hope is not in the folly of man, but in God's Kingdom, which is within me. I may have to remind myself of that every minute of every day, but that's okay, *"for when I am weak, then I am strong"* (2 Corinthians 12:10).

I'm not the first parent who's had to let their child go into the hands of God when it went against everything they believed. Take Mordecai, for instance. Esther didn't rebel against him, but how in the world could sending Esther into the decadence of a pagan palace for a year, possibly to become the wife of the pagan king, be God's will? This went against the very core of God's chosen people. Mordecai didn't try to avoid this fate by hiding or disguising Esther; he trusted in God's will for her. His faith resulted in the salvation of his people.

Daniel, as well as my oldest son, are covered by God's hedge, and God will have His way in their lives. Amen.

Thank you for your continued prayers.

God's grace and peace be yours,

Rebecca

*H*ow easy those words came. But saying and doing are two different things. My initial instinct was to drop this new blog, stop everything, curl up in my bed with as much chocolate as I could find, eat myself into a coma, and sleep until Jesus came. The pain in my heart radiated to every part of my body, and I just wanted it to go away. My mind raced day and night. What had I done wrong? How could my own child hate me so much? Getting out of bed each morning took every ounce of my strength, and getting through each day was like wading through quicksand.

One day, as I lay sprawled across my bed, trying to pray, I thought about the blog.

"I guess it's just not the right time," I told myself. "I'll get back to it when I feel better. There's no way I can finish it now."

That's just what the enemy wants.

I knew that voice. And His words flipped a light switch in my brain. Suddenly I saw clearly that this wasn't about my son at all. This was about me putting my money where my mouth was. Now I was angry. Angry and determined. If Satan went to such extremes to keep me from my commission, this blog must have the potential to cause him a world of hurt.

I pulled out my computer and fired it up. My body fought me the whole time. but my heart knew that the same God who gave me the words to write would give me the strength to finish what He'd started in me.

Still Here
Monday, May 23, 2011
Blessings, Friends,

Today's promise is Colossians 1:26–27: *"The mystery that has been kept hidden for ages and generations, but is now disclosed to the Lord's people. To them God has chosen to make known among the Gentiles the glorious riches of this mystery, which is Christ in you, the hope of glory."*

I'm still trying to get used to not having my son live with me. He doesn't want anything to do with us, but I'm praying this will change. My medication reduction isn't helping matters. I still have three weeks until I'm off Neurontin, and it hasn't been easy. But I'm determined. My pain has increased, but I'm trusting God this will diminish in time. Whenever I start getting discouraged, I just remember where I was a year ago, and I can't help but praise the Lord!

I finally launched my companion blog site, WatchGodWork.com, last week! I've been working on this for some time, and though I'm not thrilled with the program and will be changing it soon, I'm pretty excited it's finally out there. This site is all about encouraging a closer walk with Christ, so while my CarePage will still be for my personal updates, I'll be posting my messages on the new site. Some posts will be from my CarePages, but I'll let you know the subject of the posts here, in case you want to check them out.

Today's post, by the same name as this one, is about the rapture that was supposed to take place last Saturday.

God's grace and peace be yours,
Rebecca

Gifts
Monday, June 6, 2011
Blessings, Friends,

Today's promise is Matthew 5:19: *"Whoever therefore breaks one of the least of these commandments, and teaches men so, shall be called least in the kingdom of heaven; but whoever does and teaches them, he shall be called great in the kingdom of heaven"* (NKJV).

Kind of makes you want to take inventory, doesn't it?

Boy, what a week! God has been so good in sustaining me and giving me the strength not only to endure but also to enjoy some very long days. Friday, Rachel graduated from high school, and yesterday, she graduated from college with her associate's degree!

As most of you parents out there know, this has been a time filled with joy, pride, and the realization that my baby is not my baby anymore. But with graduating classes of nearly 500 and 900, it was also a time of extreme testing for my tender surgical site. Ouch.

I got a gift from my Father last week, that was a wonderful reminder of His love for me. Just when I needed it most, I received a phone call telling me that my story, "The Uninvited Guest," was a finalist in the contest I'd entered! The winners are announced at a writers' conference in August, so I'm praying God provides the means for me to attend. It's a bit rich for our budget, but I know God will provide. I'd been questioning my writing ability just days before I got the news, but God knows just what we need and just when we need it. I'm so excited!

Chuck says I'm being rewarded for my faithfulness. I don't know if he's right, but it felt really good to not let my circumstances dictate my ability to accomplish the task God set before me. I'll continue to pray for the grace to be an overcomer. It isn't easy, and it certainly isn't fun, but it's so worth it, robbing the enemy of one more victory.

Please keep me in your prayers for the final withdrawals from Neurontin and the upcoming court battle over my son. May God's will be done. You remain in my prayers every day, and I hope you feel the presence of the Holy Spirit carrying you through each day.

God's grace and peace be yours,

Rebecca

Perfect Peace
Monday, June 20, 2011
Blessings, Friends,

Today's promise is Isaiah 26:3: *"You will keep him in perfect peace, whose mind is stayed on You, because he trusts in You"* (NKJV).

Boy, do I need that! It's not that my mind isn't stayed on God; I guess I'm just afraid of botching things up. I'm talking about my son, of course. Even though I had a word from God last week, basically saying, "I'm in control; you can't screw this up no matter what you do," I'm still struggling with how much, if anything, I should do. As my ex's attack heats up, with threats of child abuse charges, the same son who was wanting to cuddle with me last month, now won't even talk to me on the phone.

The mother bear in me wants to fight to the death for my son. But, the servant in me knows Daniel belongs to God, not me, and He knows him far better than I do. I don't want to get in the way of God's plan for Daniel, but I also don't want to stop being a mom, if that makes any sense. He is only 13, after all.

I know it sounds silly in light of the word I received from God, but while I can have perfect peace about the outcome, I still dread the battle ahead. I'm physically, mentally, and emotionally drained, and I just want peace. If, in fact, I am strong when I am weak, then at this point, I'm invincible! Praise the Lord!

As ever, I'm praying for you.
God's grace and peace be yours,
Rebecca

The Prize
Monday, June 27, 2011
Blessings, Friends,

Today's promise is 1 John 5:11: *"And this is the testimony: that God has given us eternal life, and this life is in His Son"* (NKJV). Amen!

I taught on Philippians 3 yesterday—on pursuing Christ. It struck me doing this study that there was a time in my early walk with Christ that I thought the "prize" that Paul talks about in this chapter was eternal life. I thought that is why we do what we do: so we wouldn't have to die. I now know that we are all in fact eternal beings, created in God's likeness. The question is not if we will live forever, but where we live. Daniel 12:2 says, *"And many of those who sleep in the dust of the earth shall awake, Some to everlasting life, Some to shame and everlasting contempt"* (NKJV).

But Heaven is no more the prize than everlasting life is. That has no more meaning than aspiring to retire at fifty or to save a million dollars by forty. Yes, there is a sense of mission in the race, but once you reach a finite goal such as this, you tend to say, "Okay, now what?"

Paul was a man beyond reproach in the eyes of men. He had attained everything a Hebrew could aspire to in his life. Yet, when he met Jesus face to face, he realized that all of his great works didn't amount to anything. He called it all "dung." From the moment he met Jesus, that was all he wanted—more of Jesus. This is what we were created for—intimate communion with our Creator. What never ceases to grow, change, and evolve? What are constant sources of stimulation? Living, breathing relationships. And, in the case of relationship with Christ, a constant source of life, joy, and peace. An eternal source. This is the prize.

I'm not sure at what point in my walk I realized this, but I do know it was at that point when my belief became faith, and my faith became action. Like Paul, I found myself wanting more of Jesus and willing to give up everything to get it. My prayer for my family and all believers is that we, like Paul, *"may know Him and the power of His resurrection, and the fellowship of His sufferings, being conformed to His death"* (Philippians 3:10 NKJV). He is the Living Water—the only thing that satisfies.

Please, be praying for God's will to be done in our upcoming hearing regarding our son on July 5th.

God's grace and peace be yours,

Rebecca

Chapter 33

REFINER'S FIRE

Supernatural
Wednesday, July 6, 2011
Blessings, Friends,

Today's promise is Psalm 32:7: *"You are my hiding place; You shall preserve me from trouble; You shall surround me with songs of deliverance"* (NKJV).

Boy, do I need that today! I spent yesterday morning taking a beating in court. You'd think by now I'd be used to being dragged through the mud, but I haven't quite learned how to turn off my heart yet. I know the things that are said about me are lies, and I know God knows, but it doesn't make it hurt any less. In fact, it's even worse coming from your own children.

But, I'm keenly aware I'm not battling against flesh and blood. This is a spiritual battle designed to keep me from the path God has set before me. So, I pray for my accusers' forgiveness. Please, pray for me. The joy of the Lord is my strength, so please pray I can bring Him joy—because I really need strength. I'll be going to court again before this is over. Not that it will ever be over until Jesus returns.

I'm reading a book right now called *23 Minutes in Hell*, by Bill Wiese—a must-read—and, as amazing as Bill's journey to Hell was, what was so exciting to me was the time he got to spend with Jesus after he was brought out of Hell. Most exciting were Jesus' words to Bill: "Tell them I am coming very, very soon!"

Satan knows his time is short, too. Never before have I witnessed such widespread demonic attack within the Body of Christ. Yet, I don't give Satan credit for the work of God. What Satan is working in his effort to steal the faith of the weak, God is using to hone His swords to razor sharpness, stripping away our impurities so we may stand in His power, undefeatable.

I know the key to not just surviving—but thriving—in the midst of God's holy flame, is to remember I am no longer merely human. I have been made superhuman through the blood of Christ, and though my flesh wants to curl up in a fetal position and wait out the storm, I have the Spirit of the Living God within me. As long as I choose to submit to Him, He will be my power and strength to keep running for the prize, to keep encouraging others, and to continue witnessing to His goodness.

We are blessed to have each other to pray for, and love, and encourage. How we need each other now! And, how we need to draw from the eternal well of love that is Christ Jesus so we may all continue to run the good race and, more importantly, finish strong.

My prayers continue for you all!

God's grace and peace be yours,

Rebecca

Choices

Monday, July 11, 2011

Blessings, Friends,

Today's promise is Proverbs 16:23: *"The heart of the wise teaches his mouth, and adds learning to his lips"* (NKJV).

Those of you who follow my blog site at www.WatchGodWork.com will know that I post a new promise every day (which you can receive in your inbox by subscribing). But lately, the promises I've been given have been speaking specifically to the struggle I've been going through with my sons. Take today's promise, for instance. And, yesterday's was Luke 6:35: *"But love your enemies, do good, and lend, hoping for nothing in return; and your reward will be great, and you will be sons of the Most High. For He is kind to the unthankful and evil"* (NKJV).

Ouch. I think, at least for myself, that is the hardest thing Jesus asks me to do. Nothing stirs up my pride more than injustice, betrayal, and lies. I want right to prevail—and I want it now! Gosh, I wonder what this trial is all about?

The need for justification is so very human. But, like I've said so many times before, we are not called to be human, but superhuman. I am justified by Christ alone. Pride serves me no purpose anymore; it's all about Him. So, why do I still struggle with it? And, when I say "struggle," I mean knock-down, drag-out fight.

So, what would a superhuman (like Jesus) do? The opposite of what is human, of course. If my instinct is to repay evil for evil, I repay good instead—relying on God's grace to do so, of course. Jesus said, *"Therefore, submit to God. Resist the devil, and he will flee from you"* (James 4:7 NKJV). By zigging when everything in you wants to zag, you strip evil of its power. Like everything else, it all comes down to making a choice—my way or God's way. And He has promised, *"Humble yourselves in the sight of the Lord, and He will lift you up"* (James 4:10 NKJV). Do I believe His promises? Yes. Can I lift myself up any higher than He can? No. I choose God. And I have to say, once I resolved to do things His way, I finally had peace. God is good.

Sunday, I taught on the first 2 two chapters of Colossians. In them, Paul tells us how important it is that our faith be evident to others through our love for one another, for this is how the Gospel spreads. We must be in prayer for all Christians to increase in their knowledge of God, that our eyes and hearts be fixed on that one goal, knowing Him. It is only in this knowledge that we are able to trust in His will and endure and grow through any trial. It is only in the knowledge of Him that we find true peace.

I hope you are all enjoying your summer... except Barrie and Muriel, who are hopefully enjoying their winter down under. You all remain in my prayers. God's grace and peace be yours,

Rebecca

Boldness
Monday, July 18, 2011
Blessings, Friends,

Today's promise is John 6:35: *"And Jesus said to them, 'I am the bread of life. He who comes to Me shall never hunger, and he who believes in Me shall never thirst.'"* Amen!

What a week it has been! The court ruled that my son will stay at his father's through the summer, and I don't expect that to change come fall. But

I know people are praying for my son and me, because I just have that peace and joy that can only come from above. So, thank you!

Rachel is off on a camping/college visitation trip with friends in Montana, and I'm missing her. Please keep them in your prayers. And Aaron is learning to drive—'nough said.

The really exciting part right now is what God is doing in my husband's life. I have to share. Not to brag on Chuck, although if you'd have known him ten years ago, you'd know just how big this is. No, this is totally a God thing. Chuck has been a counselor for a local grief camp for kids for nine years. He always knew it was God who put him there, and it is a really big part of his life. In the last couple of years, he has felt God telling him to lead a prayer group for the camp staff after their meetings. This was a huge step for Chuck, but he finally did it and was excited about how the group was growing. But this isn't the exciting part.

Recently, Chuck has been reading *Jesus Freaks*, put out by Voice of the Martyrs, which tells the stories of martyred saints from the Apostles to modern-day saints. It has really inspired him to pray for more boldness in his faith— I know what you're thinking—and you're right. Wednesday night, he called me from his camp meeting and told me that it has hit the fan (so to speak). He has been told that he can't invite people to pray for the camp anymore because it makes them "uncomfortable." The kids and I started praying, of course. Chuck said he was shaking the whole time, but he told them that the Jewish leaders had told the Apostles that they couldn't talk about Jesus anymore, and the Apostles told them that they had to do what God told them to do, not man, and that was just what he was going to do!

At the end of the meeting Chuck invited those who wanted to come outside to pray for the camp and campers, and several joined him. He told them he had been forbidden to do that, and they prayed for their persecutors as well. During this prayer, Chuck said he felt the Holy Spirit come down on him, and he had perfect peace. Afterward, he went back in for his "meeting" with these leaders (among whom were an Episcopal minister, the son of a Lutheran minister, and two professed Christians!), and Chuck said he literally lived Luke 21:13-15: *"But it will turn out for you as an occasion for testimony. Therefore settle it in your hearts not to meditate beforehand on what you will answer; for I will give you a mouth and wisdom which all your adversaries will not be able to contradict or resist.*" No anger or raised voices, just a joyful witness.

They told him he could just pray to himself, and he said, "I do. But 'where two or more are gathered in His name, He is there,' and I want Him there."

He told them that God had put it on his heart to do this, and he had to be faithful to his God. They told him maybe God had told them to tell him not to, and he said, "Oh, I know He did. God is control of all things, and I truly believe He told you to do this because I have asked Him to make me bolder in my faith, and you can't get much bolder than being confronted. I believe you are being faithful to what God has asked you to do, and I praise Him for it!" He told them about Jesus Freaks and that what he was doing was illegal in 52 countries, and that he would be dead for what he was doing in over 30 of them, and he praised God for the freedom to do what he was doing.

Chuck told them he would ask God if there was another way He wanted him to go about the call for prayer, and that he would know before the weekend was out. Because, though he didn't hear a voice, God always answered and gave him clear direction. One of the leaders commented that they wished God answered them like that! Anyway, he made it clear that, regardless of the venue, he would continue to be faithful to God—even if that meant not being allowed to participate in the camp. And he had total peace about that.

I'm telling you, he was so high on the Spirit when he got home; we were up most of the night! It was awesome! We don't know if Chuck will be going to camp next weekend, but we are certain God's will will be done.

I can't wait to see what's next! I hope Chuck's story encourages you to step out of the boat and watch God work. What a ride! You are all in my prayers.
God's grace and peace be yours,
Rebecca

Complete
Monday, July 25, 2011
Blessings, Friends,

Today's promise is 2 Corinthians 13:11: "*Become complete. Be of good comfort, be of one mind, live in peace; and the God of love and peace will be with you*" (NKJV).

What an action-packed week! My greatest praise to report is that Chuck and I have been walking 3-4 miles in the mornings! Even though my body is hurting, I feel so blessed to be doing this, it makes me want to cry! This was only a dream not that long ago when I was confined to bed, and my oncologist fully expected me to be paralyzed after the last surgery! So praise GOD! And may I take full advantage of His blessing to bring Him glory! I certainly have been working on it. I've been up to my elbows preparing manuscripts and book outlines for my upcoming conference, working with a design team at Blogging Bistro to get WatchGodWork.com back up and running, and trying to negotiate with very difficult people to be able to see my son. I know people are praying for me, because I'm still relatively sane. So, thank you!

Chuck was "allowed" to attend camp. He felt God wanted him to approach people about prayer time individually, and the powers that be were all right with that. He ended up having people approach him for prayer, which is really cool. He was even given two opportunities to share his testimony with counselors who had both lost spouses and wanted to know how Chuck was able to move on and be so happy after his loss. He was really blessed to see a total transformation in his camper during the weekend, which was a first for him and meant so much. He usually doesn't get to see the effects of camp until their reunion in February. He came back from camp very tired and very blessed. Thank you for your prayers.

Rachel also came back from her trip to Montana very refreshed and excited about her college life ahead. She is beginning to stress, however, about her plans to return to India to do missions work. Besides fund raising, she still wants to find a group to travel with, and so far we haven't found anything that will work. She has an orphanage to work in once she gets there, but none of us want her traveling alone. Please keep her in your prayers.

I have been so blessed by my study in Colossians. Much of my time has been spent judging and condemning myself for my failure to live up to Christ's example, but Colossians 2:8-10 has made me realize how vain I have been. It says: *"Beware lest anyone cheat you through philosophy and empty deceit, according to the tradition of men, according to the basic principles of the world, and not according to Christ. For in Him dwells all the fullness of the Godhead bodily; and you are complete in Him, who is the head of all principality and power"* (NKJV).

I have been so hard on myself, thinking I was disappointing God. But this scripture opened my eyes to the fact that, in God's eyes, I am already complete in Christ. In my time, I'm still on the journey, but by choosing to humbly submit to God's working daily in my life, in God's time I'm already there. Not by my effort, but by the power of Christ in me. He doesn't require perfection of me—only faith and obedience, and then again, not by my own power, but by His. How liberating!

You remain in my prayers, for healing and provision, but above all else, that you will grow in your knowledge of our great and loving God each step of your journeys.

God's grace and peace be yours,

Rebecca

Chapter 34

LIVING THE DREAM

The Priesthood
Monday, August 1, 2011
Blessings, Friends,

Today's promise is 1 Peter 2:9: *"But you are a chosen generation, a royal priesthood, a holy nation, His own special people, that you may proclaim the praises of Him who called you out of darkness into His marvelous light"* (NKJV).

This morning I had a dream that Gracie and I were standing outside a beautiful, old, abandoned church. I remember telling her what a shame it was that there are so many "condemned" churches out there when there are so many people in need of God's truth and salvation. A couple of "educated" men came our way and overheard me. They tried to warn me against going into the church, telling me that some churches just had to be condemned to "protect the people." But this church was made of stone. It was solid and built to last. All it lacked was someone to preach the Word, and people to receive it. Determined that their warning to stay out wouldn't deter us, I took Gracie's hand, and we went in.

The impression I got was that the condemned church represented all the churches out there that are diluting the Gospel to make it more palatable to people—the "feel-good" churches. As we were looking around on the inside, an older woman, holding the hand of a child, passed us. They were singing a Sunday School song I can't remember now, but Gracie and I began singing, too. And, as we walked on, singing, I began to see more and more children in the church.

I asked the Lord what He was showing me, and He said, "This is the generation that will usher in My Kingdom." Wow.

It does make sense because children's hearts are the most receptive to Jesus. If they are trained up in the truth early, God promised they will not depart from it when they are grown. Children are the future of the Gospel. It's important we do all we can to see they know Jesus loves them and has a future for them. Not just our children, but all children. "Jesus loves the little children of the world."

We've also been told by Jesus that unless we become as little children, we will not enter His Kingdom (Matthew 18:3), so . . . .

Well, I have orders from my other boss (Chuck) to finish what I need to do for the writers' conference. I still have to polish my query and synopsis and get everything organized before we leave on Wednesday. Please keep us in your prayers for safe travel, and that God's will be done through it all. Chuck, Gracie, and Aaron will be hitting the zoo and other fun things while I'm working, so I'm sure they'll have a ball.

Oh, and WatchGodWork.com is almost up and running again. I'm so excited! I'll keep you posted. In the meantime, you are all in my thoughts and prayers.

God's grace and peace be yours,

Rebecca

What a Conference!
Wednesday, August 10, 2011

Blessings, Friends,

Today's promise is Isaiah 26:12: *"Lord, You will establish peace for us, for You have also done all our works in us"* (NKJV). Amen!

I'm back from the most amazing writers' conference ever! My short story "The Uninvited Guest" won first place in the literary contest! I just about passed out when they announced my name. Out of about 1,000 entries, they narrowed each category down to eight or nine finalists. From there, the entries were sent out to agents and editors to choose the runners–up and winners.

God was there with me all the way, opening the way to share Him with many people. I'm so thankful for Laura Christianson and her team at Blogging Bistro for getting my site up in time for the conference. I had no idea so many people would actually check it out during the conference! You should check it out. They really did a beautiful job.

So much happened over the weekend; my head is still reeling. They had a special reception for the winners, agents, and editors, so I got to pitch my mystery and memoir to even more people. Four agents asked to see chapters, so hopefully one of them will want to represent me.

The most exciting part for me was that we got to read our winning entries to an audience, and the response to my story blew me away! I was still trying to digest the fact that I'd won, but when people were asking me where they could read more of my work, I suddenly felt very overwhelmed. After a lifetime of programming to the contrary, I was looking into the faces of people wanting to hear what I had to say.

That's why today's promise is especially meaningful to me. It was God who made me a writer, and He has already given me all I need to fulfill that purpose. As long as I remember that, trust in that, I'll have His peace. And, boy, do I need that.

As I looked out over Bellevue from the windows of the hotel, I couldn't help but remember that I'd soon be back, looking out the windows of Seattle Cancer Care Alliance, waiting to take another claustrophobic ride in the torpedo tube. I have to confess that the thought makes me want to cry, but I hope the trip in September is as jubilant as this one has been.

Though I haven't had much time for keeping up on your updates, you've remained in my prayers. I hope you're feeling them.

God's grace and peace be yours,

Rebecca

With the winnings of that contest, God had provided the money needed to cover the remaining cost of the new blog.

I'd soon learn it was only the beginning.

Standing on the Promises
Monday, August 15, 2011
Blessings, Friends,

Today's promise is Deuteronomy 31:8: *"The Lord himself goes before you and will be with you; he will never leave you nor forsake you. Do not be afraid; do not be discouraged."*

I'm really needing that one today. With the adrenaline of the conference and winning the contest over, I'm back to having to face the situation with my son. I must say the pain is all-consuming at times, and it's all I can do to hang on to God's promises. I'm just asking for prayer for wisdom and peace. I know God's in control; I just wish it didn't hurt so much.

I know I'm going through this trial for a purpose. I just have to pray God will show me what it is I need to learn, and then praise Him for it. I can be pretty dense sometimes, limited to my scope of understanding and the baggage I drag along with me. I know He knows my pain, and so much more so, having sacrificed His only Son for the world and having that gift thrown back in His face. So, I know He will carry me through. I also know He knows and loves my son better than I ever could, and He has a plan for him. I can trust in that.

So, maybe my focus shouldn't be on Daniel. Maybe this is about my relationship with God. At a time when my life experience is screaming, Save yourself! Protect your heart! Reject those who reject you!

Perhaps this is an opportunity for me to experience life in the supernatural. Perhaps this is my opportunity to be the love of Christ. But, in order to receive a gift, I first have to empty my arms of my old baggage. I may have to do this minute-by-minute, but I don't have to do it by my own power. He promised me that. So, Father God, help me lay down my fear, my pain, and my pride that I may be a vessel of your infinite love. Amen.

In the meantime, I forge on. It's almost school time again, which I can't believe, and my chapters are just about ready to send to the agents. Thank you for your prayers and words of encouragement.

God's grace and peace be yours,

Rebecca

Promise of Peace
Friday, September 16, 2011

Blessings, Friends,

Today's promise is Philippians 4:7: *"And the peace of God, which surpasses all understanding, will guard your hearts and minds through Christ Jesus"* (NKJV). Amen!

It's been a while since my last post, though I've been writing about adversity in my blog, WatchGodWork.com, and for good reason. Today's promise is especially meaningful to me at this time. My days seemed to be filled with battles concerning my wayward son. If I'm not in court, I'm in my attorney's office or opening mail filled with yet another volley of false accusations and personal attacks.

The prayers of my faith family have sustained me, and though I have my days when I feel the hot breath of the enemy on my neck, I am claiming this promise in Philippians and daily submitting my fear, anger, and weakness to God, Who alone is capable of carrying it.

Thank God, He provides reminders of His presence and love each day and things to focus on to take my mind off the pain and help me continue in the work He gives me.

I've had an awesome testimony come from WatchGodWork.com, which I'm sure God sent me to encourage me through this difficult time. I know in my heart I'm doing what God wants me to do, but when I hear from readers, it's like an affirmation from Him, and it makes me want to press on.

Please remember us in your prayers. Although I've been somewhat overwhelmed lately, I never forget to ask for God's peace, healing, and joy for you. I hope you are feeling it.

God's grace and peace be yours,

Rebecca

Rest in the Lord
Tuesday, October 4, 2011
Blessings, Friends,

Today's promise is 2 Corinthians 9:10: *"Now may He who supplies seed to the sower, and bread for food, supply and multiply the seed you have sown and increase the fruits of your righteousness"* (NKJV). Amen!

What a blessing to know that God provides all we need! All we have to do is sow the seed, and He is faithful to do the rest. I used to get hung up on the outcome of my sowing, thinking it was my job to "save" people. (Like I could save anyone—I couldn't even save myself!) But, how liberating it is to know my responsibility ends with sharing the good news! Of course, if the seed does take root, I'm more than happy to disciple. I do love to teach.

My scans and appointment are scheduled at Seattle Cancer Care Alliance for October 14th. Chuck and I will drive up on the 13th, and come back home on the 15th. We're mixing business with "pleasure" this trip as we visit some manufacturers. We have dinner reservations in the Space Needle to celebrate our eighth anniversary, so if I don't totally freak out (heights), we'll have some fun, too. Gracie is so excited to spend a couple nights with her favorite cousins!

I wish I could say I don't have any scan-ziety, but I can't. I trust God completely with the outcome, and even the process, but . . . I just don't like it.

You're all in my prayers daily, and you are held in the Father's loving hands always.

God's grace and peace be yours,

Rebecca

Free!
Monday, October 17, 2011
Blessings, Friends,

Today's promise is 1 John 5:14–15: *"Now this is the confidence that we have in Him, that if we ask anything according to His will, He hears us. And if we know that He hears us, whatever we ask, we know that we have the petitions that we have asked of Him"* (NKJV).

Praise the Lord! I'm free!

Yes, my scans looked even better than last year, and I was told I don't have to come back next year unless I want to! The doctor said I could come back any time I experienced symptoms, or just for my own peace of mind, and I'm thrilled!

The funny part is they still can't explain what happened to me. Not the rapid onset of symptoms and growth of what they are now calling a "cyst," nor its equally rapid shrinkage and release of my nerves. Of course, even though she isn't sure of anything else, this doctor remains adamant that it was never malignant. One of the best oncologists in the country must have been mistaken. It's just too difficult for an educated mind to grasp that the God of all creation can manipulate the very flesh He created according to His will and purpose.

But, you know, even if the skeptics are right, and it was never cancer, God still wins. Because the true miracle wasn't what He did with the tumor, but what He did with my heart. I'm not the same person I was in 2009. I thought I was a Christian most of my life. But, when God put that tumor in me, He stripped me to my core. He put a mirror up to my face, and all illusion fell away.

I don't understand how He did what He did; I only know I can no longer serve a God of my own making, on my own terms. I must possess Him—in Spirit and Truth. He has started a fire in me that nothing on earth can quench, a fire I must share. I tremble in my flesh because I know He is stretching me far beyond my perceived limitations, but I can't go back. To deny Him would be death for me. Far worse than the fires of Hell, would be the absence of Him. I could not bear it.

I pray that all Christians receive the fire that makes them step away from a Jesus who fits their lifestyle and embrace the true Jesus of the Gospel. The Way, the Truth, and the Life. What a different world it would be if we all did!

So, cancer or not, it wasn't the surgery on my backside that revealed God's greatest miracle in me. It was the surgery the Great Physician performed—and continues to perform—on my heart. The rest is just frosting on the cake.

Thank you for your prayers!

God's grace and peace be yours,

Rebecca

Chapter 35

LIFE AFTER CANCER

Since writing the first edition of *Loved So Much It Hurts*, *I've had readers wanting to know how I'm doing, now. Certainly, the end of that first edition was not the end of my story, but the beginning of a new chapter.*

I'll begin with my health. You may recall, in Chapter Eighteen, I write that my doctor told me I would be on thyroid medication for the rest of my life... I'm happy to report that the Great Physician had other plans. By the end of that year, Dr. Monroe was baffled by the results of my blood test. I was being *overmedicated*. Though he would never admit it, just as he would never admit that God healed me of cancer, my thyroid was working perfectly on its own. This was something I had been told was a medical impossibility. But praise be to God, "impossible" is not a word in His vocabulary.

I'm not going to tell you that my health is perfect, and I've gone on to win Olympic gold for eight years running—though it would be nice. The truth is, between my illness and all the medication, my immune system, strength, and endurance were greatly depleted. Chuck says he's amazed at how much stronger I've grown and how much more I'm able to do, though I still get frustrated with myself. But, as God once told another of His servants, *"My grace is sufficient for you, for My strength is made perfect in weakness"* 2 Corinthians 12:9. Therefore, like Paul, I will boast in my infirmities, that the power of Christ may rest upon me. In other words, I'm still learning patient endurance. My flowerbeds aren't restored to their former glory—but potted plants line my front steps each year, and Chuck and I put in a vegetable garden, which is mostly well-maintained. The restoration of our century-old home has resumed, though Chuck does the heavy lifting, and we've been able to start entertaining again. I've been able to teach writing and drama at our local homeschool co-op one day a week, which I love, and Chuck and I have become 4-H leaders and support staff for Gracie as we travel the Pacific Northwest showing her beautiful Jersey Wooly and Holland Lop rabbits. I feel so blessed to be taking a more active part in Gracie's activities after missing so much with my older kids. The rare occasions when pain confines me to my bed are well worth watching my baby grow into a beautiful, confident young woman.

Many people have asked about our older kids, wanting to know if I ever reconciled with my estranged sons. I'm sorry to say that, despite my efforts to reconcile, my oldest and youngest sons still want nothing to do with me. Sadly, our oldest daughter also turned from the Lord and, consequently, from us. Unfortunately, the church made the choices of our kids too easy. It is not a new phenomenon by any means. I was once a young adult, trying to understand what it means to be a Christian, having only the witness of other "Christians" to go by. I now appreciate how difficult it is to justify my faith to kids (or any non-believers) who see the same the ugliness and hypocrisy in the church that they see in the world. This was, after all, what drove me from the church in my youth. The old adage, "Do as I say, not as I do" just doesn't work in the Kingdom of God. Anyone who has raised teenagers—and survived to tell about it—will tell you our words mean nothing. Our labels mean nothing. Jesus said, *"A tree is known by its fruit." Matthew 12:33.* And, two thousand years later, nothing has changed.

I would be lying if I said the alienation of my children didn't hurt—a lot—but we do not get to Heaven on the coattails of our parents or grandparents. Ultimately, we must each take responsibility for our personal relationship with Jesus Christ. Only we can choose to accept or reject His gift of life. That said, I rebelled against God, too, and look what He did with me! I still believe with all my heart that they were God's children before they were mine. I know God has a plan for each of them. I know He'll never give up on them. Neither will I.

Our middle son, Aaron, left our home under better terms. We don't see as much of him as we would like, but I'm thankful for his hugs when we do. He still has relationships with his siblings, which I am also grateful for.

As for Gracie, now a teenager herself, the abandonment of her older siblings has had a profound effect on her young heart. But she remains steadfast in her faith and passion for the Lord. She is a mighty prayer warrior and continues to amaze and inspire her father and me, and so many others.

God also dealt with me about my ex-husband. Yet one more trial-by-fire. A condensed version of this story, called "Set Free," was published in the online magazine, *Now What?* But you can read the full account, "The Color of Forgiveness," at www.watchgodwork.com.

Most amazing to me is what the Lord has done in and through me since writing the first edition. Watch God Work Ministries is read all over the world now, and I am privileged to pray for those who reach out to me. Through fasting and prayer, the prophetic side of my ministry has grown considerably as the Lord continues to reveal Himself to me and speak to me about the church through dreams and visions.

I will soon be releasing a one-year devotional based on my Promise of the Day blog, as well as taking it to the airwaves on a podcast called "Promise of the Day." My writing has also found homes in publications such as *The Upper Room*, *Live*, Focus on the Family's *Clubhouse, Jr.*, and *Now What?*

My greatest joy has been the privilege of interceding for the church and for the individuals who contact me. One of this ministry's commissions has been to establish a prayer booth at our community 4th of July celebration in the park, which we have been doing for four years as of this writing. God has been so faithful in answering the prayers we have offered for help and healing.

I will end this chapter with a request that you include me in your prayers as I continue to do the work God sets before me. As far as I've come, I know the Lord is not finished with me yet. It comforts me to know that I am being held up before the Throne of God. Thank you, and God bless you on your own journey!

A TRIBUTE TO MY HEROES

Daniel Saenz

August 28, 1995 – July 23, 2010

Daniel was diagnosed with acute lymphatic leukemia on May 13, 2005. He was nine years old. Daniel was in remission after the first twenty-nine days of chemo, and after enduring three years of chemo, he enjoyed three months of freedom. In October of 2008, Daniel had a testicular relapse and began a new treatment, which included high-dose chemo and radiation. A year and one month later, Daniel relapsed again. Daniel received a stem cell transplant on February 25, 2010, and though the cells grafted fully, Daniel suffered multiple organ failure and went home to be with the Lord five months later at the age of fourteen.

The first thing that drew me to Daniel was his name. I also have a son named Daniel. But I quickly fell in love with his big heart, his great sense of humor, and his playful spirit, which was evident in every picture posted to his CarePage, and I soon nicknamed him "Handsome." It may sound strange to miss someone you've never met, but that is the impact this guy had on me. When he went home, he took a big piece of my heart with him.

"Daniel Saenz, Jr. was a very charismatic and loving young boy. He loved to please others and always had joy in his heart. As loving and caring as he was, he loved having the attention of others, and he had his ways of getting it. Even though Daniel went through so much in his short time, his faith was anchored to the '"Rock,"' Jesus Christ.

He never feared the battle he confronted. Daniel Saenz, Jr. is missed here on Earth tremendously, but Daniel lives forever in our hearts... until we meet again!" – Maria Saenz (Daniel's mom)

Camilla Andrea Duarte

December 13, 2007 – February 14, 2010

Camilla was diagnosed with acute monocytic leukemia on June 18, 2009. She was one-and-half years old. After enduring multiple chemo and radiation treatments, Camilla received a stem cell transplant from her six-year-old brother, Sebastian, on October 24, 2009. Three months later, Camilla relapsed, and, after numerous radiation treatments, she passed peacefully in her mother's arms on February 14, 2010, at two years of age.

What a sweetheart! Camilla amazed me with her tender heart and her refusal to allow cancer to rob her of the joy of childhood. She reminded me so much of my daughter, Rachel, at that age, who was always more concerned with comforting others than focusing on her own pain. When I think of Camilla now, I always see her dancing with the angels.

"Camilla touched many hearts at Texas Children's Hospital with her abundant energy. Her favorite pastime in the hospital was to ride her red car all over the hallways even after receiving chemotherapy. She fought a great battle and never gave in. And even though she endured so much pain, she would always be smiling and making everything okay. She taught me to never give up, no matter how hard and painful things may seem, and to always smile, even in my worst moments in life. Her favorite TV show was Barney. She loved to dance with her dad and listen to all kinds of music while lying in bed with her brother. Her brother was her hero. We have

unforgettable memories of Camilla that we shall cherish and treasure forever!" – Elena Duarte (Camilla's mom)

Kathy Dulski

Kathy, a busy single mom of three, was diagnosed with soft tissue sarcoma of the right thigh in March of 2006. After many radiation treatments and surgery, multiple nodules were found on both of her lungs in June of 2007. After a clinical trial, the nodules were removed in 2010. But more nodules were found in 2011. Kathy endured six cycles of one of the worst chemo treatments, known by patients as the "Red Devil." She began a second clinical trial in May of 2015. At this writing, Kathy is on an immunotherapy that has recently come to trial, and her tumors are stable.

Kathy was the first CarePager to reach out to me. After reading her story, I was amazed that a woman going through so much would take the time to encourage and comfort me. I soon realized that I wasn't alone. Kathy's name seemed to appear on every page I visited. After following Kathy's journey for a while, I came to refer to her as "Wonder Woman." I'm still amazed by her endurance, tenacity, and faith. She's an awesome mom and a selfless friend.

"Twice during this journey, I heard the words, '"There is nothing that will help you.'" Twice during this journey, I was led to an option by the grace of God. I advise any cancer patient to not give up. It's easy to become war-weary, but miracles do happen, and I've been shown twice now not to go out with a whimper, that maybe the lemon I've been handed in the form of sarcoma can be made into lemonade by testing

these treatments and leaving behind an option I didn't have for the next generation. That may be my purpose through the pain." – Kathy Dulski

Vinny DiGerolamo

October 9, 2003 – February 18, 2013
www.caringbridge.org/visit/vinnydigerolamo
www.kidsofchildhoodcancer.org

Vinny was born with severe cleft lip and cleft palate and diagnosed with valvular pulmonary stenosis on October 9th, 2003. Much to the surprise of his cardiologist, he survived heart surgery at five days old. When Vinny was three, an unsuccessful cleft-related velopharyngeal flap surgery caused two weeks of bleeding and mucus discharge. Exploratory surgery revealed a 7 cm tumor extending from his palate, behind his eye, into his left temporal lobe, and down to the base of his tongue. At four years of age, Vinny was diagnosed with embryonal rhabdomyosarcoma, a rare childhood cancer that affects three hundred children per year. Vinny was given less than a fifty percent chance of living five more years. They obviously didn't know Vinny. After nearly a year of chemo and radiation, Vinny "won" his cancer. Over the next five years, Vinny would relapse three times, each time being counted out by health care professionals. But Vinny continued to beat tumors in his lungs, eye, and sacrum, as well as a collapsed lung. At the age of nine, Vinny relapsed again in his spine. Vinny lived for three days after his fifth-year-anniversary of his initial diagnosis, beating the "less than 50 percent chance of living only five more years." He defied the odds the way only Vinny could and earned his wings on February 18, 2013.

I first met Vinny when I read on his CarePage that he'd had his scans done without his "sleepy drink." Being severely claustrophobic myself, I instantly dubbed Vinny "My Hero." And the more I read of his incredible spirit, endurance, and faith, the more I fell in love with him. Vinny had a gift for putting things into perspective for me. He was a huge heart in a small package, and it's no surprise to me that the angels were drawn to him.

"Vinny began to question me about God, angels, dying, and Heaven. He felt the angels on our ward and could perfectly describe the ones he had never met before. He felt them, giggled at them, and when I cried, he would comfort me and tell me the angels were happy in Heaven. Vinny was not taught much about God or Heaven before his cancer years, but he was very well-connected to God, and through his funny antics and stories, he made my own faith stronger. He was the reason I started believing that Heaven is real and that angels are all around us.

"Vinny continued to beat the odds over and over, being placed on hospice twice. But God and Vinny had their own plans. Once, when we thought he had 'one good month' left, Vinny laughed and said he was really cancer-free—and he was! Vinny loved life and playing pranks. He lived more life in his short nine years than most adults live in a lifetime. Vinny was a miracle, a lesson, and an inspiration to thousands of people who followed his CaringBridge site or met him in person.

"In November of 2012, a friend of ours did Healing Touch on Vinny's favorite teddy bear and told Vinny to hug the bear whenever he was in pain. Vinny's sister, Desiree, took a picture of him hugging his bear in the car on the way to the beach. (See the left picture.) After texting the picture to two friends, they wrote and asked if we had seen the picture. An angel in a blue robe appeared in the top corner, behind Vinny. We had the picture analyzed by two IT tech firms that clearly showed the angel and two faces behind the angel. What was the message it was trying to send? Was Vinny going to live, or was this a comforting way to prove that he would have a life in Heaven if he did not survive?

"Vinny was sent home on hospice once more on December 21st, 2012, and we were told he would not live through the weekend. Instead, paralyzed, back in diapers, and

weighing 29 pounds, Vinny lived nine full weeks, building Legos with me, watching Disney Channel, and having lengthy talks to me about what awaited him in Heaven, about the angels he felt, about his private talks with God, and what signs and messages he would bring us when he earned his wings. Vinny fought hard, stumped the hospice workers again and again, and continued to live even while his tiny body kept failing.

"I asked over and over, what was keeping him here, and told him again and again that it was okay to go be with God and our little angels.

"He would just smile and say, 'I want to spend more time with you, Momma.'

"Within two weeks of Vinny's death, we received our first message from him. And three years later, we laugh, smile, and cry whenever he sends the promised signs, knowing in our hearts that it's him." – Sarah DiGerolamo (Vinny's mom)

Joshua Dean Mueller

April 4, 1989 – October 16, 2008

Josh was told he had cancer on his nineteenth birthday, April 4, 2008. On April 17th, he was told it was rhabdomyosarcoma, and then on April 23rd, that he had Ewing's sarcoma. On April 30th, after beginning chemo, Josh received a new diagnosis of malignant spindle cell, epithelioid neoplasm, and possibly myoepithelthial. Josh underwent new chemo treatments through July 20th, and then, after a break from chemo in August, radiation to his left sinuses and lymph nodes in his neck in September. During his break from chemo, the cancer exploded in his lungs and spread undetected to his brain. Josh fought to the last, surrounded by family and friends.

I came to know Josh late in both of our journeys, but let me tell you, I will never forget him! What can you say about a guy who calls chemo treatments "BORING?"? Who can be tranquilized, bolted to a table, irradiated, then get up and run errands with his mom and sign up for college classes on the same day? What can you say about a guy who removes his own feeding tube, puts in a new one, and describes it as "Blah. Gross!"? Rambo on Xanax. That's how I pictured Josh. Josh seemed to live as though this cancer thing was just an inconvenience to be endured on his way to something greater. His ability to make light of the worst of situations inspired me to see beyond my circumstances.

"*Pray for me. Be strong for me. But remember those who care for me. Do the same for them. I know my mom, dad, and sisters could really use your thoughts, too.*" – Josh Mueller, April 22, 2008

Tyler Fisher

April 17, 2000 – December 23, 2017

Tyler was diagnosed with Ewing's sarcoma in October of 2006. He was six years old. He began chemo aggressively and had reconstructive surgery on his right tibia in February of 2007, then spent a year in a wheelchair. Tyler was pronounced NED (No Evidence of Disease) after a year of chemo, in October of 2007, but six years later was diagnosed with cardiomyopathy due to the damage to his heart caused by chemo. In August of 2014, Tyler relapsed in his rib and lungs, at fourteen years of age, and had surgery to remove his left 5th fifth rib. Once more, he began aggressive chemo and then radiation in November of 2014. Tyler began to experience major issues with his heart and severe weight loss in February of 2015, and his treatment was ended that May, when he was diagnosed with heart failure. His heart failure symptoms worsened in December 2016, and he was sent to Duke University Hospital for four months where he received a LVAD, a "bridge to heart transplant," until he could be considered for a new heart, once after being five5 years had passed since his most recent from cancer treatment. On December 23, 2017, Tyler passed peacefully due to a blood clot and brain hemorrhage. His body could no longer fight the illnesses that had invaded it.

I connected with Tyler the first time I read his story. Perhaps it's because his gentle spirit and love for life reminded me so much of my own sons. I was thrilled when Tyler was pronounced NED, and so angry when I learned he had relapsed. Tyler's eyes truly were the windows to his beautiful soul. He wasn't a guy who craved the limelight, so his allowing me to share his story speaks volumes of his heart for others in need of encouragement. Not a day goes by that I don't thank God for Tyler.

"Though Tyler was sick for most of his life, he tried to enjoy every moment. He had a great personality, and he was a jokester and always wanted to make others laugh. His positive outlook helped many '"cancer newbies'" of all ages. He was a hero to many, and we will sure miss his contagious smile. Tyler was an inspiration to so many people. His "Never Give Up" attitude and wonderful smile moved more people than he will ever know. He is still inspiring others, and he is still my hero." – Wanda Fisher (Tyler's mom)

Brian Ernst

March 11, 1991 – March 16, 2010

http://www.godtube.com/watch/?v=7KPGD7NX

Brian was diagnosed with Ewing's sarcoma on March 11, 2008. He was seventeen years old. Brian was treated with fourteen rounds of chemo and seven weeks of radiation therapy, but surgery was not an option in his case, due to the size and location of the tumor. He had numerous hospital stays due to blood and platelet transfusions, chemo-induced fever, and other complications. In December of 2009, no active cancer cells were found, and just a few weeks after chemo, Brian had gained all his weight back, looked great, and had actually grown an inch. In January of 2010, Brian relapsed, and a large tumor pressing on his spine required immediate surgery. The cancer had spread throughout his body and to his bone marrow, and the tumors proved to be treatment-resistant. Brian went to be with the Lord shortly after his nineteenth birthday.

I loved reading about Brian's mischievous antics and love for others. Just thinking about him brings a smile to my face. As with so many of my heroes, Brian had a supernatural gift to reach beyond his own pain to comfort and cheer others. I will always be grateful to him for that.

"In high school, Brian was an excellent baseball player. At 6' 4" and 220 lbs., he was already a Division I college prospect. Playing collegiate baseball was one of his goals. And his strength and faith in God were unwavering.

"Upon learning of his diagnosis, Brian said, 'If I can help or inspire just one person through my journey, then I've done my job, it will all be worth it.'

"Brian reached and quickly surpassed that goal. From one simple DVD, made by his high school FCA (Fellowship of Christian Athletes), about how God helped him through fighting cancer, to followers of his CarePages, Brian touched and inspired hundreds of lives. Brian received letters from children admiring his faith in God through so much suffering, many from broken homes or foster homes. They wanted to renew their relationship with Christ because of Brian's testimony. Brian turned the focus away from himself and allowed God to use his adversity to honor and point others to Him.

Brian always had a smile on his face and an incredible sense of humor. His laughter was infectious. He never met a stranger and could easily warm someone up with his compassionate, caring heart. He loved his friends and family and shared a very close bond with his older brother. They weren't just close brothers, they were best friends. His family finds solace in the fact that his "Heaven Date" correlates to John 3:16, one of the most well-known verses in the Bible." – Donna Ernst (Brian's mom)

"For God so loved the world that He gave His only begotten Son,
that whoever believes in Him should not perish, but have everlasting life."
John 3:16

Derrick Ide

September 8, 1973 – November 26, 2009

Derrick was diagnosed with urachal adenocarcinoma, a very rare cancer, on May 26, 2006. Because this is a cancer of something from gestation that should go away after birth, it is diagnosed extremely late. Because it's not an organ we use, symptoms aren't noticed until it has spread. That, combined with its rarity, makes it deadly. Derrick had an initial surgery to remove the tumor and a portion of his bladder. Tragically, his urologist discouraged Derrick and his wife, Rachel, from consulting other doctors, and though some scans were done, he was refused chemo. Six months later, the cancer was back with a vengeance and had spread to his liver, lungs, and lymph nodes. Derrick finally received chemo, as well as a liver resection and lung ablation surgery, and was put on many different clinical trials. His pain was excruciating for the last fourteen months of his life, despite a pain pump that served as a direct spinal twenty-four seven, and huge amounts of oral pain medications. He received limited radiation at the very end. Derrick wanted to be able to die at home, and though it was an uphill battle, Rachel was able to fulfill his last wish.

I never got the opportunity to get to know Derrick, except through his beautiful wife, Rachel, but I connected with Rachel instantly, and I wasn't the only one. It was a connection only God could make, and it drove me to my knees. Her strength and honesty inspired me, and even in the midst of her own pain, she never ceased to ask for prayers for others in need and to champion her daughter. She's an amazing woman who has blessed so many, and I will always count her as a friend.

"Derrick was the most amazing friend, husband, and father. He was extremely adventurous—he loved skydiving, mountain biking, and surfing. He liked everyone he met, and he was the most positive person I've ever known, even in the face of adversity and the torture of constant chemo and many surgeries. He never lost his positive attitude. Derrick was always helping someone—friends, family, and neighbors. When we received an unfair assessment of our home, he researched the assessments of our neighbors as well. Derrick fought for and won a reduction for an elderly widowed neighbor. He used to take her vegetables from our garden, and she called him her prince. Derrick loved his daughter like nothing else. In fact, he saved her life. She, too, had a urachal remnant, the thing that had caused Derrick's cancer. We would never have known. She had surgery six months after Derrick died to remove it. A blessing in disguise. He has been gone six years now, and not a day goes by that we do not miss him." – Rachel Ide (Derrick's wife)

Jonathan O'Malley

Jonathan was diagnosed with acute myeloid leukemia on August 25, 2008. He was sixteen years old. After nine months of treatment, Jonathan was pronounced in remission in 2009, but the cancer recurred three months later. On February 5, 2010, Jonathan received a double cord blood transplant. The next two years brought trips to ICU, time on a ventilator, hip transplants, internal bleeding, partial loss of his palate and jawbone, heart problems, memory loss, and more. But Jonathan is so much more than a survivor.

How can you not love a guy who'll get out of his own hospital bed for a tea party with his three-year-old neighbor on the cancer ward? Jonathan reminded me constantly of the important things in life. And reading about his antics, I couldn't resist nicknaming him "O'Malley Cat." His faith still encourages me to keep my focus on Jesus and trust in His plan. We continue to pray for Jonathan, knowing that God will complete the work He began in him.

"Jonathan still has a few health problems that he will deal with over time, but he is diligent about living a normal life and never using his past battle with cancer to stop him from doing what he wants to do with his life. He is overall healthy, working full-time, going to college and will take any opportunity to encourage kids with cancer that

no matter what the outcome may be, you can't let cancer take away the smile on your face and the happiness you find in each moment. *That was always Jonathan's motto. He was one of the "big" kids on the cancer floor, but we had little kids knock on our door to play with Jonathan because he gave them his time and would even play tea party with one of the little 3three-year-old girls on the floor. He played pranks on nurses, doctors, pharmacists, and everyone else because it made people smile. But when some of his darkest times of pain came, he asked some of those same nurses and doctors to pray with him as he cried out to God in pain, with them gathered around his bed holding his hand and begging for mercy. These are the things that Jonathan used to get through his journey with cancer.*

"Jonathan's illness was a defining moment in our lives that changed everything. Nothing would ever be "normal" again. But our family's faith is the stronghold of all that we do. We chose to stand together as a family and fight with Jonathan and follow whatever God's plan was, whether it was what we wanted or not. We have moved forward with life with that same belief and faith. Though we go through hard times that sometimes leave us heartbroken, confused, or angry, God is there with the reassurance of His mercy and grace, which we surely do not deserve. These are the lessons we carry with us along with the images of the families we met along the way who will be forever engraved on our hearts." – Melanie O'Malley (Jonathan's mom)

David Buck
August 5, 1988 – July 30, 2010

David was diagnosed with embryonal rhabdomyosarcoma of the maxillary sinus, intermediate-risk, May 14, 2008. His 6 cm tumor was inoperable because of its location near critical arteries and nerves. He underwent forty-three weeks of chemo, May of 2008 through February of 2009, and twenty-eight sessions of radiation in July of 2008. This killed only half of the tumor, which began to grow again when treatment ended. David then underwent salvage treatment of eleven cycles of chemo, June through December of 2009, of eleven cycles of chemo, which kept the tumor stable but did not shrink it. Surgery was still too dangerous. When the salvage treatment ended, the tumor again began to grow. David then participated in a Phase I/II clinical trial, February and March of 2009, but despite that treatment, the tumor continued growing, and the cancer spread. No viable options for treatment remained.

Reading about David was like watching one of my favorite superheroes. He never played by the rules. He had his own rules, and every time he zigged when he was supposed to zag, I cheered. Yes! You go, David! His hunger for life was rivaled only by his appetite for ice-cream pie and pierogi, prompting the salutation that ended his mom, Lori's, later updates, "Peace, Love, and Ice cream." I can't think of that phrase without thinking of David and being reminded that life is a feast to be savored—not a diet plan.

"At diagnosis, David was a chemical engineering major at the University of Delaware, pursuing minors in physics and mathematics. He liked to refer to himself as a '"Renaissance Man,"' proud of his diverse intellectual and artistic interests. In early elementary school, he was identified as a divergent thinker; his curiosity led him in all sorts of directions. Quantum physics, the Manhattan Project, and the National Parks all fascinated him. David loved beauty in the natural world and spent many hours seeking it out to photograph. His pictures reveal a keen and attentive eye with an unusual perspective. He also had a soft spot for harp seals, and loved every kind of music, playing percussion in the high school marching band and wind ensemble, and singing tenor with the vocal jazz ensemble.

"David was fond of puns and had a quick wit that would crack you up on the spot. He seemed to possess an inner knowing or wisdom beyond his years, tempered by a guarded vulnerability. He was pragmatic and sensible and didn't suffer fools gladly. He knew what he wanted from life and was purposeful about going after it. He loved UD [the University of Delaware] and returning to campus after treatments was always uppermost in his mind and is what drove him to minimize the effects of pain, nausea, and hair loss. He was at ease with people of all ages, counting among his peers UD students who were decades older, but he was most comfortable with his beloved black cat, Sophie. David spent three semesters at UD and was named to the Dean's List each time. His family established a memorial fund at UD in order to award scholarships to other chemical engineering students who demonstrate his kind of intellectual curiosity." – Lori Buck (David's mom)

Mikayla Rietgraf

Mikayla was diagnosed with Ewing sarcoma with stage IV metastatic lung disease in February of 2009. She was eight years old at the time. Her primary tumor, the size of a baseball, was in her left hip. She had six lung tumors, one being as big as her hip tumor. Her treatment was fourteen rounds of inpatient chemo, and after six rounds, she went to MD Anderson in Houston, Texas for three months, where she received thirty-six rounds of proton radiation, and then returned home to Iowa to finish her chemotherapy. She completed her chemo treatments in February in 2010, and then went back to MD Anderson and finished with ten rounds of radiation to her lungs. Mikayla reached remission status in March of 2015. Her late-term side effects have been varied. She has kidney disease and is on multiple medications to keep her kidneys from producing stones and overworking. She has painful arthritis in her left hip, which requires aqua therapy, and her pelvic bone quit growing sometime after radiation. She's had neuropathy since August of 2015 and is on pain medication for that.

This young lady's faith and strength still inspire me. Whenever I was tempted to whine about my own pain during my treatment, I could think of Mikayla's smile and know the same God giving her the strength to endure and joy in the midst of it was with me as well. Her spirit is contagious, and I know I wasn't the only one infected. It's exciting to be able to watch the Lord continue to work in her life, and I look forward to seeing His grand plan revealed in her.

"When Mikayla was diagnosed, we were devastated. We didn't know if she would live and how she would get through such horrible treatment. Although it was harder than we imagined for her, God was always faithful and showed us His plan over and over. He cared for her with such depth, love, and gentleness. There is always hope even when the odds look overwhelming. God isn't concerned with statistics, and He proved with her that He gets the last word!" – Deanna Rietgraf (Mikayla's mom)

*W*ere I to include all of the tests, treatments, and surgeries these heroes endured in their valiant battles against this demon called cancer, it would fill another complete volume. These are only a handful of my heroes. These individuals and their families are true testimonies of God's grace. Their full stories can be found at the CarePage and CaringBridge addresses listed under each name. I pray that readers will be blessed by these lives as I have been, and that we may ever be reminded of the need to support the fight for a cure, and to pray for those engaged in the battle, and for those suffering the pain of loss.

Over one million people in the United States alone are diagnosed with cancer each year. Over 12,600 of them will be children. Our children. We are at war, and we can't wait until this demon knocks down our front door and claims one of our loved ones before we take up a weapon and fight. This is not a war that can or should be fought from the infirmary. It must be fought by the healthy and strong. What can we do? So many things:

·   First, as I mentioned before, pray without ceasing.

·   Then give: time, money, emotional support... there are so many good organizations out there for research and support. Find one that strikes a chord and make it a part of your monthly giving.

·   Be proactive in supporting the rights of alternative treatment providers to practice in the U.S.

· Find a family in your area battling on the frontlines—you won't have to look far—and send them a gift card every month, or cook them a meal, or offer to babysit, or help in some other way. Cancer is not only physically devastating, but emotionally and financially as well.

· Family members need caregivers, too. Just to be there for them and listen.

· And don't forget those who lose their loved one—talking about their loved one can mean so much to a grieving parent, child, or spouse.

· Give blood. Cancer patients are the number one group as a whole who needing blood products.

· Take part in fundraisers, or toy, hat, or blanket drives.

· Send cards.

· Visit patients in hospitals....

One person can have an enormous impact. One person can save a life.

This is not a war we can afford to sit out. We must fight with everything we've got until we can raise a generation of kids who will one day ask, "Mom, Dad, did you ever know anyone who had cancer?"

And we will answer, "No, hon. That was long before my time."

THANK YOU!

*I*f my story has blessed you, please take a moment to post a review. Every review this book receives makes it more visible to more readers. Thank you so much for your support!

One of the most amazing revelations I have received in my pursuit of God is that of Heavenly visitation. There are sights, sounds, even smells in Heaven there are no words to describe. They must be experienced to believe, and, as believers, they are ours to discover. I share what I've learned in my book, *3 Practices of People Who Visit Heaven*, and you can get your copy free by visiting my website, **www.WatchGodWork.com**. Also available is my new book, *Break Free! Your Personal Guide to Forgiveness.* By joining the Watch God Work family, You can receive the "Promise of the Day," in-depth Bible studies, and prophetic words in your inbox, as well as access to my prayer hotline and dream interpretation. I hope to see you there!

God bless!

ABOUT THE AUTHOR

Rebecca Olmstead is an award-winning author and founder of Watch God Work Ministries. She writes fiction and non-fiction, and her work has appeared in publications such as Focus on the Family's *Club House, Jr.*, *The Upper Room*, *Live*, *Now What?*, and *Houseboat*. Her award-winning short story, "The Uninvited Guest: A Short Story," is available on Amazon as an ebook. You can get it free when you subscribe to her author newsletter at **www.rebeccaolmstead.com**.

Currently, Rebecca is working on a devotional based on her "Promise of the Day" blog, due for release the first of 2021...if not sooner. She is also preparing to launch a podcast for Watch God Work Ministries and has a Youtube channel, "Rebecca Olmstead," that you can subscribe to for teachings and special messages.

Other books in the works are a collection of short stories and the first in her clean mystery series, featuring Walla Walla, Washington boutique owner, Gabrielle Dorian. If you're a fan of mysteries, great short stories, and non-fiction, subscribe to her newsletter to receive updates and share some of her adventures, or misadventures, as the case may be. Follow Rebecca on:

www.rebeccaolmstead.com

www.watchgodwork.com

Parler:

https://parler.com/profile/WatchGodWork/posts

https://parler.com/profile/RJO26/posts

Linkedin:

https://www.linkedin.com/in/rebecca-olmstead-9bb30972/

Made in the USA
Columbia, SC
08 December 2022

525352e7-0063-418e-aa88-2e619a2a7d00R01